CAESAR AGAINST THE CELTS

CAESAR
AGAINST THE
CELTS

by
RAMON L. JIMÉNEZ

SARPEDON
New York

Published in the United States by
SARPEDON
166 Fifth Avenue
New York, NY 10010

ISBN 1-885119-20-8

Library of Congress Cataloging-in-Publication Data

Jiménez, Ramon L.
    Caesar against the Celts / by Ramon L. Jiménez
        p.   cm.
    Includes bibliographical references and index.
    ISBN 1-885119-19-4. — ISBN 1-885119-20-8 (pbk.)
    1. Gaul—History—Gallic Wars, 58–51 B.C. 2. Caesar, Julius.
3. Great Britain—History—Roman period, 55 B.C.–449 A.D.
4. Germany—History. 5. Celts—History. I. Title.
DC62.J56   1995
936.4—dc20   95-25429
                                                       CIP

10 9 8 7 6 5 4 3

MANUFACTURED IN THE UNITED STATES OF AMERICA

This is for
Joan Leon

CONTENTS

LIST OF MAPS

PREFACE

Unlike many readers, it was not until my adult years that I first read a certain remarkable account of military campaigns in ancient Europe. It was perhaps because of that circumstance that I found it so compelling and developed such a craving for something more about the subject. The author of the work was Julius Caesar, and its title was *Commentaries on the Gallic War*. When I investigated further, I found that there was little else available to augment Caesar's bare and limited paragraphs, and nothing that explored the background, the motives, or the arresting sidelights of this major piece of Latin literature.

It almost seems that Caesar, by leaving behind a lucid and detailed history of his military campaigns, demanded, in a sense, that they be studied and elaborated upon. By never alluding to the political intrigue that absorbed him in Rome, he seemed in invite further investigation. This book is my attempt to respond to that invitation and, using the fruits of modern scholarship, to retell the story for today's reader.

In the following pages readers will not find a comprehensive history of Caesar's Rome or of Celtic civilization. Instead they will find a narrative that emphasizes those elements of the story that compelled me to embrace it in the first place. I have purposely, and with the cooperation of my editors, not attempted to include every event, individual and location that is mentioned in Caesar's account, or that has since been revealed. That information is available elsewhere to those who wish it. My aim, instead, has been to relate, for those readers who share my curiosity, how one man, in the century before Christ, took hold of European history and bent it to his own will.

Although many writers have treated Caesar's political career in Rome, my purpose has been to focus on his war against the Celts. That the Celts, "that mysterious people," as John Keegan refers to them in *A History of Warfare,* once dominated all of Western Europe may come as a surprise to many.

The reader will also find that this work leans to the British perspective of Celtic life and history and to Caesar's adventures across the Channel. This has always seemed to me the most extraordinary episode of the Gallic War. That Rome would, eventually, under one great commander or another, conquer Gaul and its Celtic tribes, rings, in hindsight, with a certain inevitability. But when Caesar "leaped" to the unknown island, risking himself and his army, he wrenched his nation in a new direction, one that it followed with determination a century later.

In the postscript, "The English Search for Caesar," I have sought to examine the record of Caesar's invasions from other than Roman perspectives, especially those of the Celts and their descendants. Since the ancient Celts did not write, their perspective is difficult to ascertain. Nevertheless, we can be certain it exists, whether hidden in song, story or in centuries-old manuscripts written by later occupiers of Britain. My other objective has been to explore the fascination with Caesar that persists to this day in every locality to which the Gallic War took him. Archaeologists, historians and linguists continue to unravel mysteries and dazzle us with their findings.

Grateful acknowledgment is made to Professor Barry Cunliffe of Oxford University for permission to use several copyrighted photographs and descriptive captions.

By way of acknowledgment, I am sincerely grateful to Cisna Baun, Linda Gelnaw and Jan Vetter for patiently reviewing the manuscript for errors and omissions and for their helpful suggestions. All remaining shortcomings are entirely my own responsibility. For custom translations I thank George Cozyris, Susan O'Hara and Helga Roth. For encouragement, support and inspired ideas, my gratitude to my wonderful wife, Joan, is endless.

Ramon Jiménez
Berkeley, CA, 1995

CHRONOLOGY

3000–2000 BC	Migration of Celtic peoples into Europe
c. 750	Founding of Rome
c. 600	Celts reach Britain, Ireland and Scotland
390	Movement of Celts into Italy
325	Voyage of Pytheas
c. 200	Roman control of all of Italy
100	Birth of Caesar; *Histories* of Polybius
82	Dictatorship of Sulla
c. 80	*Histories* of Posidonius
61	Caesar Governor of Further Spain
59	Year of Caesar's Consulship
58	Caesar's first campaigns in Gaul
55	First expedition to Britain
54	Caesar's invasion of Britain
51–50	Completion of conquest of Gaul
c. 51	Publication of Caesar's *The Gallic War*
49	Caesar crosses the Rubicon
44	Murder of Caesar; writings of Diodorus Siculus
30	Suicides of Antony and Cleopatra
c. AD 10	Strabo's *Geography*
43	Invasion of Britain under Claudius
c. 90	Tacitus' *Dialogue on Oratory*
110	Plutarch's *Lives*
116	Tacitus' *Annals*
120	Suetonius' *Lives of the Caesars*
c. 400–425	Romans abandon Britain
c. 450	Anglo-Saxon invasion of Britain

NOTE

The Romans customarily used three names to formally identify themselves, such as Marcus Tullius Cicero. In the interest of clarity and brevity, the names and spellings used in the narrative are generally those most recognizable to the modern reader, such as Mark Antony, Pompey, etc.

For ease of understanding, the system of denoting years as BC or AD is used, as are the modern names of the months. With respect to particular dates, only two—the dates of Caesar's first departure for, and landing in, Britain—have been converted to the modern calendar. All other dates are those used by the Romans at the time, and have not been converted. These may be from three to eight weeks ahead of the same date in the Julian Calendar, which was not adopted by Caesar until 45 BC, a year before his death. After being modified slightly by Pope Gregory XIII in the sixteenth century, this calendar remains in use today.

Distances given by Caesar are in Roman measurements. The Roman foot (*pes*) was 296 millimeters, or slightly over 11 inches, five of which made one *passus*. The Roman mile (*mille passus*) was 5,000 Roman feet, equalling 92 percent of an English mile.

CAESAR AGAINST THE CELTS

Now in the names of all the gods at once,
Upon what meat doth this our Caesar feed
That he is grown so great?

Cassius, in
Shakespeare, *Julius Caesar* I, ii

GAUL IN CAESAR'S TIME

HELVETII Tribal names   • Oppida or towns   ✕ Battlefield

0   50   100   150   200   250   Roman miles

0   50   100   150   200   250   300   350   Kilometres

GERMANS

UBII

SUEBI

CHERUSCI

GERMANY

Danube

DACIANS

HARUDES

Danube

Gaul

Cisalpine

Po

Po

Aquileia

Northern Italy

Illyricum

ITALY

Rome

PROLOGUE

In the middle of a late-summer morning about two thousand years ago a band of British Celts stood on the chalk cliff coast of England overlooking the narrowest part of the English Channel. Through the cool mist they could see a group of long and narrow warships, each with a high deck crowded with soldiers, and with three rows of oars along each side pulling it steadily toward the shore. The ships flew a strange flag and were unlike any the Britons had ever seen, but they were not surprised. They had known for some weeks that their island was about to be invaded by an army that had swept back and forth across the country opposite them for the past three years, defeating their brother tribes and chieftains, one by one.

They had even sent envoys to the leader of this army, offering to submit to his authority and to send hostages to guarantee their allegiance. He had sent them back with his own envoy, Commius, a Gaulish chieftain who had defected to him, to negotiate a peaceful occupation. He had promised them leniency if they did as he proposed. But the invasion would proceed.

On board the leading trireme the fleet commander, the Roman Governor of Gaul, may have been surprised that the large number of men on the cliffs were armed for battle with swords, shields and spears, and clearly intended to oppose his landing. If the Roman governor's emissary, Commius, chief of the Belgic continental tribe known as the Atrebates, had been successful, there would now be one or more small boats rowing out to meet him. He would be able to land unopposed, occupy the nearby harbor and use the massive hillfort visible on the cliff as a base from which to march inland.

Instead, there were no boats and no sign that there would be anything but the fiercest opposition. The commander noted the narrowness of the beach below the cliffs and the menacing spears of the Celts, and decided it was too dangerous to land. He gave the order to anchor, and waited over the next six hours for the remainder of his fleet to arrive.

Thus began the first Roman invasion of Britain, a military feat that dazzled the ancient world and caused a twenty-day thanksgiving celebration in the streets of Rome. It was led by the forty-five-year-old Gaius Julius Caesar—not only one of the Republic's most prominent politicians, but its most illustrious general, and one of the greatest in history. It took place in what is now called 55 BC, but was then the Roman year 699, that being the number of years since the legendary founding of the city of Rome. The day was in the fourth week of the month of *Sextilis*, today called August, after Augustus, Caesar's grand-nephew and successor only eleven years later.

By about three o'clock in the afternoon an additional eighty vessels, huge flat-bottomed transports, as well as numerous smaller boats, had joined the group of warships off the British coast. When it finally assembled, the fleet stretched for more than a mile along the shore of the Dover cliffs.

Caesar's invasion force comprised two Roman legions, the VIIth and the Xth, each numbering close to four thousand infantrymen. With them were cadres of auxiliary troops to carry out special functions, such as artillery bombardment, for a grand total of about ten thousand men. Many of them were Gaulish Celts or Germans who had been recruited to fight for Rome. Most were seasoned soldiers, having fought with Caesar throughout Gaul since his arrival there as Governor three years before.

The main body of the army was carried on eighty massive cargo vessels commandeered from the seagoing Gallic tribes. These were built of heavy oak timbers, and had deep drafts of at least five feet. Each was fitted with a single square sail of rough linen, and carried at least a hundred legionaries, along with their weapons, provisions and bag gage, and towed one or more small boats behind. They were clumsy and slow and, lacking oars, barely adequate to navigate the choppy waters of the Channel. Because of strong tides and unpredictable winds it was, as it is now, a hazardous place for sailing ships.

Experienced Gaulish seamen piloted all the vessels in the fleet; the Romans were not sailors.

On board the smaller high-decked triremes—Caesar's warships—were the army high command, the quartermaster's corps and the Roman artillery. Among the artillerymen were slingers, or *funditores*, recruited from the Balearic Islands, who carried a deadly ancient weapon: a cord of leather or sinew about three feet long with a flat pouch in the center in which they put a rounded stone the size of an egg. Holding the two ends of the cord, they whirled it around their heads and then released one end, propelling the stone as far as two hundred yards with tremendous force and accuracy.[1] Also among them were the *sagittarii*—expert archers conscripted from Crete and from Numidia (modern-day Algeria).

Other men on board the warships operated elaborate catapults that shot javelins or heavy arrows as far as five hundred yards, much like modern field guns. The catapults were like giant stationary bows fitted with thick ropes of hair or sinew that produced torsion when twisted, and then a tremendous thrust of energy when released. They were mounted on the decks of the warships in raised wooden turrets to give them greater height and protection from enemy fire.

Caesar had no cavalry with him. At the time he was assembling his fleet, bad weather had prevented eighteen of his transports from reaching the port of departure in time to leave with him from Gaul. Before sailing, he had dispatched all his three hundred cavalrymen to the port where their transports were waiting, six miles away, and directed them to follow him across the Channel. But by the time they got underway, they were too late to join Caesar and the rest of his fleet below the cliffs. A storm drove them back to the mainland port and they never reached Britain at all.

While he waited for the rest of his fleet to join him, Caesar summoned his officers to his flagship and gave them what information he had about the coastline and the currents in the Channel. He explained what he intended to do, and told them that because of the hazards of landing such a large number of ships they must carry out his orders instantly and without question. When both the wind and the tide were in his favor, as he later wrote in *The Gallic War,* "I gave the signal for the anchors to be weighed. We moved on about seven miles and ran the ships aground on a flat and open beach" (IV, 23).*

Over the next several hours, as the summer afternoon passed, the fleet edged along the shore, while a parade of long-haired and mustachioed warriors, on horseback, on foot, and in light two-wheeled chariots, followed it on the cliffs. When the ships reached their landing place, the Celts were waiting. A mass of horses, chariots and armed warriors was spread along the beach, and for the first time in Britain, Roman and Celt faced each other.

Caesar's seaborne expedition to Britain was the most dramatic military feat of his war against the Celts. It was also the most dangerous. By attempting a hurried Channel crossing at the end of the sailing season, he put ten thousand men, a quarter of his army, in double jeopardy—both from the capricious Channel weather and from the unknown number of hostile Britons waiting to resist them. And if he thought his lack of cavalry was bad luck, in a few days he would see much worse.

It was also the most frivolous. Of the many needless battles in a meandering war with no clear purpose, the attack on Britain was the least justified. But it brought Caesar what he wanted most—the acclamation due a daring commander and public approval of a war that took on aspects of a traveling circus and big-game hunt. He also became the first Roman to land on Britannia, an island that the rest of the world was not quite sure existed.

Nevertheless, the British landing was not unusual for this soldier, politician, historian and priest, whose arrogance and ambition were nearly matched by personal charm and proven courage. Beginning with his desperate flight as a teenager to avoid execution by the dictator Sulla, Caesar's lifetime was a series of rash adventures and narrow escapes. But his military genius and political brilliance saved him time and again and produced a nearly unbroken record of successes both on and off the battlefield. And for the ages yet to come he left his own unique chronicle of one of the remarkable careers in ancient history.

*Translated as *The Battle for Gaul,* by Anne and Peter T. Wiseman, 1980. All subsequent quotations from and references to this work will be identified in parentheses in the text by "Book" and "Chapter" number rather than cited at book's end.

CHAPTER I

⟨⟩ · ⟨⟩

CAESAR IN ROME

I n the fall of the year 82 BC a young man of eighteen, already a husband and father, and the last male in one of Rome's ancient patrician families, fled on horseback into the mountainous country east of the city, where he sought refuge from government police pursuing him with orders to kill. He paid for his food and lodging in a different rural household each night, but the price on his head forced him to pay even steeper amounts, to ensure that he was not betrayed.

A short and bloody civil war between Rome's two political factions had just ended. The victor was Lucius Sulla, an ambitious general returning from a series of military successes in Greece and Asia. When the Senate insisted that he disband his army, he invaded the Roman homeland instead, and appeared at the outskirts of the capital with forty thousand infantry. In a ferocious battle at the Colline Gate, on Rome's northeastern wall, he crushed the forces of the governing faction, the *populares*, and began a brutal purge of its supporters. The fortunate he banished from the country; the rest he had murdered and their heads nailed up for public display. Those senators who survived proclaimed him dictator for the indefinite future.

Although the young Julius Caesar had taken no part in the fighting, his prominent family was aligned with the losing cause, and it was his cousin Marius who had led the opposition to Sulla. After losing the brief war, Marius had killed himself. But what caused Caesar to be condemned was not his family's politics. It was his bold refusal of the dictator's order that he divorce Cornelia, his sixteen-year-old wife of two years and the daughter of another politician in the former government. Sulla also stripped him of his inheritance and of the dowry paid him by Cornelia's family.

After several weeks of eluding his pursuers, Caesar took ill with malarial fever and was captured. Even then, however, a large bribe allowed him to escape. Finally, acting on the pleas of Caesar's relatives, Sulla removed his name from the "wanted list," but not before predicting that the stubborn boy would one day be dangerous.

The incident was doubly prophetic. It was the first and perhaps the finest example of Caesar's courage—and of his loyalty—in a lifetime filled with risks and alliances of every kind. And for those who opposed him, and many who did not, he would indeed become the most dangerous man in Roman Italy—a country bred to war and conquest, and nurtured on political intrigue.

During the sixth century before Christ the people known as Romans were one of several tribes in the area of Latium on the west coast of the Italian peninsula who lived under the rule of Etruscan kings. Toward the end of the century, Roman families of the aristocratic class joined together to overthrow the monarchy and establish an independent republic. They adopted a form of government comprising a Senate, an Assembly of citizens, and a hierarchy of elected magistrates, or administrators, headed by two *consules*, or consuls. This arrangement was an attempt to balance the interests of the patrician aristocrats, the merchant class, and the remain-ing citizenry by dividing political power in such a way that no group could persistently dominate the others. To guard against a new monarchy and to reduce any monetary incentive, the magistrates and consuls were unpaid and their terms limited to one year, each consul having veto power over the actions of the other.[1]

Wielding a combination of aggressive diplomacy and military strength, the Romans, over the course of the next two and a half centuries, gradually subdued and absorbed the various tribes around them, until by 266 BC they controlled the entire Italian peninsula below the Po River. During the next sixty years, after three successful wars against the Phoenician empire of Carthage—the last against its legendary general, Hannibal—Rome took Sicily, Sardinia, Corsica and most of Spain and made them its provinces.

During the entire second century BC the Romans failed to send an army abroad in only three years. By 120 BC they had conquered and established provinces in Macedonia, Africa (modern Tunisia), Asia (western Turkey), Cilicia (southern Turkey) and Further Gaul (the southern coast of modern France and the Rhône Valley). Their domination of the Mediterranean world was such that they called its sea "*mare nostrum*," or "our sea."

At the time of Julius Caesar's birth in 100 BC the Roman state had been a republic for more than four hundred years. The collection of primitive huts on the hills overlooking the Tiber River had evolved over the previous six centuries into the largest city the world had yet seen. As the capital of the Republic, and then the Empire, Rome remained the center of trade, culture, religion and government in the West for over a thousand years. Besides its native population, the overcrowded city was home to large numbers of immigrants, refugees and adventurers from all parts of the known world. The great majority of its nearly one million inhabitants lived in crowded and squalid tenements of two or three stories and had only the meanest necessities of life. Their diet consisted almost entirely of vegetables, lard, and bread or porridge made from wheat. As much as a third of the city depended on subsidized grain from the government; another third, also dependent, were slaves.[2]

Toward the end of the second century BC, the republican system of shared rule was shaken by popular uprisings, especially of slaves, and by several foreign and civil conflicts that introduced a military factor into the political arena. The established processes for governing were repeatedly breached, and the practice began of assigning important military commands to particular men by vote of the Assembly. This led to a disorderly competition among ambitious patricians, supported by their hired gangs, to use any means to capture votes. The gamut ran from propaganda and ordinary bribes to violence and outright murder. Among the least reprehensible were subsidies and entertainments, the classic "bread and circuses."

Although there were no organized parties in the modern sense, political activities tended to polarize into two opposing groups: the conservative *optimates* ("the best men"), who endorsed the status quo and supported the prerogatives of the Senate, and the radical *populares* ("men of the people"), who demanded change and sought to exert power through the citizens' Assembly. Within these groups, the schemes of perennial office-seekers, supported by family and clientage ties, marriage alliances and ad hoc agreements, created an atmosphere of constant political intrigue.

Caesar's forebears on his father's side, the Julii, came from one of Rome's thirty or so original patrician families, and claimed descent not only from the founders of Rome, Romulus and Remus, but also from the Trojan Aeneas, and ultimately through him from the goddess Venus. Caesar's mother, Aurelia, was a forceful and independent woman from a wealthy family, the Aurelii Cottae, who boasted consuls and other influential men in their lineage; her father and three of her cousins were consuls in her own lifetime.

Caesar's Aunt Julia, Aurelia's sister, was the wife of Gaius Marius, a plebeian from the country who had made the army his career and then, in the decade before the turn of the century, became Rome's most celebrated military hero. Under his command a Roman army defeated two large tribes of invading Germans, the Cimbri and the Teutoni, who had reached the Po river valley, less than three hundred miles from Rome. Despite a law forbidding it, Marius was elected consul four years running, and in 100 BC was serving his sixth term.

During his time in power, Marius reorganized the Roman army and removed the last property requirement for enlistment, thus opening the ranks of the legions to any citizen who wished to volunteer. As the population increased and opportunities for individuals to farm their own land declined, more and more unemployed and landless men were willing to become soldiers in return for wages. But because the Senate made the crucial mistake of refusing to pay for a standing army or to provide for veterans discharged after a campaign or retired after long service, soldiers had to look to their own commanders for their security.[3]

To guarantee the loyalty and effectiveness of his troops, Marius increased their pay and promised free land to those who served until a campaign was completed. Subsequent military commanders took the same course. The natural result of this arrangement was that, upon induction, a soldier swore an oath of allegiance to his general rather than to the Roman government. This became the common practice whenever a new legion was created, ceding independent power to individual generals, and was a crucial factor in the civil war that brought down the Republic some fifty years later.

Although Caesar's father was a senator, the Julii were far from wealthy, and lived in a small house in a crowded and noisy section of the capital. When Caesar was nine, his father was elected a *praetor*, six of whom made up the second rank of magistrates of the Republic; he later served for a year as Governor of the province of Asia.

As was customary for the male children in patrician families, Caesar's parents spared no expense for his education, which was grounded in rhetoric, philosophy and law—most of the texts being Greek, a culture greatly admired by the Romans. One of his tutors was Antonius Gnipho, a Latinized Celt who had studied in Alexandria, and became a celebrated grammarian. The boy displayed an interest in literature, an avocation he never abandoned; but the examples of his father and uncle inevitably led him into politics. At an early age he learned the importance of public opinion and the value of good political connections. Friends of his Uncle Marius arranged for him to be made a priest of the Sacred College of Jupiter at the age of fourteen. When he was fifteen his father died, and the next year he married Cornelia, the daughter of the patrician Cneius Cornelius Cinna, a colleague of Marius and one of the leaders of the *populares.* Within another year Cornelia gave birth to Julia, Caesar's only certain child in a lifetime of sexual promiscuity.

Despite his pardon by the dictator Sulla, Caesar decided that it was time to leave Rome and become a soldier. The son of a senator, he easily obtained appointment as an officer, and was assigned as aide-de-camp to Marcus Thermus, Governor of the province of Asia. An assault on the province by the powerful Mithridates, King of Pontus, another Anatolian kingdom, was the occasion for two incidents that became part of Caesar's legend.

The first occurred just months later, when the Romans laid siege to Mytilene on the island of Lesbos, the last Greek city to support Mithridates. Caesar was dispatched to Bithynia on the southern coast of the Black Sea to persuade King Nicomedes II to make his fleet available for use by Marcus Thermus in the Aegean. In return for the use of the fleet, Nicomedes desired that Caesar share his bed and, reportedly, Caesar complied. Although sexual encounters of this kind were commonplace in the Mediterranean world, the idea of a patrician playing the role of a male prostitute caused a scandal in Rome. This was the only alleged occasion of this sort in Caesar's life, and he always denied it; but the incident dogged him throughout his career and was often alluded to by his enemies. Even in his later eminence, the matter was brought up more than once in the Senate, where he was occasionally referred to as "the Queen of Bithynia."[4]

In the next year, when the siege of Mytilene reached its climax and the Romans stormed the city, Caesar saved the life of a fellow soldier. For this he was decorated with the Civic Crown—a wreath of oak leaves that he was allowed to wear for one day, and thereafter on festive occasions. With the crown came a small badge, like a modern medal, that the recipient could wear permanently as a symbol of his courage. There is ample evidence that Caesar set great store by bravery and competence on the battlefield, and repeatedly demonstrated it himself. Presumably, he wore his decoration at every opportunity.

Meanwhile, Sulla, after two years of absolute rule in Rome, revealed a personality like that of no other dictator. He disbanded his legions, reestablished consular government and abandoned his dictatorship. A lifelong epicurean and art collector, he retired to his villa on the coast to write his memoirs and indulge himself in the pleasures of private life. Although he escaped the violent death of many of his peers, he succumbed only two years later to liver failure brought on by alcoholism.[5]

Caesar hastened back to Rome on the death of Sulla in 78 BC, and was invited by the *populares* to take part in their attempt to return to power. But he was not impressed with their leaders, and declined, the effort eventually failing. He took up the practice of law and, in the course of several highly visible trials, distinguished himself as a formidable advocate and orator. Over the next two decades he earned a reputation as an orator second only to Cicero's. He is said to have delivered his speeches in a high-pitched voice accompanied by impassioned gestures. Unfortunately, none of them has survived. By now he had also demonstrated an athletic gift with a flair for the dramatic. He was known to be a skillful swordsman and so accomplished on horseback that he could ride without a saddle at full gallop with his hands behind his back.

In 75 BC Caesar traveled to the Greek island of Rhodes to study oratory under Apollonius Molon, earlier the instructor of Cicero, and reputedly the best living exponent of the art. On his way across the Aegean Sea his ship was attacked and boarded by pirates. The story was recounted two centuries later in *The Lives of the Caesars* by the biographer Suetonius:

> Winter had already set in when he sailed for Rhodes and was captured by pirates off the island of Pharmacussa. They kept him prisoner for nearly forty days, to his intense annoyance; he had with him only a physician and two valets, having sent the rest of his staff away to borrow the ransom money. As soon as the stipulated fifty talents arrived (which make 12,000 gold pieces), and the pirates duly set him ashore, he raised a fleet and went after them. He had often smilingly sworn, while still in their power, that he would soon capture and crucify them; and this is exactly what he did.[6]

Caesar proceeded to Rhodes, but soon after arriving learned that King Mithridates had again attacked the Roman province of Asia. Not one to lose a chance for glory on the battlefield, Caesar abandoned his studies and crossed to the mainland to join the Roman defense. Though only a junior officer, he raised an army of volunteers that helped drive out the invaders. When he returned to Rome in 73 BC, he carried with him the aura of a soldier who was also a leader of men. The Assembly voted him the rank of colonel, and the twenty-six-year-old aristocrat plunged into the politics of the disintegrating Republic.

The best surviving physical description of Caesar is also from Suetonius:

> Caesar is said to have been tall, fair, and well-built, with a rather broad face and keen, dark-brown eyes. His health was sound, apart from sudden comas and a tendency to nightmares which troubled him towards the end of his life; but he twice had

epileptic fits while on campaign. He was something of a dandy, always keeping his head carefully trimmed and shaved; and has been accused of having certain other hairy parts of his body depilated with tweezers. His baldness was a disfigurement which his enemies harped upon, much to his exasperation; but he used to comb the thin strands of hair forward from his poll, and of all the honors voted him by the Senate and People, none pleased him so much as the privilege of wearing a laurel wreath on all occasions—he constantly took advantage of it.[7]

Caesar has been rightly called the most compelling personality in Roman history. No other Roman succeeded so thoroughly as both a politician and general, and no one who excelled in those pursuits achieved, as he did, literary immortality. In the way of many accomplished men, he displayed contradictory traits—generosity alternating with cruelty, wild ambition with utter realism, and profligacy with Spartan living.

Fine dining did not interest him and he was never more than a moderate drinker, but in other respects—clothes, money, women—he indulged himself to the fullest. His choice of attire ran from the unorthodox to the flamboyant. In Rome he affected a loose belt around his waist, and fringed sleeves reaching to the wrist; on the battlefield he was usually seen in a bright red cloak. Even before he entered politics and had access to any substantial wealth, he incurred enormous debts to buy the best slaves and collect the most expensive sculpture, carvings and gems. On borrowed money he had a villa built for himself on a lake in the hills south of Rome and, when he found it not entirely to his liking, had it torn down. In the year of his first consulship he presented to his mistress, Servilia, a pearl costing sixty thousand gold pieces, reportedly to atone for his marriage to a much younger woman when Servilia was available.

The mutual attraction between Caesar and women of every sort quickly became notorious. Throughout his life, whether in Rome or abroad, in provincial capitals or on the march, he made time for sexual encounters. The attractive young officer and pleasure-loving aristocrat was a natural magnet for women, and Suetonius describes his affairs as "numerous and extravagant." Nor did he hesitate, apparently without great difficulty, to seduce the wives of his colleagues, even those of his political partners, Pompey and Crassus. His foreign mistresses included Eunoë, a Moorish queen, and, near the end of his life, the most famous of all—the young Queen Cleopatra of Egypt.[8]

Considering his reputation as a rake and a spendthrift, it is not surprising that when he first sought public office Caesar's peers did not take him seriously as a politician.[9] But they were soon confronted with an ambition they had not suspected and, more important, a genius for politics. This included not only skill at public relations and deal-making, but also a capacity for rough tactics. As a well-connected patrician, Caesar easily found support for his first campaign and, in the year after his return from Asia, he won election as one of the twenty-four military tribunes of the Republic. He was elected by the Assembly, the democratic institution established in the early days of the Republic to balance class interests and prevent rule by the privileged few. Despite this professed purpose, however, the Roman political system excluded the great majority of its citizens from participation in the government, and functioned as an oligarchy in all but name.

Membership in the Assembly, and therefore the right to vote, was limited to male citizens over the age of fifteen. Neither slaves nor freed slaves were citizens. The Assembly was organized into thirty-five groups of different sizes based on wealth, and voting was by group rather than by individual. The poorer citizens were crowded into a small number of groups so that the vote of the richest citizens was always the majority. A further requirement for voting was that citizens attend meetings of the Assembly in Rome in person, thus disenfranchising those in outlying areas who could not make the trip to the capital. Moreover, the Roman conduct of government allowed no woman to take part, either as voter or office-holder.[10]

By the first century BC, the original Assembly had been supplemented by two others that were intended to spread voting power more equitably. But they also favored landowners over the landless and the urban poor. The result was that the selection of the two consuls and the remaining magistrates of government was generally in the hands of the nobles and property owners who resided in Rome.

As a military tribune, Caesar was an officer in one of the Senate's legions, and probably took part in the campaign against Spartacus, a former gladiator who raised a rebel army of ninety thousand slaves and renegades, and held out against the government's army for more than two years until his defeat in 70 BC.

In the next year the Assembly elected Caesar as one of the twenty *quaestoris*—administrators who assisted provincial governors with judicial and financial duties. For Caesar, the election was doubly important. All *quaestors* were entitled to membership in the Senate, a privilege they retained, whether in Rome or abroad, for the rest of their lives. In Caesar's time the Senate had become a privileged body of five to six hundred ex-magistrates who were almost all nobles or wealthy landowners—the cream of Roman society. As symbols of their exalted rank they wore red leather shoes and tunics with a broad purple stripe. There had been senators and magistrates in their families for centuries, and nearly every senator walked in his father's and grandfather's footsteps.

It was in the Senate, presided over by a consul, that most new laws and other matters of national interest were customarily brought up and discussed. Once the Senate had agreed on a piece of legislation it was sent to the single Assembly that excluded patricians, the *concilium plebis,* which alone had the authority to approve or veto it. Although the passage of legislation was thus in the hands of an Assembly of the People, it was in the Senate that nearly all legislation was introduced, debated and approved before it was sent to the Assembly. Because of the wealth and influence of its members, and because it controlled the army, the treasury and the conduct of foreign affairs, the Senate, over the last decades of the Republic, gradually came to control the conduct of government.

Caesar's assignment as *quaestor* was to carry out judicial responsibilities for the Governor of Further Spain—the western half of the Iberian Peninsula. But before his term started, at the beginning of 68 BC, Cornelia, not yet thirty and Caesar's wife for more than fifteen years, suddenly died. Despite Caesar's womanizing, it is likely that his marriage to Cornelia was based on genuine affection. Although it was not the custom at funerals of young women, Caesar took the opportunity to deliver a moving tribute to the bride of his adolescence. The public reaction was one of widespread approval and sympathy.

In Further Spain, Caesar carried out his duties for less than a year before traveling to southern Gaul, where the provincial colonists were demanding Roman citizenship. He thought he saw an opportunity to embarrass the ruling *optimates* by organizing an armed revolt, but the Senate responded by sending two legions to the area, and the effort came to nothing. Back in Rome in 67 BC, Caesar married Pompeia, granddaughter of his old enemy Sulla. Despite her antecedents, Pompeia was the right woman at the right time—she possessed great wealth.

Two years later Caesar was elected *curule aedile,* an official responsible for order in the capital, and charged with organizing the public games held on religious holidays. He made the most of this by staging, partially at his own expense, the most lavish and elaborate displays ever seen in the city, including gladiator fights and wild beast hunts. He assembled so many gladiators for one brawl that the Senate became alarmed and passed a law limiting the number of armed men that anyone might bring to Rome.

To finance his expensive style, he made an alliance with Marcus Crassus, reputedly the richest man in Rome, who agreed to guarantee Caesar's debts, and thus became indispensable to his career. In return, Caesar supported Crassus' ambitions for political power, and especially his opposition to Gnaeus Pompeius, today known as Pompey, a successful general who was a dominant figure in the *optimate* party. A remark by Crassus suggests the mix of money, politics and the military that prevailed in Rome in the first century BC: "A man whose income is insufficient to support an army can never become a leading statesman."[11]

A sign of Caesar's growing importance was his election by the Assembly in 63 BC to the lifetime post of *pontifex maximus,* or chief priest, the highest religious office in the Roman state. Building on his already widespread popularity, Caesar clinched the election by bribing large numbers of voters, and was himself the object of an unsuccessful bribe to withdraw his candidacy. A well-known anecdote has it that Caesar told his mother on leaving their home on election day that he would either return as chief priest, or not return at all, having had to flee the city to escape his creditors. Once elected, he took great satisfaction in the prestige and privileges of the office, which allowed him to move into a luxurious official residence and to wear sumptuous robes on public occasions.

Nevertheless, the role of *pontifex maximus* was probably never borne so lightly. In the way of many politicians, Caesar observed the niceties of religion when it suited him; otherwise, in the words of Suetonius, "No regard for religion ever turned him from any undertaking, or even delayed him."[12]

One of the consuls in that same year of 63 BC was a man whose ambition and brilliance equaled those of Caesar, and whose letters, speeches and other writings have illuminated the affairs of the Republic more than any other: Marcus Tullius Cicero. Six years older than Caesar, Cicero was the son of a well-to-do businessman who moved to the capital from a small country town so that his sons, Marcus and Quintus, could receive the best possible education.

The young Marcus took up the practice of law and then spent two years in Athens and Rhodes studying philosophy and rhetoric. By the time he was elected to the office of *quaestor* at the age of thirty he had earned the reputation of a skillful advocate whose oratory was equally persuasive whether he was defending or prosecuting. By hard work and cultivation of influential friends Cicero overcame the tradition that limited political office to men of noble families, and at the age of forty-two was elected consul. It was in the last month of his term, during an emotional debate in the Senate about the fate of five conspirators against the government, that he had occasion to come to the defense of Caesar, whose political ambitions he would alternately support and oppose for the next two decades.

Lucius Catiline, a patrician who had lost the election for consul, organized a group of disaffected senators and noblemen to assassinate Cicero and seize control of the government. After an informant betrayed the plot, five of the conspirators, all prominent men in Roman politics, were arrested while carrying incriminating letters, and then declared guilty by the Senate. In the meantime, Catiline and his supporters had encouraged slave rebellions, and then raised a renegade army in the countryside north of Rome under the banner of agrarian reform and the abolition of all debts. Two days later, tension and fear swept the capital as crowds of citizens pressed against the troops surrounding the Temple of Concord, where the Senate was deciding the conspirators' punishment.

As presiding consul, Cicero called first on one of the next year's consuls, Junius Silanus, who urged the "ultimate penalty." All the following speakers agreed with him until it was the turn of Caesar, who had, a few months before, been elected Governor of Further Spain for the following year. In a short and conciliatory speech Caesar urged the senators to consider the matter carefully and to act without emotion. He argued that the death penalty would alarm the public; it would be taken as a rash act and reflect badly on the Senate. It would not be expedient. Life imprisonment and confiscation of all the conspirators' property would be an even sterner penalty, but would not violate the law that forbade execution of a citizen without a trial. Even Caesar's enemies acknowledged that his gifts as an orator were second only to Cicero's. The finely drawn phrases and reasoned arguments gradually persuaded the hundreds of senators that the course of moderation was best.

The following speakers supported Caesar's proposal, and Junius Silanus returned to the rostra to assert that what he meant by the "ultimate penalty" was life imprisonment. But there was one who was not swayed, one with such a hatred of the free-wheeling Caesar that he opposed him at every chance, no matter what the issue. This was Marcus Porcius Cato, called "the Younger" in deference to his famous great-grandfather of the same name. The younger Cato was distinguished by a long neck, a wedge-shaped head and a reputation for obstinacy that arose from his own rectitude and conservative Stoicism. But it was widely thought that his persistent opposition to Caesar was motivated not so much by his stern moralism as by the fact that his married stepsister, Servilia, was Caesar's most enduring mistress.

Cato lost no time contradicting every phrase in Caesar's argument. The public would not be alarmed if the conspirators were executed. On the contrary, there would be great disappointment if they were spared, and the rebellion would spread. Imprisonment was a sham;

they would be released in a month by some trick vote in the Assembly. In his wrath Cato quickly went beyond the issue and ad hominem, to the man, suggesting that Caesar was part of the plot.

Again the Senate was moved, this time to the opposite position. Cato's last remark was provocative. Caesar must have been party to the conspiracy. Cicero quickly called for a vote, but there was no need to count. The vote seemed to come in one loud shout and was all but unanimous: the prisoners would be executed. Because they had changed their minds twice, the senators were all the more certain. Many of them stood up and began milling around in agitation, staring and pointing at Caesar, waving their fists at him. When he turned to leave his seat, some moved to block his passage, and as he made his way out of the Temple, only a last-second signal from Cicero prevented the consul's bodyguards from attacking him.

On Cicero's order the five conspirators, including Lentulus, an ex-consul, were led out. Within the hour they were taken one by one into the prison opposite the Forum and down into its deepest cell, where each was strangled. The grim deed would later cost him dearly, but for the moment Cicero was hailed as the courageous defender of the Republic.[13]

Within a few weeks the Senate sent a legion against Catiline, and the entire rebel army, including its patrician leader, was annihilated. Caesar absented himself from the Senate for the rest of the month, and prepared to assume the governorship of Further Spain for the year to come, 61 BC. But before leaving for his province he became embroiled in another incident, this time involving his wife, Pompeia.

The annual celebration of the festival of the Bona Dea, the women's goddess, was held at the end of the year in the home of Caesar, the chief priest, with his wife presiding. Although only women were permitted to attend, a young nobleman, Publius Clodius Pulcher ("the Handsome"), contrived to enter the house disguised as a woman. He was discovered and then escaped, but the sacrilege was quickly known throughout the city, and he was accused of seducing Pompeia.

When the story reached Caesar he promptly sent a declaration of divorce to Pompeia by messenger. Clodius was arrested and tried for immoral conduct, but Caesar made no formal charge against him, and he was acquitted. When Caesar was later asked why he had divorced his wife, he made the notorious remark that Caesar's wife must be above suspicion.

Caesar's departure for Spain was further complicated by the enormous debts he had incurred during several years of expensive politicking. His creditors demanded repayment before he took office as governor and became immune from a suit for indebtedness. Again, Crassus guaranteed a large part of what was owed, and bound Caesar even more strongly to him.

As Governor of Further Spain, Caesar had his first military command and his first chance to display his flair for tactics on the battlefield. More than that, it was an opportunity to keep his name before the voters in preparation for his campaign for consul in the following year. He immediately increased the size of his army by half and moved quickly against bandits harassing a region just outside the border of the province. When some of them fled to an island off the western coast, he put his army on boats, landed on the island and captured them. Afterwards, he sailed to the northwest corner of the Peninsula and crushed a rebellion in the city of Brigantium, eventually pacifying the entire region of Lusitania, today Portugal.

Several ancient historians record an incident in Spain that illustrates Caesar's growing ambitions. Coming upon a statue of Alexander the Great in Gades, modern Cádiz, the almost forty-year-old Caesar is said to have sighed impatiently and remarked that he had accomplished nothing noteworthy so far in his life, but at a lesser age Alexander had already conquered the world.[14]

Warring in Spain produced considerable plunder for Caesar, and he was accused in the Senate of even sacking cities that offered him no resistance. Still, after helping himself to enough to repay his debts, he saw to it that his soldiers shared in the spoils, and then sent large sums to the treasury in Rome. Along with the booty went his dispatches to the Senate describing his successes over rebels and criminals, as well as the glorious deeds of the Roman troops. Dominated by Caesar's supporters, the Senate voted him a formal *triumphus,* or triumph.

The triumph was an honor granted to a victorious general that allowed him to enter Rome in a chariot and parade through the city to the Capitoline Hill accompanied by his soldiers, his prisoners and samples of his booty. The *triumphator* wore a wreath and triumphal dress; his face was painted red and he carried a scepter. The ceremony was followed by public celebrations for the number of days the Senate decreed.[15]

Although Spain was paying his debts, Caesar hurried back to Rome in June of 60 BC to claim his political reward even before his two-year term as governor was over. A long-standing law required candidates for the consulship to appear in Rome in person. But another law obliged a returning general to wait outside the city until his formal triumph was arranged. Because election day had already been announced and there was no time to hold the triumph prior to it, Caesar was faced with the choice of either standing for consul or celebrating his triumph. He tried to persuade the Senate to change the law, but was thwarted, largely because of a filibuster by his tireless enemy Cato the Younger. Finally Caesar gave in, waiving his triumph, and entered the city to declare his candidacy.

Although he had a substantial following, Caesar realized he could not win unless he spent generously among the voters. Forming an alliance with another candidate, Lucius Lucceius, a wealthy friend of the popular Pompey, the two of them campaigned together, using Lucceius' money for extravagant bribes. This tactic was only partially successful: Caesar was elected as one of the consuls, but those opposing him were able to elect one of his enemies, Marcus Bibulus, as the other.

Even as co-consul, however, Caesar could not be assured of the complete power he wanted without substantial support in the Senate and the money to buy the votes of the Assembly. He now made one of the imaginative moves that distinguished him as the most astute politician of his time. He approached the two most powerful men in Rome, Crassus and Pompey, and proposed that they join with him in a secret alliance—a pact that would give each of them an immediate benefit and make all three invulnerable to any political or military opposition for years to come.

Marcus Crassus, fifteen years older than Caesar and the son of a consul, had made a fortune in real estate by buying up the properties of nobles murdered by the dictator Sulla twenty years earlier. After leading the Senate's legions in the defeat of Spartacus in 72 BC, he shared an uneasy consulship with Pompey two years later. Jealous of Pompey's popularity, he had since then been trying to buy his way to a position of equal influence.

Pompey, also the son of a consul and a partisan of Sulla, had become a popular hero, and had amassed his own fortune with a series of extraordinary military campaigns in Spain, Africa and the eastern provinces. When he returned triumphant from Africa in 81 BC, he was hailed by Sulla as "Pompeius Magnus" in a clear reference to Alexander the Great, and he later adopted the surname permanently. The dictator allowed the general, then only twenty-four, to celebrate a triumph, the first ever for a general whose family was of the middle class. Pompey's ambition and popularity repeatedly tempted him to use his legions to seize control of the government; but so long as there was the slightest chance of failure he would not take the risk.

Caesar's proposal was this: as consul, he would see to it that legislation favorable to his partners' interests was passed—for Pompey, a land grant to accommodate his veterans, and for Crassus, a revision of tax collection laws. In return they would support his own program with money, votes and influence. Caesar had become such an effective politician that Crassus and Pompey knew their ambitions would go unrealized without his support. They also knew, according to Suetonius, that Caesar had already seduced their wives, and Pompey had divorced Mutia for that very reason. Nonetheless, they agreed to his scheme, with the understanding that none of them would take any political action that did not suit each of the others.

With this deft maneuver Caesar formed the so-called "First Triumvirate," a nearly impregnable alliance that stifled opposition and guaranteed him a free hand, provided only that he first convince his two partners. The Triumvirate set the course of Roman politics for the next decade, until a collision between Pompey's jealousy and Caesar's ambition brought down first the one, then the other, and finally the Republic itself.

Taking office as consul in January of 59 BC, Caesar attempted to assure the Senate that he would act legally and only for the benefit of the State. As evidence of his good faith, and at the same time hoping to embarrass his opponents, he ordered all transactions of the Assembly and Senate to be written down and published, the first time in Rome's history that this was made a routine practice. But when he introduced his legislation to distribute public land to Pompey's veterans, his old antagonist Cato attempted to kill the measure with a personal fili-buster. Caesar immediately ordered him arrested by the Senate's offi-cers and taken to prison. Cato continued to speak as he was being hus-tled out, and most of the senators rose to accompany him. In a rage, Caesar shouted at one and demanded to know why he was leaving; the senator replied that he preferred Cato's company in prison to Caesar's in the Senate. Caesar was shamed into halting the arrest and adjourn-ing the Senate.[16]

Taking advantage of a little-used legal procedure, Caesar then introduced the bill in the Assembly, which had the authority to enact it without the Senate's concurrence. But when his co-Consul, Marcus Bibulus, attempted to veto it, Caesar's henchmen emptied a basket of dung over his head, beat up his escorts and then had the bill's oppo-nents dragged out of the building. With Pompey's soldiers in evidence all around the Forum, the Assembly enacted the law providing them with land. Using the same strong-arm tactics, Caesar kept his agree-ment with Crassus by pushing through the tax collection law, a law from which he, too, profited. Then, to strengthen his alliance with Pompey, Caesar altered his will to make him his heir and, further, gave his seventeen-year-old daughter, Julia, to him in marriage, even though she was engaged at the time.

Although the Triumvirate was successful with these and other mea-sures, the opposition continued to resist them, and the Senate was often the scene of filibustering, flying debris, physical threats, expul-sions and arrests. Marcus Bibulus tried by every means to halt or obstruct the barrage of legislation favoring Caesar and his partners, but he was outnumbered and outspent. After a few months he withdrew to his home and refused to appear in the Senate for the rest of the year. Cicero simply left Rome. Caesar exercised such authority that a remark commonly heard was that the year's two consuls were Julius and

Caesar. Another saying, referring to the rumors about Caesar and King Nicomedes, was that Pompey was the King of Rome and Caesar the Queen.

When the truth of the secret alliance became known and its actual impact could be fully seen, there was great resentment and anger, not only among the *optimates*, but throughout the capital. In a letter to his friend Atticus, Cicero railed against the *tres homines* and complained that "the present regime is the most scandalous in history, the most disgraceful and universally hated by all sorts, classes, and ages of man. . . . The *populares* have taught even sober citizens to hiss."[17] The "three-headed monster," as it was called in pamphlets circulated among the senators, had the effect of restricting to only three men the decisions of a government that still claimed to be representative.

Caesar's tactics were clearly illegal, but the strength of the Triumvirate was enough to prevent the opposition from stopping him. As consul he was legally immune from prosecution, even if the votes could be found to convict him. Only after his one-year term ended could he be brought to trial and, to forestall this, he laid the groundwork for his appointment as a provincial governor at the end of his consular year. In such a position he could not be prosecuted until he returned to Rome as a private citizen.

He now nominated two of his allies for consulships in the following year, and married Calpurnia, the eighteen-year-old daughter of one of them. Another of his supporters, Vatinius, successfully carried a bill in the Assembly that gave Caesar, immediately, the governorships of both Illyricum (Dalmatia) and Nearer Gaul, or *Gallia Togata* ("Toga-wearing Gaul"), in northern Italy, for five years. With the office came the control of three legions of infantry—perhaps fifteen thousand men—and the right to found colonies and appoint his own generals. This gave Caesar control of the two provinces closest to Rome, and a substantial army to do with what he pleased.

Events in Further Gaul, Rome's province on the French side of the Alps, soon gave Caesar a chance to take more territory under his control. In the previous year, news had reached Rome that the Helvetii, a large Celtic tribe occupying the area of modern-day Switzerland, had made known their intention to abandon their homeland because of increasing harassment by German tribes on their northern border. They and several smaller tribes planned to migrate across Roman territory and into western Gaul. The memory of waves of barbarism— *"barbariae fluctibus,"* in the words of Cicero[18]—from the north just forty years earlier persisted in the minds of many Romans, and the Senate voted to allow the Governor of Further Gaul to recruit additional troops. Then, in early April of 59 BC, this governor, Metellus Celer, suddenly died, and Pompey proposed that the Senate add this territory and an extra legion to Caesar's command. The supporters of the Triumvirate bulldozed the senators into granting him the additional province, but for only one year. Thus, almost by accident, the last piece of Rome's northern frontier fell into Caesar's hands.

In the autumn of Caesar's year in office his two nominees were elected consuls for the following year. When his own term ended in December, his opponents immediately sought to declare invalid all his acts as consul and to prosecute him for treason. Caesar participated briefly in the debate, but even before it ended in his favor he prudently moved beyond the city limits, thus legally assuming his new office, and ensuring his immunity from criminal charges.

For fifteen years he had devoted his enormous energy and talents to the primary tasks of the politician: raising money and running for office. Using every tactic but outright murder, he had put himself among the most powerful men in Rome, and forged a coalition like none ever seen before. To preserve it he had spent his year as consul securing his future and placing his allies where they could protect him. He was to spend the next nine years with his legions in Gaul battling the Celts—still the most formidable politician in the Republic, but a virtual exile from Rome.

CHAPTER II

⟨꙰⟩ · ⟨꙰⟩

THE CELTS IN EUROPE

Quintus Sulpicius stood in the middle of the square, watching grimly as his men struggled to lift the heavy ingots of gold and bags of jewelry onto the primitive scale. Surrounding him were hundreds of vicious-looking light-skinned men, all brandishing swords and daggers, and dressed in outlandish costumes, some in *bracae*—strange garments that enclosed each leg separately. Beyond the circle of ruffians stretched the remains of the burned and devastated capital: skeletons of buildings surrounded by piles of smoldering debris, and everywhere the stench of death. In front of him stood the barbarian chieftain Brennus, a huge, red-eyed creature wrapped in a dirty woolen cloak, haranguing him in a barking staccato language that his interpreter only haltingly translated.

When the Roman tribune saw that the scale had not moved, he pointed to it and protested that the counterweight was incorrect. As soon as this complaint was translated, Brennus shouted an oath to the crowd and hurled his sword onto the scale with a great flourish. The mob roared its approval and repeated the words again and again to the banging and clanking of weapons. The interpreter hesitated briefly, and then in a low voice uttered them in Latin: "*Vae victis*"—"Woe to the vanquished."

Sulpicius clamped his jaws together and said nothing. There was nothing he could say, or do. Those Romans who had not fled, starved to death or been slaughtered were barricaded in the citadel on the Capitoline Hill behind him, along with what was left of the Roman army. For weeks they had cowered in their stronghold, gradually consuming all the food they had brought with them, while the barbarian army rampaged through the city, pillaging, destroying and burning. It was not until they too had used up every scrap of food that they had agreed to lift their siege and depart. But there was another price to be paid: a thousand pounds of gold.

The tale is told by Titus Livius, the Roman historian of the first century BC, and the personal details may be his invention.[1] Although there is no archaeological evidence of the destruction of the city, the literary evidence leaves no doubt that marauding Celts overran Rome in about the year 386 BC. It would be another eight hundred years before an enemy army again entered the capital, but this painful and humiliating calamity lingered in Roman memories for centuries. It was inflicted by a people they called Celtae or Galli; the Greeks called them Keltoi or Galatae; they both called them barbarians.

The people we today call Celts were one of several great prehistoric societies that flourished on the European continent during the first millennium before Christ. Together with the Dacians, Illyrians and Thracians, they pressed on the northern frontiers of the more advanced societies that developed first in Greece and then in Rome. Traditional theory holds that ancestors of the Celts accompanied the Italic ancestors of the Romans in the westward migration of Indo-European peoples from the steppes of Eurasia in the third millennium BC. Archaeologist Colin Renfrew and others have asserted recently that this migration originated in Anatolia and took place with the spread of farming, far earlier, in about 6500 BC.[2]

Although the date remains in dispute, it is agreed that when they arrived in Europe the forebears of the Celts settled in an area extending southeast and east from what is now France through modern Switzerland, Bavaria, Austria and the upper Danube Valley. In this region rose the continent's three great rivers: the Rhône, the Rhine and the Danube, the last two of which still bear Celtic names.

In the late 1840s, excavations on a slope above the village of Hallstatt in the Austrian Alps revealed that an aristocratic iron-using people had flourished there in the decades before 700 BC. This Hallstatt culture, as it came to be called, quickly spread to the north and west, and reached as far as Britain, Ireland and Spain during the following century. Several decades after the discoveries at Hallstatt, archaeologists in France and Switzerland found evidence that a second and more sophisticated iron-using culture had arisen in the fifth century BC in the area between the Middle Rhine and the Seine. They called it the La Tène culture, after the site in Switzerland where it was first uncovered, and it too spread—both west and east—over the next few centuries. The Hallstatt and La Tène cultures are both attributed to the Celts on the basis of ethnographic evidence and the literary testimonies of classical writers.

The first references to Celts occur in the works of the Greek historians Hecataeus and Herodotus in the sixth and fifth centuries BC, where they are described as fierce warriors who fought with a seeming disregard for their own lives. In the *Nicomachaean Ethics*, Aristotle wrote, "Anybody would be mad or completely bereft of sensibility if he feared nothing; neither earthquake nor wave of the sea, as they say of the Celts."[3]

Despite a deserved reputation for volatility and aggressiveness, the Celts were also skilled artisans and enterprising farmers. They were especially adept at smelting and forging iron; at the major ironworking site of Manching, near present-day Ingolstadt in Bavaria, archaeologists have identified some two hundred different types of iron implements, including chisels, needles, keys and surgical instruments.[4] The Celts also produced superbly crafted artifacts of stunning beauty in gold, silver and bronze. They started settlements throughout Europe based on agriculture and stockraising, and developed advanced farming implements such as the plow, the harrow and even a reaper. The Celts were also traders, and from the earliest days they bartered their cattle and hides, as well as commodities from the earth—gold, silver, lead, iron and salt—to the Romans and Etruscans for such items as fine pottery and luxury goods, particularly wine.

Neither a race nor a nation, the Celts were a broad ethnic group whose dozens of tribes shared a common culture and spoke closely related dialects of a single language. But throughout their long history they maintained their tribal separateness, and never developed a central government or anything resembling an empire.

In about 400 BC, several Celtic tribes pushed through the Alpine passes at the southern edge of their territory and invaded northern

Italy. Ancient historians say they were attracted by the wines and fruit, such as figs and grapes, introduced to them by Roman and Etruscan traders.[5] It is also likely that because of increasing population they were covetous of the fertile lands of the Po Valley. Over the next several decades they overran the city-states of the Etruscans and founded their own colonies throughout the region, notably on the sites that later became Milan, Turin and Bergamo.

In 386 BC it was a tribe called the Senones that fought its way to Rome, which they besieged for several months, sacking and burning most of it before they were paid a large ransom of gold to depart. Several tribes continued down the Apennine Peninsula, establishing colonies as far south as Apulia and Sicily. Their roving armies remained a threat for nearly another century and a half, until the Romans subdued them everywhere south of the Po and absorbed them into their own expanding state.

Alexander the Great received a deputation of Celts in what is modern Bulgaria in 335 BC, and fifty years after his death they reached the Black Sea and entered Greece. They attacked the sacred Temple of Apollo at Delphi in 278 BC, but were repulsed. In the same decade three Celtic tribes made their way into Asia Minor, where they founded the kingdom of Galatia in what is now central Turkey. More than three centuries later, Saint Paul addressed one of his epistles to the "foolish Galatians."

At the time of their greatest expansion, during the third century BC, Celtic tribes occupied over 800,000 square miles of the European continent, from Ireland and Scotland to the mouth of the Danube on the Black Sea. But within a few decades the Romans began a steady incursion into their territory, and over the next four hundred years gradually reduced all but a few outlying tribes to the status of Roman subjects.

In 225 BC, two Roman armies trapped and decisively defeated a tribal coalition of seventy thousand Celtic warriors at Telamon, an Estruscan town on the northwestern coast of Italy. The account of this battle by the Greek historian Polybius contains the earliest-surviving description of Celtic appearance and dress. The men of the local tribes, he wrote, wore light cloaks, and trousers that he calls *bracae*—from which the word "breeches" derives. The Gaesatae, a group of mercenaries brought in from beyond the Alps, fought naked in the forefront of the battle line, adorned only with gold armlets and gold torques around their necks.

Polybius also mentions the Celtic tactic of noisemaking on the battlefield to frighten the enemy: "There were countless horns and trumpets being blown simultaneously in their ranks, and as the whole army was also shouting its war-cries, there arose such a babel of sound that it seemed to come not only from the trumpets and the soldiers but from the whole surrounding countryside at once."[6]

Large numbers of Celts joined the army of the Carthaginian general Hannibal when he marched through the south of Gaul on his way to Italy during the Second Punic War. But his withdrawal in 203 BC only left them more vulnerable to Rome's increasing power. In 192 BC, the Romans overwhelmed the Boii tribe at their stronghold, today's Bologna, and finally took control of all of northern Italy, which they called "Nearer Gaul." During the first century BC, incursions by German tribes from across the Rhine and Iberian peoples over the Pyrenees gradually pushed the Celts into the corner of Europe known as Gaul.

The Gaul of Caesar's time, which he describes in the opening words of *The Gallic War*, was indeed divided into three parts. He distinguishes the Gauls occupying the central part of modern France from the Belgae in the northeast, and the Aquitani in the southwest. The Gauls were Celts, the Aquitani were Iberians, and the Belgae were probably a mixture of Celts and Germans. Caesar considered the Celts and Germans two distinct peoples, describing the Germans as more warlike, uninterested in agriculture, and worshiping only gods "that they can see," such as the sun, the moon and fire. But some scholars maintain that the difference was one of degree only, the Celts being more culturally advanced than the Germans.

What Caesar called Gaul was about 15 percent larger than the France of today, and the most reliable estimate of its population is about nine million people.[7] Besides the accounts of classical writers, our knowledge of the Celts and their society comes from archaeology and from certain legal documents and hero-tales that were preserved orally for hundreds of years, and then set down in Ireland in the sixth and seventh centuries after Christ.

The Stoic philosopher and historian Posidonius, a native of Syria, traveled throughout the Mediterranean, and visited Gaul about fifty years before Caesar. His account of the Celts, although now lost, survives in part in the works of the Greek writers Diodorus Siculus and Strabo, among others. In *The Gallic War,* Caesar drew on Posidonius and added observations of his own. The archaeological evidence derives primarily from graves and artifacts, and is supplemented by the results of linguistic analysis. The material from the Irish texts is the only description of Celtic society articulated by the Celts themselves.

Diodorus Siculus, a Greek from Sicily who traveled widely in Europe and Asia in the first century BC, tells us that the Gauls were ". . . tall in stature and their flesh is very moist and white, while their hair is not only naturally blond, but they use artificial means to increase this natural quality of color. . . . Some shave off the beard, while others cultivate a short beard; the nobles let the moustache grow freely so that it covers the mouth."[8] He adds that "the Gauls are terrifying in appearance, with deep- sounding and very harsh voices."

Several writers have noted that in preparing for battle the Celts often coated their hair with clay and lime and combed it into stiff spikes to emphasize their fearsome looks. But once off the battlefield they were preoccupied with the idea of physical beauty and took great pains with their appearance. Both sexes were exceedingly conscious of their hair and wore it long and in plaits. Furthermore, it was considered a disgrace to become fat, and young men might be fined if their waistlines exceeded a certain limit.

Athenaeus, a fourth-century Greek writer, quotes Posidonius on their eating habits:

> The Celts sit on dried grass and have their meals served up on wooden tables raised slightly above the earth. Their food consists of a small number of loaves of bread together with a large amount of meat, either boiled or roasted on charcoal or on spits. They partake of this in a cleanly but leonine fashion, raising up whole limbs in

both hands and biting off the meat, while any part which is hard to tear off they cut through with a small dagger which hangs attached to their sword-sheath in its own scabbard. Those who live beside the rivers or near the Mediterranean or Atlantic eat fish in addition, baked fish, that is, with the addition of vinegar and cumin. They also use cumin in their drinks. They do not use olive oil because of its scarcity, and because of its unfamiliarity it appears unpleasant to them. When a large number dine together they sit around in a circle with the most influential man in the center, like the leader of a chorus, whether he surpass the others in warlike skill, or nobility of family, or wealth. Beside him sits the host and next on either side the others in order of distinction. Their shieldsmen stand behind them while their spearsmen are seated in a circle on the opposite side and feast in common like their lords. . . . The drink of the wealthy classes is wine imported from Italy or from the territory of Marseilles. This is unadulterated, but sometimes a little water is added. The lower classes drink wheaten beer prepared with honey, but most people drink it plain. It is called corma. They use a common cup, drinking a little at a time, not more than a mouthful, but they do it rather frequently.[9]

Many ancient writers remarked on the Celts' fondness for alcohol. They considered them naïve because they drank wine without mixing it with water as the Greeks and Romans did. The wine of ancient times was a thick liquid, often filled with impurities. In another passage in his *World History,* Diodorus Siculus writes:

The Gauls are exceedingly fond of wine and sate themselves with the unmixed wine imported by merchants; their desire makes them drink it greedily and when they become drunk they fall into a stupor or a madness. And therefore many Italian merchants with their customary greed look on the Gallic love of wine as their own godsend. They transport the wine by boat on the navigable rivers and by wagon through the plains and receive in return for it an incredibly large price: for one amphora of wine they receive in return a slave, a servant in exchange for a drink.[10]

From these and other comments, it is clear that the introduction of wine had a significant impact on Celtic society, and both Caesar and his contemporary, Strabo, the Greek geographer, record instances of individual tribes banning its use. One beneficial result of the Celts' fondness for wine was their invention of the wooden wine cask, a convenient substitute for the amphora.

The ordinary clothing of a Celtic man consisted of close-fitting trousers, often in a plaid or checkered pattern, a dyed or embroidered long-sleeved tunic of linen, and a cloak fastened by a safety-pin brooch of bronze. Women wore longer tunics pulled in at the waist, perhaps with a gold- or silver-decorated belt. The Celts were accomplished sheep herders and weavers, and both sexes wore long woolen cloaks that might also be colored with dye. Their custom of wearing trousers, which the Romans found strange, may have come from contact with the horse-riding Thracians and Cimmerians on their eastern frontiers.

The Celts were much attached to ornament. Men and women who could afford them wore splendid gold and silver bracelets, and rings on their fingers. The men wore neck-rings or torques of gold, silver or bronze. Leather shoes and sandals were common, and sometimes linen shoes with soles of leather. Headgear was not popular because of their preoccupation with their coiffures.

The position of Celtic women in their society was of great interest to the Romans because they appeared to have equal status with men, which Roman women did not. Some tribes were headed by women, the most noteworthy being Boadicea, who led her Iceni tribe in a bloody revolt against the Romans in Britain in AD 60. There is evidence that the Celts were the first people in Europe to manufacture soap, and that Celtic women used tweezers and makeup. The Roman poet Propertius is said to have chided his mistress for "making up like a Celt." One writer claimed that Celtic women were the equal of their husbands in both size and strength, and added that ". . . although their wives are beautiful, they pay very little attention to them, but rather have a strange passion for the embraces of males."[11]

As did many preliterate peoples, the Celts placed great importance on memorization and speaking ability. In order to preserve and transmit their knowledge and traditions, they reduced them to forms that were easily recalled, such as poetry or repetitive sequences. Because they depended on the spoken word, they cultivated eloquence and artistry in speaking—traits that have persisted among their descendants. Their distinctive habits of speech were noted by more than one observer. Diodorus Siculus reported: "In conversation they use few words and speak in riddles, for the most part hinting at things and leaving a great deal to be understood. They frequently exaggerate with the aim of extolling themselves and diminishing the status of others. They are boasters and threateners and given to bombastic self-dramatization, and yet they are quick of mind and with good natural ability for learning."[12]

Celtic society, in the words of one modern scholar, was "tribal, rural, hierarchical and familiar."[13] It was grounded on relationships of family, clan and tribe, and on obligations based on economic needs and personal loyalties. The common political unit was the tribe, which could be as small as a few thousand people or as large as several hundred thousand. The tribe settled, farmed and defended a specific geographical area. Kingship was the oldest and most customary form of governance of the tribe, the king being elected from among the young males of the previous king's extended family. However, as Caesar notes, many of the tribes in and near the Roman provinces had abandoned kingship in favor of a *vergobret*, an annually appointed or elected magistrate who ruled in conjunction with the aristocracy. Sometimes a separate leader was selected for a particular military campaign. Surrounding the king or *vergobret* were the nobles, a warrior aristocracy that Caesar calls *equites*, or knights. A noble often had clients or retainers who volunteered him allegiance in return for support and protection. The Druids, a combination of seer, scholar and priest, were recruited from the noble class.

Besides the nobles and Druids, Caesar observed only one other class—the *plebs*, or common people—most of whom he describes as "crushed by debt or heavy taxes or the oppression of more powerful men" (VI, 13). However, it is certain that Celtic society was more complex than this, and that several social levels based on wealth or skill were ranked below the nobles. The range of professions included farmers, shepherds, doctors, artists, bards, public workers, craftsmen and merchants. Most land was the common property of the tribe and what was privately held was taxed. Farmworkers, servants and herdsmen were hired by those who could afford them. The lowest class—outcasts, bankrupts and law-breakers—was only one step removed from slavery, a practice that was not customary among the Celts. Although the Celts conducted a considerable slave trade with the Romans, they were not guilty of the organized and pervasive slavery on which Roman society was based.

Of prime importance to the Celts, and especially to the warrior aristocracy, was the horse. Probably first domesticated on the steppes of southern Russia, the horse was already in use in Europe when the Celts arrived, and it gradually became central to their society. Every form of Celtic art depicts the horse and its symbols, and the stylized image of a horse became a favorite design when the first Celtic coins were struck. Throughout the ancient world the Celts were known as expert horsemen, and particularly as fierce cavalrymen. Greeks, Romans and Carthaginians recruited Celtic cavalry as mercenaries, and Strabo wrote that the best of the Roman cavalry were Celts. The Greek historian Xenophon mentioned javelin-carrying Celtic cavalry in his description of the defeat of Sparta by Thebes in the fourth century BC.[14] When Caesar arrived in Gaul, he quickly recognized the value of Gallic horsemen, and used them throughout his campaigns.

The horse indeed had a role in every part of Celtic life, from the farm to the battlefield, and even to the grave. For the warrior, the horse was not only his transportation and his means of fighting, but also a symbol of his wealth and status. The remains of horse trappings of every kind, with the exception of stirrups, have been found in the tombs of Celtic nobles, including bridle bits, armor, spurs, rein-rings and harness fittings, many decorated with red, yellow and blue enamel. It is almost certain that the Celts introduced a primitive saddle to Europe and possibly the horseshoe, both later adopted by the Romans. Stirrups were invented in the Far East and not used in the West until the seventh century after Christ.

It is likely that the Celts or their ancestors also introduced the wheeled vehicle to Europe. In addition to horse trappings, many of the early Celtic tombs contained the remains of heavy four-wheeled ceremonial carts or carriages that later evolved into the light two-wheeled chariots used expertly by the Celts on the battlefield. Linguistic evidence indicates that the Romans also borrowed the chariot from the Celts; the Latin words for wheeled vehicles, *carrum* and *carrus*, were of Celtic origin, and are the roots of the English "car," "cart," "chariot" and "carriage."

The war chariots of the Celts had spoked wooden wheels with iron treads and were pulled by two small horses linked by a yoke to a wooden pole. Each chariot carried a warrior and a charioteer, who rode into battle together, the warrior hurling his spear from the chariot and then dismounting to fight with his sword and dagger. The charioteer would remain in the rear until the warrior was ready to be carried again.

The nature of the Celtic religion has been the subject of extensive speculation by both ancient and modern writers. The archaeological record sheds little light on the matter; the main evidence is literary, and is found in passages from more than a dozen classical writers beginning as early as the second century BC.

The religion of the Celts was based on the worship and appeasement of a great variety of gods and goddesses who influenced all aspects of their lives. The Celtic pantheon comprised a kind of family of supernatural beings who controlled such matters as war, agriculture, the weather and the household. The names of more than four hundred deities have been identified, although only a quarter of them occur more than once, suggesting that the majority were local or tribal. Caesar reports that the Celts worshiped Mercury above all, and also Apollo, Mars, Jupiter and Minerva, but it is clear that he was merely substituting the names of Roman gods for those of the Celts.

In contrast to the Greeks and Romans, the Celts believed strongly in the reincarnation of the soul in another body or, in effect, another life after death. So strong was this conviction that they were known to throw letters on funeral pyres so that the deceased might deliver them to those already dead, and they sometimes made loans of money that were to be repaid in the next life. This belief must have contributed to their widespread reputation for reckless bravery in battle and apparent disregard for human life.

An important aspect of the religion of the Celts, and permeating their entire culture, was their attitude toward the human head. They believed that the head was the seat of the soul and possessed special properties that could avert evil and foretell the future. The head is a recurring theme in most forms of Celtic art, and there is substantial evidence, both archaeological and literary, for their use of skulls in religious ceremonies.

As did many prehistoric peoples, the Celts cut off and preserved the heads of their enemies. They believed that by possessing a person's head they controlled his spirit in the afterlife. According to Diodorus Siculus:

> They cut off the heads of enemies slain in battle and attach them to the necks of their horses. . . . They embalm in cedar oil the heads of the most distinguished enemies, and preserve them carefully in a chest, and display them with pride to strangers, saying that for this head one of their ancestors, or his father, or the man himself, refused the offer of a large sum of money.[15]

A warrior's collection of severed heads not only proved his skill in battle, but protected him and his household from evil, and ensured good luck and success.

To classical observers the most striking phenomenon of Celtic society was a distinct category of priests known as Druids. Again, there is virtually no archaeological evidence for Druids or Druidism; what is known is derived from literary sources. Although Druidism was known to the classical world as early as the third century BC, and the first recorded contact with Druids was by Posidonius, it is Caesar's account of them that is the most extensive and authoritative. He describes them as custodians and arbiters of spiritual matters as well as judges in earthly disputes. Other writers call them prophets, healers and magicians.

In their priestly function the Druids were intermediaries between the people and the gods. They conducted religious rites and ceremonies, and controlled the sacrifices, human and otherwise, the Celts continually made to learn the future and secure divine approval and success. As natural philosophers, in Caesar's words, they held ". . . long discussions about the heavenly bodies and their movements, about the size of the universe and the earth, about the nature of the physical world" (VI, 14).

It was also the responsibility of the Druids to commit to memory the collective knowledge and learning of their society, and transmit it to students who came to them for this purpose. Caesar explained this as a function of a Druidic monopoly: "They do not think it right to commit their teachings to writing. . . . I suppose this practice began originally for two reasons: they did not want their doctrines to be accessible to the ordinary people, and they did not want their pupils to rely on the written word and so neglect to train their memories" (VI, 14).

Another earthly duty of the Druids was arbitration of disputes:

> If a crime is committed, if there is a murder, or if there is a dispute about an inheritance or a boundary, they are the ones who give a verdict and decide on the punishment or compensation appropriate in each case. Any individual or community not abiding by their verdict is banned from the sacrifices, and this is regarded among the Gauls as the most severe punishment. Those who are banned in this way are reckoned as sacrilegious criminals. Everyone shuns them; no one will go near or speak to them for fear of being contaminated in some way (VI, 13).

The name "Druid" is thought to come from the Greek word *drus*, or oak tree, which refers to the reported use of oak groves as religious sanctuaries throughout the Celtic world. The second syllable may be related to the Indo-European root word *wid*, "to know."[16] It appears that Druid priests were allowed to marry and raise families, but they lived in sheltered retreats away from ordinary people and were exempt from taxation and military service. According to Caesar, they all congregated on a fixed date each year in the vicinity of what is today Orléans, an area that was supposed to be the center of the country, where they passed judgment on disputes brought to them from all over Gaul. References to Druids are exclusively to men, and it is not clear that women were allowed to become Druids.

It is likely that Caesar exaggerated the power and unity of the Druids, and that by the time he encountered them in Gaul they no longer wielded the political influence they had in previous centuries. After describing them in several short paragraphs in Book VI of *The Gallic War*, he never mentions them again. The invasions of the Cimbri and the Teutoni, and indeed the Roman incursion into southern Gaul may have tended to consolidate more authority in the tribal *vergobrets*, and thus diminished the secular role of the Druids.

The function of the Druids that attracted the most attention of the ancient writers was their supervision of human sacrifices. Ritual killing was apparently widespread among the Celts, and seems to have been carried out both to appease the gods and to prophesy the future. Diodorus Siculus wrote: ". . . they devote to death a human being and stab him with a dagger in the region above the diaphragm, and when he has fallen they foretell the future from his fall and from the convulsions of his limbs and, moreover, from the spurting of the blood, placing their trust in some ancient and long-continued observation of these practices."[17]

Both Caesar and Strabo describe the case of a huge wickerwork shaped like a man, that was of such a size that cattle, wild animals and human beings were thrown into its hollow limbs and the entire structure then burned to the ground. According to Stuart Piggott, the foremost authority on the Druids, this bizarre rite remains "unexplained and unparalleled."[18]

Caesar also tells us that the Celtic gods delighted ". . . more in the slaughter of those taken in theft or brigandage or some crime, but when the supply of that kind runs short they descend even to the sacrifice of the innocent."[19] Caesar and other Roman writers made much of the Celtic customs of headhunting and human sacrifice, but their own society was only one step removed from such practices. The Romans were no less cruel and superstitious than the Celts, but limited their sacrificial killing to animals. Even so, human sacrifices were not formally outlawed by the Senate until the first century BC, and the heads of defeated enemies were presented to the Emperor Trajan as late as the second century of the Christian era. One other phenomenon of Celtic culture, however, had no counterpart among the Romans: at least four classical writers say that the Celts consumed the flesh or blood of their dead captives and sacrificial victims.[20]

The Druids also functioned as astronomers, and were responsible for the maintenance of the calendar. As an agricultural society and prone to superstition, the Celts were particularly attentive to the seasons of the year and the best times to undertake certain activities. Religious rituals, celebrations and even war-making were all governed by the calendar.

The Celtic calendar divided the year into lunar months and counted time by nights instead of days, a custom that survives in the use of the fortnight in England and France. One half of the month was "bright"—when the moon grew larger; and the other "dark"—when it waned. The months were of thirty and twenty-nine days, the former being considered auspicious, and the latter not; particular days in each month were also considered lucky. The year was also divided into a dark and light half. The dark half, and the new year, began with the festival of Samain on November 1st, and the light half with Beltine, celebrated on the first of May.

Evidence of this is the remarkable bronze calendar found in fragments in a vineyard near the French town of Coligny, north of Lyons, in 1897. When pieced together, the calendar consisted of a huge bronze plate about three by five feet. The days and the names of the months are engraved in Roman letters and the numerals in columns that depict a period of five solar years. The lunar year was adapted to the solar year by insertion of an extra month of thirty days every third year.

Dating from the first century BC, the Coligny calendar was a Celtic refinement of a primitive calendar based on the seasons that was used throughout Northern Europe at that time. It was similar to the Roman calendar, but developed independently of it. The sixty or so words on the Coligny calendar are the oldest surviving example of the Celtic language in any form. The letters and numerals are Roman, but the language is Gaulish, the Celtic dialect of Gaul.[21]

Although the Celts never developed their own system of writing, their spoken language was, with Greek and Latin, one of the three great tongues of European antiquity. Celtic and Italic, Latin's ancestor, were two of the eight "proto-languages" that evolved from the parent tongue of the Indo-European peoples after they migrated from Eurasia. As they spread into Eastern and Southern Europe, they divided into smaller groups, and the language of those who settled north of the Alps became Celtic. Italic evolved among those who migrated southward into the Apennine Peninsula.

One of several descendants of Italic, Latin was overshadowed by Celtic until the third century before Christ. At a time when Latin was no more than a dialect in a minor province in central Italy, Celtic was spoken by millions from Normandy to the Black Sea. Ironically, it was the verbally facile Celts who, once the Romans occupied their territories, learned to write and speak Latin and spread it across Europe. Today, Latin is survived by its grandchildren, the modern Romance languages, several of which have evolved through Gaulish and other Celtic dialects. The great scholar of Celtic culture, Henri Hubert, once wrote that "French is Latin pronounced by Celts, and applied to the needs of Celtic minds."[22] Aside from Basque, the modern forms of Celtic are the oldest languages in Western Europe and are spoken today by about four million people in parts of the British Isles and in Brittany.

Despite their acknowledged facility for the spoken word, or perhaps because of it, the Celts never developed their own alphabet or written language. Except for the mysterious Ogham script, and the occasional use of Greek letters, the only written Celtic was in the Latin alphabet, and there are only scattered examples of that before the sixth and seventh centuries after Christ. Ogham first appeared in Wales and Ireland several centuries into the Christian era, and the few extant examples are exclusively of names. It consisted simply of straight or diagonal strokes drawn in relation to a central vertical or horizontal line. Thus it was easily incised on a hard surface, and is found only on wood or stone.

Without a written language, the Celts devoted their considerable creative energy to the plastic arts, primarily metalwork, sculpture and pottery. Celtic art has been called "the first conscious art style to be created in Europe north of the Alps."[23] Thousands of objects have been excavated, from tiny crude figurines of bronze to intricately crafted gold cups from chieftains' graves in Germany.

At first an isolated luxury of the wealthy class, Celtic art gradually became a part of everyday life, and finally, in some areas, took on the aspects of an industry. Over a period of more than a thousand years it exhibits a developing series of styles and techniques reflecting the oriental influence of the Near East as well as the classical style of the Greeks and Etruscans. The Celts combined these imported models and motifs with the abstract geometric forms of their Bronze Age ancestors, and used them to express their own restless and paradoxical temperament.

By the time it reached its creative height, in the third century BC, Celtic art had become fanciful, ambiguous and symbol-loving—the very character traits that distinguished the Celt from his neighbors. In the words of the art historian Paul Jacobsthal: ". . . the Celts, after the end of the fourth century, closed their eyes to foreign arts and resisted temptation . . . the foreign borrowings have undergone a deep change and are handled with sovereign freedom: there was no need any longer to look for models and inspiration."[24]

Where the classical approach had been realistic and representational, Celtic artists used geometric forms—boxes, chevrons and discs; and floral patterns—serpentines, scallops, comma leaves and palmettes. Where classical art had celebrated the natural beauty of the human form, the Celts turned faces into spirals, and limbs into curving tendrils. Their intense and sweeping designs are marked by flowing patterns and an absence of symmetry. At least two styles or schools are so distinctive that they appear to be the products of individual masters or workshops.

Caesar and other writers commented on the numerous images of Celtic gods, but for the Celts art was basically decorative. They used it to express their feelings, and to demonstrate their wealth and ingenuity. Within a narrow repertory they brought imagination and variety to ordinary things. Their favorite objects for decoration were their own ornaments—their combs, mirrors, bracelets and rings; their weapons of battle—swords and daggers, shields and helmets; and the implements of their households—flagons, cauldrons, cups and bowls. They made masks of their gods and heroes, which they attached to skulls and then displayed on poles. They decorated their chariots with gold and silver, and crafted elaborate bronze and iron trappings for their horses.

Their workshops also produced items of amber, glass, enamel, wood and graphite. The surviving examples of their stone sculpture are few, and are mostly of human heads and highly stylized animals. They never mastered the art of stonecutting, and their statuary is clumsy and unrefined. But the Celts excelled at soldering, embossing and inlaying, and invented the technique of coral encrustation. They used lathes and drawing compasses, and their extraordinary level of technology and craftsmanship was unsurpassed in Europe until the eighteenth century.

Despite its simple beauty and skill of execution, Celtic art remains an enigma for many, and its startling contrasts defy interpretation. Paul Jacobsthal has written: "It is attractive and repellent; it is far from primitiveness and simplicity, is refined in thought and technique; elaborate and clever; full of paradoxes, restless, puzzlingly ambiguous; rational and irrational; dark and uncanny—far from the lovable humanity and the transparence of Greek art. Yet, it is a real style, the first great contribution by the barbarians to European arts."[25]

It was perhaps these qualities in the Celts themselves that so fascinated the Romans. They were the traits of a transitional society in continual strife among its own tribes and with its neighbors over territory and trade routes, and at the same time undergoing dramatic cultural changes. The Celts straddled the line between spoken and written history, between barbarism and civilization. After centuries of an oral tradition, their words and customs were first recorded by a foreign people. In the space of a few hundred years, the Celts in Northern Europe saw the end of the Bronze Age and the beginning of the use of iron. By the first century BC, they had progressed from a primitive bartering economy to one based on their own complex and sophisticated systems of coinage in gold, silver and base metals. By then they were also conducting an extensive trade for manufactured items and luxury goods with the more developed societies of the Mediterranean.

But even while absorbing these innovations, they were unable to withstand one crucial product of an advanced society: modern warfare. Articulate, clever and fearless, the Celts were at the same time simple, credulous and easily disheartened, and their ragged, disorganized armies were seldom a match for Julius Caesar's disciplined and persistent Roman legions.

CHAPTER III

CAESAR IN GAUL

Early on a morning in March of 58 BC, in a northern neighborhood just outside the city limits of Rome, those residents awake might have noticed a two-wheeled carriage and a small group of horsemen gathered outside the home of their newest neighbor, Julius Caesar—the former Consul and now Governor of Illyricum and both the Gauls. The party remained only briefly in the street before galloping away with an earnest alacrity that portended a mission of the highest purpose.

What occasioned the journey was the news that the tribe of Helvetii had begun their previously announced migration. An enormous caravan was now gathered on the banks of the Rhône River opposite the Roman garrison at Lacus Lemannus—Lake Geneva—the northern border of the province of Further Gaul. After two years of setting aside grain and supplies for the move, the Helvetii had burned their farms and fields to deny them to the advancing Germans and to strengthen their resolve not to be turned back. They had persuaded several neighboring tribes—the Boii, Tigurini and others—to do the same and join them. The total number of migrants and their families was later said to be 360,000, a quarter of whom were men bearing arms.

Caesar decided immediately to prevent the migration, a decision that would in a few years cost the Celts in Gaul their lands, their wealth and their independence. It would put all but the fringes of Western Europe in Roman hands, and then put Rome in the hands of Caesar. His conquest of Gaul and its occupation by Rome would shield it from invasions over the Rhine for five hundred years, and would impose a Latinate culture and language on the area that remain to this day.

When he assumed the governorship of the northern provinces at the beginning of the year, it is likely that Caesar had no such thing in mind. His immediate objective was simply to pick a fight with any convenient barbarian tribe and demonstrate that a sizable army was needed in Gaul, and that he was the man to command it. Three of his four legions were stationed *in hibernis,* in winter quarters, at Aquileia at the head of the Adriatic Sea, near the site of modern Trieste, and there is evidence that he intended to move first in the direction of the Danube. But he seized another opportunity when it came and, improvising as he went, eventually pushed Rome's frontier as far as the English Channel and the lower Rhine.

Caesar chose to interpret the migration of the Helvetii as a threat to Further Gaul, the Roman province that lay just over the Italian Alps. As early as the sixth century BC, Rome had established an amicable trading relationship with the largest and oldest city in Gaul, the Greek colony of Massilia (today's Marseilles) at the mouth of the Rhône. During the second century BC, Massilia had asked for and received aid from Rome against invading Ligurians, and again against Celtic tribes from the north. After the second rescue mission, in 122 BC, the Romans stayed in the area and built a military base at Aquae Sextiae, modern-day Aix-en-Provence.

In the next year, in the Rhône Valley, two Roman generals commanding more than thirty thousand men trapped a much larger Celtic army from the Arverni and Allobroges tribes and inflicted a devastating defeat. As a result of this battle, Rome took control of a large area of southern Gaul that would form the nucleus of its first province beyond the Alps. Over the next two decades Romans occupied and then organized the entire southern coast of Gaul, and the Rhône Valley as far north as Lake Geneva, as the new province of Gallia Narbonensis. It took its name from a new colony at its western end—Narbo Martius, modern Narbonne—which was selected as the capital. Despite its formal name, however, the Romans quickly came to call it simply Provincia—The Province. Along the coast from Arles (then called Arelate) to Narbonne they built a road and named it after one of their victorious generals, Domitius Ahenobarbus. The Via Domitia was the first Roman road in Gaul.[1]

In the fifty years before Caesar's governorship, Provincia had been the scene of continual unrest and rebellion by Celts contending among themselves and against the Roman occupation. In 61 BC the Allobroges had mounted a revolt that had taken Rome a full year to put down. Now, three years later, Provincia was to be the scene of the opening battle of the Gallic War.

The route of the Helvetii to western Gaul lay across the northern neck of Provincia—Caesar's province—and he needed no further pretext. Traveling in a horse-drawn carriage, he hurried north from Rome along the coast on the Via Aurelia, and reached the Rhône in a week. A few days later he appeared at Genava (our Geneva), where a single Roman legion occupied the port on the southern bank of the lake where the Rhône flowed out of it. At the time of their conquest of Provincia some sixty years before, the Romans had taken possession of this lakeside settlement of the Allobroges and turned it into a working port. Excavations in the 1920s and again in the 1980s have revealed the remains of a line of pilings shoring up the bank, and a dock and a thirty-yard-long pier. The garrison here controlled the bridge across the Rhône, the only easy access to Roman territory.[2]

On his way through Provincia Caesar ordered additional troops to be recruited and sent to join him at Genava. Once there, his first act was to destroy the bridge, preventing an immediate confrontation. The Helvetii then sent representatives with the message that they did not intend to attack Provincia, but only wished to cross it.

In his *Commentaries on the Gallic War*, Caesar gives two reasons for heading the Helvetii off. He recalls that the Tigurini, a sub-tribe of the Helvetii, had once routed and humiliated a Roman army, and murdered a consul, Lucius Cassius. Although this had taken place fifty years earlier, his mention of it was a calculated appeal to Roman patriotism. As his second reason he cites the need to protect the Gauls living in Provincia: "It was my opinion that given the chance to pass through our province, these people, hostile as they were, would not refrain from violence and destruction. But as I needed a breathing space for mustering the troops I had ordered, I told the envoys that I would take time to consider their request" (I, 8).

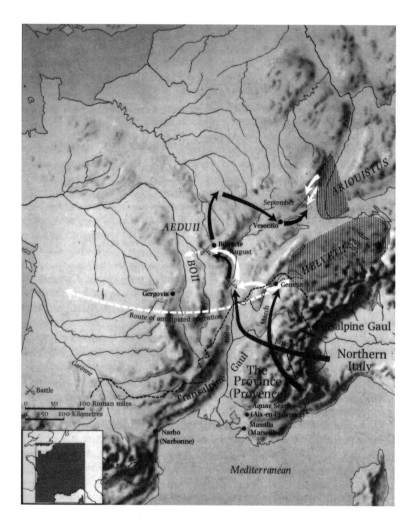

CAMPAIGN OF 58 BC

The opening events of the Gallic War took place in the spring of 58 BC at the northern edge of Rome's Provincia, also called Transalpine, or Further, Gaul. There Caesar intercepted the Helvetii and their allies attempting to migrate to the west. After defeating them decisively in what is now southern Burgundy, Caesar confronted the German leader Ariovistus in modern Alsace and drove him back across the Rhine.

What is more likely is that Caesar saw a chance for a highly visible battle that would be popular in Rome, and wanted to fight it in the best circumstances. Had he wanted, he could have required hostages from the Helvetii to guarantee their doing no damage in Provincia. Moreover, the migrants were bound for western Gaul, far outside Provincia, where they would be much less of a menace to Rome and her allies than in their original homeland.

He told them that if they wanted to raise the matter again they should come back on the thirteenth of the month, the Ides of April. In the meantime, he put the available troops to work fortifying the southern bank of the Rhône for the nineteen miles it extended southwest between Lake Geneva and the Jura Mountains to the west. Along portions of the bank they dug a deep ditch, piling up the dirt behind it, and then erected a palisade of stakes sixteen feet high on top of the bank. Soldiers were stationed at intervals along its entire length. It was the first of many such fortifications that the army, under Caesar's *praefectus fabrorum,* his chief engineer, constructed during the nine-year war in Gaul. The remains of these earthworks were uncovered in the 1860s by an excavation party sent by the French Emperor Napoleon III to locate evidence of Caesar's campaigns.

When the Helvetii returned for Caesar's answer, he invoked the "custom and precedent of the Roman people" as his reason for refusing to allow them to cross a Roman province. He told them he would stop them if they tried to cross by force. But after two years of preparation the migrants were not to be put off. Over the next several days and nights they tried by every means to get across the river. Some used boats or rafts and others simply waded through the shallows, but their enormous numbers were no advantage in a restricted river crossing. From behind their barricades the Romans pelted them with spears and stones and, when some got over, met them on the riverbank and cut them down with swords. The Helvetii pulled back, but did not change their minds.

The only other nearby route to the west lay along the northern bank of the Rhône and through the narrow Pas de la Cluse, between the Jura and the Alps, which was controlled by the Sequani tribe, the echo of whose name has been preserved in that of France's most famous river. At the northern edge of what was their vast territory the River Seine has its source, the river the Romans called "Sequana." After several days of negotiations, and an exchange of hostages, the Sequani agreed to let the Helvetii pass through, as long as they did so peacefully.

When Caesar learned of this plan, he knew that to prevent the march along this route he would need reinforcements. He left his senior commander, Titus Labienus, in charge of the troops at Genava and made a hasty trip back to Gallia Togata, his province in northern Italy, where he recruited two fresh legions. Next, he sent for the three stationed at Aquileia, and assembled all five at Ocelum, the westernmost town in the province. From there he led them up into the Cottian Alps, still clogged with snow, and through the pass at Mont Genèvre along the narrow road cut by Pompey's troops twenty years before. Besides the weather, Caesar and his cumbersome army had also to contend with hostile Celtic tribes who preyed on travelers through the mountains. Again and again along their route, marauding bands of horsemen ambushed and attacked the thin line of troops. Although the Romans beat them back, it took the five legions a week to cross the Alps.

Once in Provincia, Caesar's army marched directly to its northern border, where the troops from Genava under Titus Labienus joined them. The Helvetii, in a long file of horses, wagons and carts, had by now streamed down out of the Jura Mountains, and were crossing the River Saône north of its junction with the Rhône. The vanguard of their caravan had entered the territory of the Aedui tribe just outside Provincia, not far from the site of modern Lyons. But Caesar had come this far, and was not to be deterred by the technicality that Roman territory had not been breached. Also, according to Caesar, the thousands of swarming Helvetii were pillaging fields and homesteads along their route, and the Aedui and other tribes begged him to protect them. This he agreed to do, relying on the knowledge that the Senate had on two occasions given the Governor of Further Gaul broad authority to defend the borders of Provincia and, if necessary, protect the neighboring tribes whom Rome had befriended.

He now set up his camp on the east bank of the Saône about eleven miles south of the spot where the Helvetii were crossing. When his patrols reported that about three-quarters of the migrants had reached the opposite bank, Caesar set out from his camp with three legions soon after midnight. After making their way quietly up the valley, the Romans fell upon the remaining Celts in the early morning as they were preparing to launch their boats. Catching them unaware and hampered by their baggage and wagons, Caesar's troops butchered thousands of the migrants on the spot, chasing the rest into the woods. In his account of this battle Caesar expresses great satisfaction with the result because it was the Tigurini whom he caught at the river, and again reminds his readers of their previous insult to Rome.

The surprise attack at dawn after a forced march of three legions during the night was a tactic that became typical of Caesar's style of waging war. Throughout his campaigns in Gaul and Britain, and again in the Roman Civil War that followed, he repeatedly surprised his opponents with rapid and unexpected movements of his troops. At the time that he assumed the governorship of Gaul he was, at forty-one, well past the age when military reputations were made in the ancient world. But by then he had proved himself a natural leader—one who imparted to his men with his words and actions his own confidence and sense of urgency. According to Suetonius, "Caesar loved his men dearly," and "always addressed them not as 'My soldiers,' but as 'Comrades.'" He marched bare-headed with them, and inspired their trust and loyalty by his regular appearance among them on the battlefield.[3]

The next day, he laid down a bridge of boats across the slow-moving Saône and transported his entire army to the west bank. Shaken by the loss of a fourth of their number, and astonished at Caesar's mobility, the Helvetii sent a deputation to him headed by Divico, the aged chief who had led them to victory over the Romans and Lucius Cassius fifty years earlier. Divico proposed that if the Romans left them alone, the Helvetii would settle wherever Caesar wished, but if he attacked them they were prepared to fight. Caesar replied that he would leave them unmolested if they paid the surrounding tribes for the damage they had done, and gave him hostages to guarantee their promises. Divico answered that the Helvetii were not accustomed to *giving* hostages, but to *taking* them. He and Caesar exchanged further boasts and threats, and the peacemaking came to an end.

Nevertheless, neither army attacked. The Helvetii wanted only to reach western Gaul with the least difficulty, and Caesar, with a third of his army newly recruited, wanted a more advantageous position before he was ready to fight. The long column of the Helvetii started to move the next day, this time northward toward low-lying country that was the easiest passage around the mountains. After two weeks of following them at a distance of five or six miles, the Romans began to run short of fodder for their horses and grain for the troops. They had arranged with the Aedui and other allies to provide these, but because of the intrigues of some Gaulish leaders who supported the Helvetii, the supplies were slow in coming. When only two days' rations were left, Caesar broke off his pursuit and led his army toward Bibracte—Le Mont-Beuvray in modern Burgundy—the stronghold of the Aedui, where he knew there were ample supplies.

According to Caesar, the Helvetii either interpreted this move as a sign of weakness or thought they were strong enough to keep the Romans out of Bibracte. At the southern edge of the rugged Morvan region in Burgundy they and their allies, the Boii and the Tulingi, turned off their course and attacked the Roman rearguard. Caesar sent his cavalry to hold them at bay, and positioned the rest of his troops on a nearby hill, arranging his four veteran legions on the slope in three lines, each eight men deep. His two inexperienced legions and the auxiliary troops he placed at the top of the hill, and had them dig a trench around the baggage and supplies. By waiting until he could deploy his legions in the best position to fight, Caesar displayed the discipline and patience of a superior commander. He was not always to be so prudent, but his talent for battlefield tactics brought him repeated victories over the impulsive and poorly organized Celts.

The typical legionary in Caesar's army wore a linen undergarment next to his skin and a short-sleeved woolen tunic that reached his knees. Over this he wore a heavy leather jerkin, sometimes reinforced with metal, or a waist-length coat of mail (interlocking rings of iron wire). His legs were bare, but his calves were often protected with greaves, or shin guards, of metal or leather. On his feet he wore *caligae*, thick leather sandals that were tied with thongs to his shins. If the weather was cold he put on a heavy woolen cloak. Over an iron skullcap he wore a helmet of bronze or leather that was sometimes fitted with metal cheek-guards. The helmet would often be topped by a plume of horsehair or, for officers, red or black feathers.

While on the march each legionary carried his own spare clothing, food rations, and cooking and eating utensils, all packed in a bundle that he could attach to a *pilum,* a javelin that he rested on his shoulder. Besides this, he carried a length of rope, two short stakes, a wicker basket for carry ing earth, a shovel and sometimes a piece of chain, a hook and a saw. All this might weigh up to sixty pounds but, fortunately, when the time came to fight he could discard most of it.

The legionary's weapons were a *gladius* (a short two-edged sword), a dagger and two javelins that were simply wooden shafts extended to a length of seven feet by metal spears with barbs at the tips. He also carried a *scutum*, which was a sturdy, oblong, wooden shield about four by two feet, rimmed with iron at the edges and covered with heavy leather. On it was written the name of the soldier, his unit and the number of his legion.[4]

In the early days of the Republic part-time service in the militia was a privilege available only to those citizens who could afford the cost of their own arms, food and clothing. As the Roman state expanded against its neighbors and needed larger and more stable armies, all citizens meeting a minimum property requirement became liable for intermittent military service, compensated by a small daily wage, for up to twenty years. By the beginning of the first century BC the army was open to any citizen, solvent or not, and soldiering had for many become a full-time occupation. Even so, Caesar's legionaries were paid at a laborer's rate, and deductions were made for the cost of their food and weapons.

Caesar's army, and all those of Rome, and of Greece before them, was composed chiefly of heavily armed infantry, and relied on what has been called "edged weapon warfare." The earliest Roman armies had fought in the traditional phalanx formation, a method of infantry attack perfected by the Greeks in the seventh century BC. The usual field of battle was a level plain, on which each general deployed his entire army in close formation across his front in rows of whatever breadth he dared (five hundred men was common) and up to sixteen deep.[5] In the classic infantry attack thousands of soldiers wearing armor and wielding swords and spears advanced on foot behind a solid wall of shields. Their objective was to move their mass by sheer force across a piece of ground, often simply using their shields to push the opposing army back, killing as many of them as possible in the process. Because of the physical effort required to strike down or kill each enemy soldier, the infantry advance was slow and the battle rarely more than a few hours long.[6]

During their wars with the Celts in the fourth century BC, the Romans found that the phalanx was less than practical on uneven terrain, and too cumbersome to counter the Celts' open-order tactics. Its solid mass moved slowly and awkwardly and was highly sensitive on its flanks and rear. The middle ranks tended to stumble into each other and, for the most part, only the weapons in the first few rows could be brought into play.[7]

The Romans soon abandoned the phalanx and reorganized their armies into legions—miniature armies of up to six thousand men each. They also divided their infantry into groups according to function and experience. Over time, they increased flexibility and improved control of the legion by dividing it further into "cohorts"—ten to a legion, and "maniples"—three to a cohort—and "centuries" of eighty to a hundred men—two to a maniple. By the time Caesar took command of his

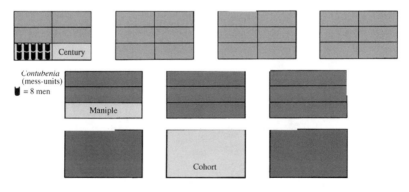

STRUCTURE OF A ROMAN LEGION

legions, this system of organization gave him the versatility to fight on any terrain and to deploy his infantry in small or large units in different directions and for different missions. Before the Gallic War was over he would become a master of legionary tactics, but in 58 BC against the Helvetii he faced the first pitched battle of his career.

Although Caesar commanded more men than ever before, the circumstances in which he preferred to fight—darkness or surprise—were absent. He writes that he spoke to his troops to encourage them, and probably also warned them, as did most Roman generals, that to fall into the hands of barbarians meant a cruel and certain death. But he took another step, one that set him apart from other commanders and pointed to his later reputation as a "soldiers' soldier." "So that the danger would be the same for everyone and no one would have any hope of escape," he dismounted, ordered his officers to do the same, and had the horses led away (I, 25).

It was early in the afternoon when the Helvetii surged up the hill in a phalanx, ranks and files close and deep, swords or spears in one hand, shields joined and overlapping in the other. When they reached a point about ninety feet away, the legionaries in the front rank hurled their javelins straight into the mass of charging men. Caesar had ordered his armorers to make the tips of the Roman javelins of soft iron that bent when they pierced a shield; and when the Helvetii were unable to pull them out, they were forced to drop their shields. According to Caesar, their phalanx was broken easily. Then the Romans, behind their own shields, charged through the enemy ranks, stabbing and slashing with their short swords and daggers. When the first line of legionaries fell back or grew tired, the second rank of eight rows stepped into their places.

The Romans steadily pushed the Helvetii back down the slope and they scrambled to retreat across the narrow valley, taking up positions on another hill a mile away. As the legionaries pursued them, the armies of the Boii and the Tulingi that had been stationed at the rear, swept onto the battlefield and attacked the Roman right flank. Caesar ordered his army to keep after the Helvetii, but detached the rear third and turned it to face the reinforcements.

All through the afternoon the valley rang with the clatter of sword against shield, with shouts of fury and screams of dying men. The tens of thousands of Celts fought like madmen, but their swarming and disorganized numbers lacked a common plan or tactic, and Caesar's disciplined troops gradually wore them down. By sunset the Helvetii had retreated to the top of the opposite hill, where they made a barricade of their wagons and carts. There they took a stand, and fought well into the night before the Romans finally broke into their camp and slaughtered all who could not escape. Those who survived fled the battlefield and marched the rest of the night without stopping.

The Romans spent three days attending their wounded and burying their dead before taking up the pursuit. In an extraordinary feat of archaeological detection, Colonel Stoffel, the leader of Emperor Napoleon III's excavators, was able to fix the location of this first major battle of the Gallic War. On the plateau of Armecy near the Arroux River in southern Burgundy he found the remains of the three-hundred-yard-long crescent-shaped trench about five feet deep that Caesar's men had dug to protect their baggage train.[8]

Although the Helvetii were clearly on the march with their entire tribe, their fighting tactics were not unusual for the Celts in the time of Caesar. A French historian has described their approach to battle as follows:

> They went out to war in large crowds, accompanied by their women and children, and carrying an incredible collection of personal property, plate and utensils of all kinds on interminable files of wagons: and, in spite of all this . . . they never succeeded in having enough provisions for a campaign of any duration.
>
> The Gauls never thought of surrounding their encampments with trenches and ramparts. A huge entanglement of carts, chariots, wagons and *impedimenta* of all descriptions was piled up at the back of the camp—their sole protection for a last desperate stand should the army flinch.[9]

The outcome of the battle persuaded the surrounding Celtic tribes to heed Caesar's warnings to refuse the Helvetii any food or assistance. Having lost three-quarters of their number, and with no way to get grain or supplies, they were forced to surrender. Their representatives met Caesar while he was on the march: "They flung themselves at my feet and . . . begged, in tears, for peace. I ordered that the Helvetian army should stay where it was and await my arrival. My order was obeyed, and when I got there I demanded from them hostages, their weapons, and the slaves who had deserted to their side" (I, 27).

Caesar also ordered that the remaining Helvetii and their allies return to their homeland because he did not want it occupied by Germans. As their food supplies had been destroyed, he told the local tribes to supply them with grain for the journey. He writes that a census of the returning migrants put their number at 110,000.

The irony of the opening battle of Caesar's war with the Celts, which brought the first Roman army into the interior of Gaul, was that it was against a trespassing tribe from across the border. But Caesar had as yet no intention of conquering Gaul: he had wanted only a military victory, and now he had it. He writes that the chieftains of the surrounding tribes gathered in his camp to thank him for turning back the intruders. At the same time, they held a council among themselves and appointed the Aeduan leader Diviciacus to speak to Caesar for them about another problem. This Diviciacus was well known to Caesar and the Romans, having personally addressed the Roman Senate in previous years seeking military assistance for his tribe, and had actually been a guest in Cicero's home.

According to Diviciacus, two large coalitions of Celts had fought for many years for supremacy in Gaul, one led by the fierce Arverni and their allies the Sequani, the other by the Aedui. The Sequani had asked a powerful German chieftain, Ariovistus, to cross into Gaul with his army and aid them against the Aedui. "But," as Caesar quotes Diviciacus, "after those uncivilized savages had developed a liking for the good land and the high standard of living enjoyed by the Gauls," they had decided to stay, and had been joined by the rest of their tribe (I, 31). The reinforced coalition had inflicted a crushing defeat on the Aedui and killed all their nobles. Ariovistus had then turned against his allies, the Sequani, and seized a third of their land, afterward demanding that they vacate another third to accommodate thousands of Harudes, another German tribe that was joining him. Now, 120,000

Germans—here for the first time Caesar uses the word "*barbari*"—occupied the area of what is modern Alsace, west of the Rhine, and more were on the way.

Diviciacus went on to call Ariovistus a cruel and arrogant tyrant, given to uncontrolled rages, who demanded the children of the most distinguished Aeduan and other Celtic citizens as hostages. According to Caesar, all the tribal chieftains at the meeting except the Sequani tearfully begged him to drive the Germans out. Because Ariovistus already occupied nearly all their territory, the Sequani were too frightened of his retaliation to ask for help. There is little question that Caesar saw an opportunity here for another campaign that would play well in Rome. It was Marius, his own uncle, who had driven back the Germans when they had threatened Rome in the previous century. He spoke encouraging words to the chieftains, and promised that he would take it upon himself to persuade Ariovistus to cease what he was doing.

Mindful that it would be a serious matter to make war on the Germans, Caesar takes several paragraphs to compose a justification. He called it "a disgrace both to me and to the state, considering the greatness of Rome's empire" that the Aedui, who had been called "Brothers and Kinsmen" in the Roman Senate, be held subject to such a fierce and uncivilized people, and their loved ones held hostage. He also noted the danger of the Germans "gradually getting into the habit of crossing the Rhine" (I, 33), and perhaps being tempted to again invade Provincia. The arrogance of Ariovistus was intolerable.

First, Caesar sent messengers to the German leader asking for a conference on an important matter of state, but the barbarian refused, demanding to know what business Caesar had in his territory. Caesar responded with an ultimatum that the Germans halt their incursions into Gaul and return their hostages, or suffer the punishment he would inflict on behalf of Rome's allies. Ariovistus rejected all of Caesar's demands and added that he was doing no more than imposing his will on a conquered people, no more than the Romans were in the habit of doing. The two exchanged more boasts and threats until, at last, Ariovistus invited Caesar to attack, adding that no one had ever fought him without being destroyed.

Flushed with a decisive victory over a massive army, Caesar lost no time in taking up the challenge. He set out with his six legions at top speed to the northeast, toward Ariovistus. After three days on the march he received word that the Germans were moving to occupy Vesontio, the principal *oppidum,* or fortified town, of the Sequani, today a hilltop citadel surrounded by modern Besançon on the River Doubs. Realizing that it would be a major undertaking to dislodge Ariovistus from this mountain stronghold, Caesar pushed his legions by night and day—and beat him there.

The ordinary day's march for a Roman legion took about seven hours and covered just under twenty miles, and forced marches of more than thirty miles a day through open country have been reported.[10] It is likely that on this occasion Caesar took no more than five days to move twenty-five to thirty thousand men and their baggage and animals more than 120 miles.

While waiting at Vesontio for supplies to be brought up, his troops suffered their first loss of nerve. According to Caesar, some of his officers believed too many of the tales they heard from the Gaulish townspeople about the size and ferocity of the Germans. The Celts claimed that when they fought them they had not even been able to bear the expressions on their faces or the glare in their eyes. Caesar's army was suddenly seized with panic. "It began with the military tribunes, the prefects of the auxiliary troops, and the other officers who had followed me from Rome to cultivate my friendship and had little military experience. They began to beg me for permission to leave, each individual giving a different urgent reason for his departure" (I, 39).

Gradually the apprehension seeped into the ranks, and Caesar was confronted with his first recalcitrant army. Wills were written and sealed, and questions raised about tactics, about the enormous forests along the route, and the problems of an adequate food supply. Caesar assembled his centurions and delivered a lengthy tongue-lashing. "I reprimanded them severely for thinking that it was their business to ask questions or even think about where they were being taken or why" (I, 40). He asserted that his demands of Ariovistus were for the benefit of the Roman people, and that the Germans were not as fierce as the Gauls claimed; they had even been defeated by the Helvetii. He reminded them that the last time Romans had faced Germans the victory had been won by none other than his own uncle, Gaius Marius. "You have nothing to fear," he assured them. "Why do you not trust your own courage and my competence?" (I, 40).

To underline his point he announced that he was speeding up his schedule—he would march out that very night against Ariovistus—and to show his scorn for the hesitaters he would, if no one else followed, take the field with only his favorite legion, the Xth, trusting completely in its valor. He writes that his words had the desired effect and that his men "were inspired with a great eagerness and enthusiasm for going into action." Caesar was not reluctant to compliment himself, but self-serving as this statement is, it is probably near the truth. And proof of it was not long in coming.

Well before dawn the next morning, all six legions set out northeastward and marched for an exceptional seven continuous days into the region of Alsace until their scouts (*exploratores*) reported that the Germans were about twenty-four miles away. Envoys from Ariovistus met the Romans and proposed a conference between the two generals. Caesar agreed, and five days later he and Ariovistus met on a hill halfway between their camps, each on horseback and accompanied by a ten-man escort. A force of cavalry from each camp stood three hundred yards on either side of the hill. Caesar relates a long conversation between them in which they exchanged rhetoric and justifications for their presence in that part of Gaul. Each asserted that he had been called to the area by the local tribes and demanded that the other withdraw. Caesar quotes Ariovistus:

> I was in Gaul before your people were, Caesar. Until now the Roman army never left the boundaries of the Roman province of Gaul. What do you mean by coming into lands that belong to me? This part of Gaul is my province, just as the other is yours. If I invaded your territory, it would be right for you to object; in exactly the same way it is wrong that you are interfering with me in a matter that falls entirely within my rights (I, 44).

While they were talking, some German cavalry began to approach the hill and threaten the Roman escort. Caesar broke off the conference and, cautioning his troops not to engage the enemy, rode back to his camp. Despite the most intense efforts by archaeologists and historians, the site of these negotiations and the subsequent battle has never been satisfactorily fixed. There is general agreement, however, that the scene was on the western plain of the Rhine just east of the Vosges Mountains, perhaps in the vicinity of modern-day Colmar.[11]

The following day Ariovistus proposed that they meet again. Caesar refused, but sent two representatives who, when they approached the German camp, were captured and put in chains. The two armies spent the next six days arranging and rearranging themselves in the best positions to fight. Caesar constructed and fortified two camps in strategic positions, and then sent his men out to attack; but after a few minor skirmishes it became clear that Ariovistus was avoiding a battle. By questioning German prisoners, Caesar learned why his adversary was hesitating: "Apparently it is the custom among the Germans for their matrons to draw lots and use other sorts of divination to decide whether or not it is advisable to engage in battle; on this occasion they had declared that the Germans were not destined to win if they fought before the new moon" (I, 50).

To use this psychological advantage, Caesar immediately forced a battle. He positioned his six legions in three lines, and took command of the right wing himself. A headlong Roman charge forced the Germans to respond, and the two armies collided so quickly that the Romans had no chance to throw their javelins. Dropping them and picking up their swords, they charged the German phalanx with a fury that Caesar notes approvingly: "Many of our men actually jumped onto the wall of shields, wrenched the shields from the enemy's hands and stabbed down at them from above" (I, 52). When the Romans on the right flank began to waver, young Publius Crassus, the cavalry commander in the rear, detached the third line of infantry and sent it in to support them.

The legionaries made short work of the Germans; Caesar disposes of this battle in two paragraphs, and records that the entire German army turned and fled all the way to the Rhine, about fifteen miles away. There, a few of them managed to find boats or to swim across, but the Roman cavalry overtook and killed the rest. According to

Caesar, both the wives of Ariovistus and one of his daughters were killed; another daughter escaped, as did the German chieftain himself.

By now it was mid-September and near the end of the customary warmaking season. In the six months since riding out to face the Helvetii, Caesar had inflicted severe defeats on two major tribes, and molded the nucleus of a devastating army. What he planned to do with it we can only conjecture. If he did not yet envision the conquest of Gaul, it is certain that his victories fed his confidence and his ambition. It is significant that although his term as governor would expire at the end of the year, he ordered his six legions to remain for the winter at Vesontio, beyond the northern border of Provincia.

Leaving Titus Labienus in command, Caesar returned to Nearer Gaul for the winter, occupying himself with administrative duties. There is no record of his political activities during these months, but he and his allies were successful in preventing the Senate from terminating his one-year command in "The Province." It was perhaps at this time that he completed the account that became Book I of *The Gallic War,* one of the most popular and enduring works to survive the ancient world. It is the greatest military narrative in the literature of Rome, and the only contemporary record of a major Roman foreign war that has come down to us.

The Gallic War is the first half of a work titled *Commentaries,* which also includes *The Civil War*—Caesar's account of his later struggle with Pompey for control of the Roman state. After the later collapse of the Roman Empire, the manuscript, which may have survived in only a single copy, was unknown to the world for more than a thousand years until it was rediscovered and printed during the Renaissance. The text as we have it now is based on the earliest extant copy, transcribed in a monastery in France's Loire Valley in the ninth century.[12]

The Gallic War is divided into eight books, one for each year of Caesar's campaigns in Germany, Britain and Gaul, and is part of a tradition of historical writing that takes the form of simple firsthand notes on events. Sober and plain, without elaboration, and offering little variety of tone or range of vocabulary, it is a model of concise narrative that is nevertheless full of drama. One modern critic has written:

"Caesar's credibility, and his claim to genius, is enhanced by a style at once lucid and precise and elegant, which he writes with the sovereign ease and the purity of diction characteristic of the literary aristocrat."[13]

It gained great popularity after its publication during the Renaissance, and in the sixteenth century the Holy Roman Emperor Charles V sent a mission into France to locate Caesar's battle sites and map his campaigns. In recent centuries it has been a staple in the schoolroom, in the libraries of generals and on the bedtables of royalty. Despite his omission of any interpretation or evaluation of historical issues, had Caesar written nothing else he would be read and remembered today as one of the three or four finest historians of the ancient world.

Caesar's style was no less admired by his contemporaries. Marcus Tullius Cicero, the most fastidious of Roman writers, said of the scenes and descriptions in *The Gallic War*:

> They are like nude figures, straight and beautiful; stripped of all ornaments of style as if they had laid aside a garment. His aim was to furnish others with the material for writing history. Perhaps he has succeeded in gratifying the inept who may wish to apply their curling-irons to his material. But men of sound judgment he has deterred from writing, since in history there is nothing more pleasing than brevity, clear and correct.[14]

The veracity of Caesar's account was not seriously questioned until late in the nineteenth century, and today most scholars agree that it is generally accurate, with some exceptions. Some of his statements about the people he encountered, especially the Germans, are questionable; and his descriptions of certain animals in the forests of Germany, such as the deer-shaped ox with a single horn, are pure fantasy. He was familiar with the travel books of earlier Greek writers, and it appears that he merely had his secretaries copy passages from them to satisfy the public's curiosity about strange people and exotic places. This was a common practice among ancient historians. In other cases he simply repeated the outlandish tales that came his way, such as the one about the elks with no joints in their legs who could not get up if they ever lay down. They were forced to take their rest by leaning against trees, and the Germans captured them by undermining trees or cutting them nearly through so that when the elks leaned against them they both fell and the animals were helpless.

The other qualification has to do with the propagandist element in *The Gallic War*. It is clear that Caesar was intrigued with the idea of creating a factual history, but a more important motive was to justify his actions to the Roman public and to strengthen his political position. In the opinion of the historian Michael Grant, *The Gallic War* is "among the most potent works of propaganda ever written."[15]

Caesar was not only the commander of the army, but his own war correspondent, editor and publisher. He alone decided what to include in his reports from the front, and what to omit. The dispatches he sent to the Senate after each battle have not survived, and there is little available elsewhere that contradicts his accounts. But there is no question that by emphasizing, omitting or rearranging the events of his campaigns he produced a narrative that served his own purpose rather than that of historical accuracy. In this respect *The Gallic War* is probably no less candid than any modern political autobiography. In some cases, Caesar was answering his critics, but he did this so cleverly that his account never seems other than a simple and objective presentation of the facts. Nonetheless, in many instances he concealed his battlefield errors and exaggerated the dangers he faced.

More than one scholar has disputed Caesar's claims for the size of the Celtic armies he fought. On two counts, for instance, the migrating Helvetii cannot have numbered the 368,000 that Caesar attributes to them. Population density figures for the civilized Roman homeland have been extrapolated for the territories of the Helvetii and their allies, and the result puts their total number at a quarter of a million at the highest. But even at that figure, the simple logistics, alone, of such a mass of people, encumbered with their supply wagons and possessions, traveling through mountain passes and along primitive trackways, make such a claim impossible to believe. (The warfare historian Hans Delbrück estimated that their baggage train would have been 180 miles long.[16]) It follows that their fighting army was considerably less than ninety thousand men, and was probably not half that number. The best estimate is that the Helvetian and Roman armies were about the same size.

Equally sound objections have been made to Caesar's figures for other engagements, and it is likely that he persistently exaggerated his enemies' strength. His reasons for this are obvious, but it is fair to mention that the Romans, like the Greeks, were accustomed to inflated reports of conquests, especially against barbarian peoples. It was a tradition dating, at least, from Herodotus and Xenophon.

One writer has opined that Caesar was too modest. In his essay "Of Books," the sixteenth-century French essayist Michel de Montaigne wrote:

> There is so much candour in his judgment when he speaks of his enemies, that, except for the false colours with which he seeks to conceal his evil cause and the ardour of his pestilent ambition, I think the only fault to be objected against him is that he speaks too sparingly of himself. For so many great exploits could not have been carried out by him unless more of his own attributes had gone into them than he sets down.[17]

The question of when *The Gallic War* was written and published has never been settled. Some scholars argue that Caesar wrote it all at the end of the seventh year of the war, and published it then to justify his actions in Gaul. But the prevailing opinion today, based on a close analysis of conflicting statements Caesar makes in several places, is that he completed each book at the end of the particular year it describes and issued it shortly afterward.[18] The scholarly officer to whom he entrusted much of his correspondence, Aulus Hirtius, wrote the eighth book after Caesar's death, covering the final two years (eight and nine) of the war.

But regardless of the time of publication, by the end of the first campaign the Roman public was fully aware that Caesar had crushed the Helvetii and routed Ariovistus, if only from his vivid dispatches to the Senate. His first year in Gaul had given both his supporters and his enemies something new to talk about, and no one, perhaps not even Julius Caesar, knew that there would soon be a great deal more.

CHAPTER IV

⋞⋟ ⋰ ⋞⋟

THE RHINE AND
THE CHANNEL

W hile I was in northern Italy for the winter . . . frequent rumors reached me, confirmed by dispatches from Labienus, that all the Belgae were conspiring against Rome" (II, 1). With these opening words of Book II of *The Gallic War*, Caesar makes his case for a second campaign in Gaul in 57 BC, asserting that the savage Belgae had brought a large and threatening army to their southern border, some 250 miles from the northern edge of Provincia. According to Caesar, their neighbors had persuaded them to join a new offensive to drive the Romans out of Gaul entirely. The numerous tribes of Belgae, whose name came from a Celtic word meaning "proud," occupied the northern third of Gaul and were reputed to be the fiercest fighters in the country.

Interpreting these reports as a virtual declaration of war, Caesar ordered two additional legions recruited during the spring in his Italian province of Nearer Gaul—the XIIIth and XIVth—asking for neither sanction nor financing from the Senate. Early in summer he sent them across the Alps and north, beyond the border of Provincia to join Labienus at Vesontio. A few weeks later he went there himself and resumed command of his army, now grown to forty thousand men in eight legions. Within days he led them out the north gate of the town, and in two weeks crossed the Marne, the southern limit of Belgic territory.

He was met in the vicinity of modern Rheims by representatives of one Belgic tribe, the Remi, who said they wanted to place themselves under the protection of Rome, and to help him against the rest of the Belgae. They told him that the other tribes had joined forces and were approaching with a combined army of nearly 300,000 men under the command of Galba, King of the Suessiones. Caesar accepted their offer of help, not without demanding the children of their leaders as hostages, and continued his march northward to the Aisne River, where he set up his camp on the north bank. Then he summoned the Aeduan leader Diviciacus, one of his Gaulish allies, and persuaded him to take his army westward and attack the homeland of the Bellovaci, the largest Belgic tribe opposing him.

Retaliating against the defecting tribe, the Belgic army now attacked Bibrax, the principal town of the Remi, a few miles to the west of Caesar's position, and about seventy miles northeast of present-day Paris. When Caesar sent a contingent of his Mediterranean mercenary archers and slingers to aid the besieged town, the Belgae abandoned their attack and turned to face the Romans. They assembled their entire army in a gigantic camp that Caesar reports as eight miles long and situated on the opposite side of a marsh two miles in front of him. With the Aisne behind them, the Romans constructed their own camp on a hill facing north, dug a ditch six yards wide and built a rampart twelve feet high around its two- mile perimeter. To prevent an attack on their right flank they dug a trench extending half a mile from the front of the camp and another from the rear back to the river; at the end of each trench they built small forts to house their catapults.

Again, Caesar had placed his army in such a position that it could readily attack or defend itself against a much larger force. The Belgae, just as the Helvetii and the Germans the year before, were gathered in a confused mass in front of him with no fortifications to protect themselves and little in the way of tactics to deal with the Romans.

Caesar now left two legions in the camp to defend it, and deployed his other six in the usual three lines on the front slope of the hill. The Belgic chieftain brought up his men in battle lines, but neither commander was willing to send them across the marsh. When it became apparent that the Belgae were not going to attack, Caesar ordered his troops back into the camp.

The next day, one of Caesar's lookouts reported a large number of Belgae circling around the Roman left flank in an attempt to cross the Aisne River and attack them from behind. Caesar sent all his cavalry and a force of infantry and archers across the bridge at the rear of his camp and along the opposite bank of the river. They caught the Belgae in the midst of crossing. In Caesar's words: "Fierce fighting ensued. My men attacked and killed a great many of the Belgae; they were trying to cross the river and so were hampered in their attempts to fight back. Others boldly attempted to cross over the dead bodies of their comrades, but we drove these men back with a shower of javelins. Our cavalry surrounded those who had managed to cross earlier and killed them" (II, 10).

It was a stinging defeat for the Belgae, who now realized that they faced an experienced and disciplined army entrenched in an impregnable position. Also, they were having difficulty feeding and supplying the thousands of troops they had collected, and the Bellovaci were alarmed at the threat to their homeland by the Aeduan allies of the Romans. The Belgae decided to abandon their camp and return to their individual tribal territories. Once there, they would all come to the aid of whichever tribe was attacked first. Writes Caesar: "Having agreed to this plan, they left their camp a little before midnight with a great deal of noise and confusion, without any proper order or discipline. Each man wanted to be at the front to get home quickly, with the result that their departure was just like a rout" (II, 11).

At dawn, Caesar sent his cavalry and three legions after them, and the Romans spent the entire day chasing and slaughtering the fleeing Belgae. He then struck his camp and led his legions on a rapid march down the valley of the Aisne against the capitals of the Belgic tribes that he had just defeated. After failing to break into the well-defended capital of the Suessiones, near present-day Soissons, his troops began filling the gigantic protective ditch in front of the town and prepared to mount an extended siege. But when the defenders saw the Romans quickly put up a pair of wooden towers against the walls of the fortress, they were so amazed and frightened that they sent envoys out to negotiate a surrender. The site of this great *oppidum*—one hundred acres in area—has been identified on a promontory overlooking the Aisne River, just outside the present-day village of Pommiers.[1]

Continuing west and crossing the Oise, the Romans entered the territory of the Bellovaci and approached their capital, Bratuspantium,

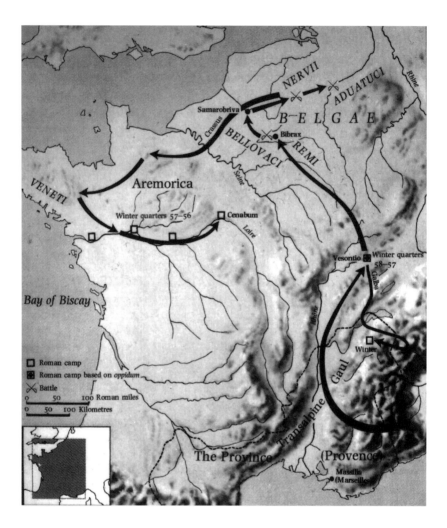

CAMPAIGN OF 57 BC

During 57 BC, Caesar took Roman legions into northern Gaul and as far as modern-day Belgium for the first time in history. His successes there and the victorious campaign of Publius Crassus in Normandy and Brittany against the Aremoricans led him to claim, prematurely, that "peace has been brought to the whole of Gaul."

now Beauvais, capital of the département of Oise. After Caesar set up his camp on the heights overlooking this *oppidum*, the Bellovaci, too, surrendered, giving up their weapons and the six hundred hostages Caesar demanded. From there he took his legions north against the Ambiani, who quickly surrendered their capital, Samarobriva—the Somme bridge—today the site of Amiens.

Over the course of a few summer weeks the greater part of the Belgic confederation had wilted before the furious assault of Caesar's smaller but highly disciplined army. But that the Belgae had been determined to deal with Caesar is evidenced by the unusual gold coins found in the area. Archaeologists have concluded that during the winter of 58–57 BC the several Belgic tribes agreed to strike a special set of coins to finance their military enterprise. They are distinguished by a blank obverse, apparently to symbolize the renunciation of separate tribal identities in the face of a common enemy. They could not have known that these battles were only the first of many, and that in a few years they would have no gold at all to use for coins. It was probably after this campaign that Caesar installed Commius, a Belgic noble who had defected to him, as King of the Atrebates, one of the tribes he defeated. Commius was later to play a part in both of Caesar's expeditions to Britain, and again in the last uprising of the Gauls.

Caesar was now in the valley of the Somme and within forty miles of the English Channel, but his next battle would be to the east, at the border of modern Belgium, and it would be the severest test of the campaign. His opponents would be the Nervii, the tribe considered the least civilized and the most warlike among the Belgae. Caesar writes that when he asked about them he was told that they were so reclusive they would not let traders enter their territory, and so Spartan they would not allow wine or luxury goods to be imported for fear that these would dilute their courage and make them "soft." Modern archaeological excavations of the settlements of the Nervii do not confirm this claim, but it was bound to impress Caesar's readers in Rome.[2]

With no more justification than a report that the Nervii had mocked their Belgic neighbors and vowed never to surrender, Caesar marched northeast for three days with his eight legions to the northern edge of modern France. The Nervii had taken a position in the woods on the north bank of the Sambre River just outside what is the present-day city of Maubeuge. It was, by now, a familiar situation to Caesar, and he sent patrols and surveyors ahead to pick the best spot for his camp. A hill overlooking the near side of the river was the natural place. On reaching it, the main body of six legions began their usual construction of ditches and ramparts while the cavalry skirmished with their enemy counterparts on a plain on the far bank of the river.

Suddenly the entire Nervian army burst out of the woods and raced across the narrow plain, sweeping the Roman cavalry in front of them and swarming across the shallow river. Occupied with laying out their camp and building their fortifications, the Romans were taken completely by surprise. Trumpeters hastily sounded the call to battle, and legionaries rushed to retrieve their swords, helmets and shields, and get into fighting formation. But within minutes thousands of the Nervii had forded the river, surged up the hill and attacked the Roman camp. They came so swiftly that most of the Roman troops had no time to find their own units, or even take off their shield-covers, before they were forced to fight. The six legions found themselves scattered across a mile-long front, each facing in a different direction—and fighting for their lives.

Caesar ran from one legion to another, first to the Xth on the left, then to the VIIIth, then to the XIIth on the right, exhorting them to keep their nerve and live up to their tradition of bravery. Brave they might have been, but the Romans suffered heavy losses. One after another, their centurions, each commanding about eighty men, were wounded or cut down. The XIIth Legion was entirely surrounded, and still the Nervii swarmed forward. Caesar records:

> I recognized that this was a crisis; there were no reserves available. I had no shield with me but I snatched one from a soldier in the rear ranks and went forward to the front line. Once there I called out to all the centurions by name and shouted encouragement to the rest of the men. I ordered them to advance and to open out their ranks so that they could use their swords more effectively. My arrival gave the troops fresh hope; their determination was restored because, with the

commander-in-chief looking on, each man was eager to do his best whatever the risk to himself. As a result the enemy's attack was slowed down a little (II, 25).

On the left, the men of the IXth and Xth managed to hold the Nervii, and then to push them back down the hill. They drove them across the river and fought their way up the hill on the opposite bank. When the Roman front began to stabilize, Caesar ordered his commanders to gradually bring the legions together and form a square so that they could attack the enemy in any direction. Each army was now fighting on both sides of the river, and the battlefield was a confused mass of men and horses struggling against each other amid mounting piles of corpses.

Finally, Titus Labienus and his Xth Legion reached the top of the opposite hill and managed to overrun the Nervian camp. The Romans now occupied the heights of both hills and began to push the Nervii from opposite sides down to the river. At this moment the last two Roman legions, which had been marching in the rear behind the baggage train, appeared on the ridge behind the battlefield. On seeing the carnage among their desperately fighting comrades, they rushed forward and attacked the Nervii from a new direction. The Romans—reorganized, reinforced and confident—again displayed their mettle in a pitched battle, steadily driving the enemy back and surrounding them. Caesar reports that the Nervii fought with enormous courage, and even stood on piles of their own dead to throw their spears; but the disciplined legionaries gradually overpowered them and, as the battle finally tilted Rome's way, butchered them by the thousands.

The fighting had taken no more than an hour, but it was a desperate hour for the Romans, and Caesar's first brush with defeat. The Nervii had taken his army by surprise, and it was only his quick action to rally his troops that saved them from a massacre. Instead, it was the Nervii who were destroyed. Those who came to Caesar to surrender told him that only five hundred of their sixty thousand warriors survived. He writes that the tribe was virtually annihilated, and that even their name ceased to be used. We may be sure that the figures cited are greatly enlarged, especially because three years later Caesar describes an attack by a Nervian army on one of his camps, and two years after that they sent five thousand men against him at the all-important battle of Alesia.

The last battle of the year was against the Aduatuci, a Belgic tribe whose army had ridden to the battlefield on the Sambre to aid the Nervii, but had then turned away and retreated to a fortified *oppidum* on the River Meuse in today's Belgian province of Liège. Arriving at this stronghold after a march northward, Caesar describes it as surrounded on three sides by sheer rocks, and protected on its fourth side by a massive wall facing a slope about two hundred feet wide.

He put his soldiers to work constructing a twelve-foot-high earth wall along a five-mile perimeter around the town, with towers at strategic places. Then, under cover of protective sheds, the Romans built a long terrace of earth leading up to the exposed wall of the *oppidum*. At the bottom of the terrace they began another siege tower—a wooden structure of several stories, similar to a scaffold, that could be moved on rollers. "When the enemy saw us building a siege-tower some distance away, they shouted down insults at us from their wall, jeering at us for building such a huge piece of apparatus so far away. Mostly the Gauls are very scathing about our small stature, contrasting it with their own great size, and now they mockingly asked us if we, little men that we were, imagined that our feeble hands and strength could set a great tower like that on a wall" (II, 30).

But their mockery turned to disbelief and then to terror when they saw the Romans roll the tower up the terrace toward the town wall. So convinced were they that such a feat could not be accomplished without some intervention by the gods that the Aduatuci immediately surrendered, asking only that they be allowed to keep their weapons for defense against their other enemies. Caesar refused the condition, and the Aduatuci threw their weapons over the wall.

This is only one of the many situations in which Caesar's bridges, siege towers or missile-throwing equipment were decisive in his battles against the less sophisticated Celts. These feats of engineering made use of the most advanced technology of the time, and were usually constructed on the spot out of whatever materials were available. Credit for them surely belongs to his chief engineers, his *praefecti fabrum*:

Mamurra of Formiae and Cornelius Balbo. But throughout the seven books of *The Gallic War* Caesar neither praises nor even mentions the two men.

Suspecting that the surrender was a trick, Caesar refused to occupy the fortress and ordered his troops to spend the night in their camp outside the walls. Soon after midnight the Aduatuci, armed with weapons they had concealed, burst out of their fortress and attacked the Roman camp. Caesar's men were ready for them, however, and let loose a shower of javelins, arrows and stones from their positions along the wall and in the towers. The ensuing battle was short. According to Caesar, the Romans killed four thousand of the enemy and drove the rest back into the town. The next morning they used a battering ram to smash open the gates, and took the entire garrison prisoner.

Caesar reports that in retaliation for their treachery he rounded up 53,000 Aduatuci and auctioned them in one lot to the slave dealers who shrewdly followed his army wherever it went. From there, the dealers would march them in chains to Rome, where there was a steady market for foreign captives, and resell them. Caesar's slave auctions during his years in Gaul were not only a major source of income, but also kept his name and exploits in front of the Roman public. His officers and soldiers, too, took their share of plunder whenever they could, and an appointment as a legionary commander in Caesar's army became known as a sure path to wealth.

Although the majority of Romans took pride and satisfaction in Caesar's victories against the barbarians, his political opponents were not alone in deploring the behavior of his rampaging army. From the hand of the young poet Catullus, born in Verona to a middle-class family of Celtic origin, came a series of biting denunciations of Caesar, sneering at him for lewdness and excoriating his officers for enriching themselves at the expense of the hapless Celts. In one notable lyric of exuberant obscenity Catullus poured out his contempt for one of Caesar's chief engineers, Mamurra, for stealing fortunes in Spain and Gaul.[3]

Before marching on the fortress of the Aduatuci, Caesar had sent a single legion into western Gaul under Publius Crassus, the son of his wealthy partner in the Triumvirate. The young man's job was to

subdue the maritime Celtic tribes along the Atlantic seaboard, especially the sea-faring Veneti, who controlled the cross-channel trade
between Gaul and Britain. The news of the defeat of the Germans and
the Belgae had spread fear of the Romans throughout northern Gaul,
and now Caesar received word from Crassus that seven tribes in the
area of modern-day Brittany and Normandy, including the Veneti, had
surrendered to Rome.

It was probably during the next few months that Publius Crassus,
who was spending the winter with the VIIth Legion near the mouth of
the Loire, undertook an exploratory voyage to Britain to find the
fabled tin mines that were thought to be there. Both Strabo and
Diodorus Siculus allude to this voyage in their later histories, but
Caesar omits any mention of it in *The Gallic War*. It is clear that by the
time Caesar published his account he was determined to be known as
the first Roman to set foot in Britain.

With the end of the fighting season Caesar billeted his legions in
camps in the Loire Valley in central Gaul and in the territory of the
Belgae, and prepared to spend the winter of 57–56 BC in Nearer Gaul.
In two seasons of campaigning he had defeated or destroyed every tribe
that faced him, and so dreaded was his army that chieftains from as far
away as Germany offered to submit to him. He writes that he told
them to come back the next summer because he was eager to return to
Italy and Illyricum. In Rome, his dispatch announcing his final victory
of the year, and the spectacle of caravans of plunder and slaves entering
the capital, caused an outpouring of public acclaim for the "Conqueror
of Gaul." The Senate was obliged to decree sacrifices to the gods, and
festivals and public holidays lasting fifteen days—a longer period of
thanksgiving than ever before accorded a Roman general.

But however gratifying they were, the celebrations did not conceal
from Caesar that new efforts by his opponents to lure Pompey from his
side were now threatening the triple alliance. The danger to Caesar was
not merely the breakdown of the partnership, but possible loss of his
Gallic command, and perhaps worse. Pompey was becoming restless
with the Triumvirate and jealous of Caesar's success and growing reputation. It appears that he took a malicious pleasure in supporting the

festivities for Caesar after the defeat of the Belgae. If the war could be shown to be over, then a case could be made for the recall of Caesar and the dismantling of his army. In any event, Caesar's five-year governorship of Nearer Gaul and Illyricum would end in two years.

Although the effort to recall him in 57 BC came to nothing, the following year brought a new threat to Caesar's position. One of the optimate politicians most strongly opposed to him was Lucius Domitius Ahenobarbus, grandson of the general who had defeated a Gallic army and claimed Provincia for Rome in the previous century. Because of his ancestor's historic association with Provincia, he aspired to be its governor, and had bitterly resented Caesar's succession to the post three years before. He now announced that in the coming election he would be a candidate for consul for the following year, 55 BC. His platform was simple: he would strip Caesar of his army and of all three of his provinces.

For more than one reason Ahenobarbus had the vigorous support of Cato the Younger. Not only had Cato opposed Caesar tooth and nail for more than a decade, he and Ahenobarbus were brothers-in-law. "We are not fighting merely for office," Cato said, "but for liberty against our oppressors."[4] More than that, there is evidence that Pompey, and possibly Cicero, covertly supported Ahenobarbus; if he were elected, Caesar would be vulnerable not only to recall but, with the loss of his immunity, possible prosecution.

In the spring of 56 BC, Caesar hastened to solidify his position. He met with Crassus at Ravenna on the Adriatic, and then with Pompey at Luca (today Lucca), just inside the southern border of his province of Nearer Gaul. Although historians still debate the content and significance of these meetings, they concur that Caesar mollified Pompey and preserved the compact by proposing a new scheme that addressed each of their ambitions. The three agreed again to act in concert, this time to divide Rome's most important provinces among them, and to insure that none of them could be dislodged from power for the foreseeable future.

With the support of Caesar, Pompey and Crassus would stand for election as consuls for the coming year. Once in office they would push through a law extending Caesar's governorship of all three of his

.nces for another five years and allowing him two additional
.ns. They would also arrange their own appointments as provincial
governors in the year following their consulships—Pompey in Spain
and Crassus in Syria—also for five years.

The renewed agreement bears the mark of political genius. By
proposing cooperation, not to mention conspiracy, Caesar removed the
threat from Pompey and splintered the *optimate* opposition—at the
same time yielding nothing and clearing the way for the doubling of
his term and the expansion of his personal army. The co-opting of
Pompey brought along his followers and left Cicero, who had been
courting him, nowhere to turn. Cicero's fortunes and those of his
brother, Quintus, now depended on the Triumvirate, and his about-
face was one of the most startling in Roman politics. "Goodbye to
honesty, truth and honor . . ." Cicero wrote to his friend Atticus in
May. "Since I am refused affection by the powerless, I shall do my best
to win it from the powerful."[5] His forthcoming speech to the Senate
was a panegyric to Caesar in which he urged that the conqueror of
Gaul be allowed to finish the job and bring the entire region under
Roman control. The Senate agreed, and rejected the proposal to recall
Caesar.

The remainder of the scheme was not so easily managed. When
Pompey and Crassus announced their intention to seek consulships,
Gnaeus Marcellinus, the consul in office, ruled that the deadline for
declarations of candidacy had passed and that they could not run as
long as he was in office. When they failed to overcome this obstacle,
Pompey and Crassus engineered a delay of the elections until after the
end of the year, when the term of Marcellinus ended. There the matter
remained throughout the rest of the year 56 BC.

Caesar mentions none of this in *The Gallic War*. After his account
of the campaign of 57 BC, he writes that he was spending the winter in
Illyricum when he received a report from Publius Crassus that three of
the maritime tribes in northern Gaul had captured and imprisoned
several of his officers. The tribes in the area of modern Normandy and
Brittany—the Osismi, the Coriosolites, the Venelli, the Veneti and
others—were known as Aremoricans, from Celtic words meaning
"people beside the sea."[6] For many decades they had acted as middle-

men in the lucrative trade between Gaul and Britain, carrying cargoes of wine, amber, ivory, fine pottery, glass and other luxury goods to British ports in Cornwall and Dorset. There they exchanged them for tin, the principal British export, as well as cattle, hides and hunting dogs. Led by the most powerful among them—the Veneti—they all now agreed to unite against the Roman occupation.

Caesar is vague about the cause of the revolt. It may have been stimulated by the voyage of Publius Crassus to Britain, which threatened to reveal the Aremoricans' trade routes and sources of goods. It is also possible, as some historians have speculated, that the maritime Celts feared a naval attack by the Romans that would destroy their ships and rob them of their livelihood. So important to the Veneti was their maritime trade that one of their earliest gold coins depicts a figure holding aloft one of their sailing ships. Because their fleet was their fortune, and their strongholds on the rocky coast were nearly impregnable by land, any attempt to subdue them would require attacks by both land and water. For this, Caesar needed a navy.

He relates that his response to the news of the revolt was to order his army in Gaul to begin building a large number of warships in the estuary of the Loire River, then called the Liger. Thousands of legionaries and Gaulish slaves spent the entire spring of 56 BC constructing a shipyard and then building the first Roman fleet to sail the Atlantic. It is likely that the ships they built were triremes—the long, narrow vessels resembling giant racing shells that had been perfected by the Athenians four hundred years before. The trireme was powered by two rectangular sails, on separate masts, and three rows of up to twenty-five oarsmen each along both sides. The Romans also commandeered at least a hundred merchant ships from the Gaulish tribes under their control, and conscripted native pilots and seamen from coastal tribes all along the western seaboard of the continent.

Most scholars agree that Caesar intended to invade Britain in the spring of 56 BC to provide a rationale for continuing his Gallic command. But in *The Gallic War* he simply asserts that the revolt of the Veneti obliged him to build a fleet to put it down. Historians J.F. Lazenby and C.E. Stevens, however, suggest that he built his fleet for the express purpose of invading Britain, and that rumors about the invasion and the obvious naval preparations were what precipitated the rebellion, rather than the other way around.[7] They accuse Caesar of reversing the cause and effect in *The Gallic War* by placing the revolt in the previous winter, when it actually occurred in the spring, after he had begun constructing his ships. Thus he justified his preparations for the British invasion on the pretext that he was defending Rome's newly won territory in northern Gaul. Evidence for a deception of this magnitude is inconclusive, but Caesar does conspicuously omit from *The Gallic War* any mention of an invasion of Britain in 56 BC. It would not have suited his political purposes to make the embarrassing admission that the Venetic revolt had thwarted his plans.

When Caesar joined his troops on the Loire in early May of 56 BC, he found all the Celtic tribes of northwestern Gaul making preparations for war. He writes that they had even obtained reinforcements from Britain. He immediately sent three legions northward under Quintus Sabinus against the Aremorican tribes in Normandy, and a force of cavalry under Titus Labienus to northeastern Gaul to prevent the Belgae from joining the uprising. To discourage the tribes of Aquitania from sending reinforcements, he dispatched infantry and cavalry south of the Garonne under Publius Crassus. As his *praefectus classis*—commander of the fleet he would send against the Veneti—he named his young protégé Decimus Brutus, the same man who was sent by Caesar's assassins a dozen years later to persuade him to join them in the hall of Pompey's theater.

Caesar himself led his remaining legions into Brittany to mount a land attack on the fortified settlements of the Veneti. These walled strongholds were situated on low-lying promontories surrounded by water and were accessible by land only briefly, at low tide. Caesar's solution to this problem was again to use the advantage of Roman engineering:

> Sometimes . . . we had the Veneti beaten by the sheer scale of our siegeworks; we managed to keep the sea out with great dams, which we built as high as the walls of their oppida. But whenever this happened and the Veneti began to realize the hopelessness of their position, they would bring up numbers

of ships, of which they had an unlimited supply, load them with their possessions and retreat to other oppida nearby, where they would once more defend themselves by the same advantages of terrain (III, 12).

The Romans spent most of the summer besieging and capturing several strongholds in this manner before Caesar decided that land attacks were useless, and that to defeat the Veneti he would first need to destroy their fleet. By now the Roman ships were ready and waiting in the mouth of the Loire. But it was one thing to build a navy and another to fight a battle at sea. The Romans were poor sailors, and had never ventured into the rough waters of the Atlantic. The Veneti, whose name derives from the Celtic word *vindu,* meaning "white" or "blond," were the most skillful seamen in Gaul and had years of experience with the tides and shallows along the rocky coast of Brittany.[8] Caesar describes their boats as heavy, flat-bottomed cargo carriers, with high prows and sterns to withstand rough seas. The hulls were of oak and the crossbeams, a foot thick, were fastened with heavy iron bolts. Their sails were made of leather, and the anchors held with iron chains. The lighter and faster Roman ships were built for war—and equipped with oars as well as sails. The Veneti were dependent on the wind.

On the day that Caesar gave the order to sail, Decimus Brutus led the Roman fleet out of the estuary of the Loire and northward along the coast. Caesar writes that the Veneti and their allies had collected 220 ships in the mouth of the River Auray, and now sailed out to meet the Romans. Although the precise location is not known, the best evidence is that the two great fleets closed on each other in Quiberon Bay, probably opposite the inlet to the Gulf of Morbihan.[9] Caesar and thousands of his soldiers witnessed the battle from their camp on the heights above the bay.

The customary Roman tactic at sea was to hurl javelins and other missiles onto the decks of the enemy ships, then ram them and use grappling irons to pull close enough to board. Caesar knew that this method would be fruitless against the heavy Venetic ships. Their size precluded ramming by the light Roman triremes, and their height prevented the use of javelins and grappling irons. He records:

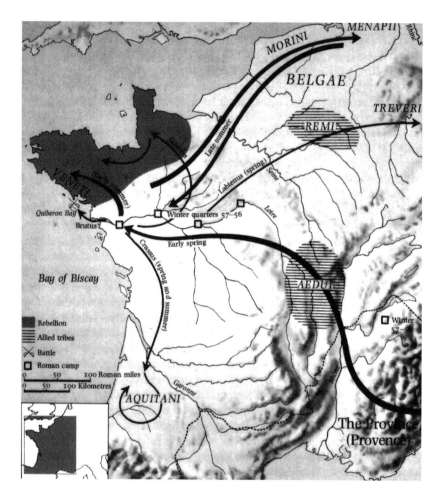

CAMPAIGN OF 56 BC

Caesar spent almost the entire battle season of 56 BC making war on the sea-faring Veneti and their allies in northwestern Gaul. After ordering a fleet of ships built in the Loire estuary, he sent his commanders out in three directions to keep the other tribes at bay. For most of the summer Caesar himself assailed the coastal *oppida* of the Veneti, but when he captured their strongholds they escaped by boat. The subsequent clash between the Venetic and Roman fleets was the first recorded battle in the Atlantic.

But our men had one piece of equipment, prepared beforehand, which proved very effective—sharp-pointed hooks inserted into long poles, rather like the grappling hooks employed in sieges. These were used to grab and pull tight the ropes fastening the yardarms to the masts of the enemy ships. The ropes were then snapped by a sudden spurt of rowing, and the yardarms inevitably collapsed. As the Gallic ships relied entirely on their sails and rigging, when they lost these they were at once robbed of all power of maneuver (III, 14).

Sending two or three ships to attack an enemy vessel, the Romans used this technique to immobilize and then set it on fire, or board it with enough men to overpower the crew. The Veneti had failed to supply themselves with missiles to hold off the Romans, and as one after another of their ships was disabled or captured they saw that they would have to flee to save themselves. The entire fleet came about and, with the wind at its back, began pulling away from the Romans. Their superior seamanship would probably have carried them to safety, but the brisk wind that had prevailed all day suddenly came to a complete stop. The skill and experience of the Veneti could not compensate for their lack of oars, and their boats were left becalmed and unable to move. The Romans in their swift galleys closed in and boarded or burned each Venetic boat, one by one. By sunset only a few had managed to escape. It was the first recorded naval battle in the Atlantic Ocean and a stunning victory for Caesar—again due to a slight technological advantage, and to his luck.

The Veneti and their allies had staked everything on their fleet, and were now forced to surrender. Still angry about their capture of his officers, and frustrated by the time it had taken to defeat them, Caesar decided to make an example of the rebel leaders. The entire governing council of the Veneti—the elders who had taken the decision to revolt—he put to death. The remainder of the tribe he sold into slavery.

At the same time he received word that Quintus Sabinus had lured into battle and then defeated a huge rebel army that had marched against him in Normandy under Virodovix, the chieftain of the

Venelli. A few days later, Publius Crassus reported that he had besieged and captured a large *oppidum* in Aquitania and that the important tribes in the area had submitted to him.

With the threat from the south removed, and in control of the coastal waters, Caesar now led his army into the territory of the Morini, north of the Somme and facing the English Channel. His pretext for this last campaign of the season was that the Morini, and the Menapii to the north of them in modern-day Holland, were the only remaining tribes in Gaul who had not surrendered. But there is little question that his purpose was to clear the area of hostile Gaulish tribes and to make it a secure base for his next campaign: the invasion of Britain.

Caesar writes that he expected a quick victory against the Morini, but when these Celts realized the folly of a pitched battle against the Romans they withdrew into the woods and marshes. From there they made such a successful surprise attack while the Romans were setting up camp that Caesar literally ordered the forest to be cut down. The Romans began clearing a wide area around themselves as they made their way into the woods, and stacked the cut timber as barriers on either side of their roadway. Although Caesar claims that he was making good progress with this method, he was forced to abandon it when the rain became so heavy that "it was impossible to keep the men in tents any longer" (III, 29). After destroying all the buildings, villages and fields they could find, the Romans marched about a hundred miles to the south and set up their winter camps in the valley of the Seine.

Caesar himself returned to Nearer Gaul and spent the winter making sure that the scheme of the Triumvirate proceeded as planned. At the end of December, when the Consul Gnaeus Marcellinus left office, Caesar and his allies arranged the appointment of a temporary consul, an *interrex*, who was friendly to their interests. On taking office in January of 55 BC, he announced that the election for consuls would take place within the month. In the meantime, Caesar had been in communication with his army in Gaul, and as polling day approached, a thousand legionaries appeared in Rome to vote for his candidates—Pompey and Crassus—the latter being the father of their commander, Publius.

Although Domitius Ahenobarbus refused to abandon his own campaign for consul, the alliance was prepared by now to go beyond merely stuffing the ballot box. The night before the election, a gang of ruffians ambushed Ahenobarbus and some of his followers and killed one of his servants. According to Plutarch, Cato was in the middle of the fracas, and was the last one to flee, after being wounded in the right arm.

A combination of these tactics and widespread bribery was successful; the Assembly elected Pompey and Crassus consuls for 55 BC. A few weeks later, legislation was introduced to appoint them, respectively, governors of the Two Spains and Syria for the five years following the end of their consulships. Cato the Younger, the most persistent foe of the Triumvirate, railed against the bill with such fervor that he aroused a storm of opposition in the Assembly. When they could not stifle him, the consuls' henchmen dragged him from the rostra and out of the building, which they then surrounded with armed thugs. According to Plutarch, the violent free-for-all that followed left many wounded and four citizens dead before the legislation was rammed through.[10]

Shortly afterward, Caesar's allies introduced a measure to extend his governorship of the three northern provinces for another five years, until 49 BC. Again, Cato opposed it, speaking directly to Pompey and warning him that he would one day regret supporting Julius Caesar and would find himself unable to be rid of him. Pompey ignored him and the bill passed. The result was that for the foreseeable future the *tres homines* would control Rome's six richest provinces and command all twenty of her legions.

The way was now clear for Caesar to undertake what he must have thought would be his most dazzling feat: the conquest of the mysterious island that many still claimed to be imaginary. But before he could start, another incident in Gaul forced him to postpone his plan. Two German tribes, the Usipetes and the Tencteri, had been driven from their lands by a stronger tribe, and crossed the Rhine where it enters present-day Holland, advancing into the territory of the Belgic Menapii. Now they began to range southward along what is today the Maas, or Meuse, River into modern Belgium and the Ardennes region, much closer to the ports from which Caesar intended to launch his invasion.

Finding it necessary to remove this threat to his base of operations, Caesar left his winter quarters for Gaul somewhat earlier in the season than usual. He joined his legions in the region of the lower Seine, and then met with the kings and tribal chieftains of northern Gaul, some of whom had begun to reconcile themselves to the Germans. He declared that he intended to repel the invaders, and ordered them to supply him with cavalry for the campaign. He then marched eastward into southern Belgium and crossed the Meuse, where he was met by envoys of the Usipetes and the Tencteri. He demanded that they return to the east bank of the Rhine, but they refused, and the two sides agreed to delay any fighting for at least three days so that negotiations could continue. Despite this, a small number of German cavalry made a surprise attack a few days later on a troop of Caesar's Gallic horsemen, killing several dozen and forcing the remainder to flee.

Caesar writes that he now understood that he faced a treacherous enemy, and prepared for a battle the following day. In the morning, however, a contingent of German chiefs and elders appeared in his camp to apologize for the attack and to negotiate further. Caesar seized and confined them, then led his legions on a rapid eight-mile march and burst into the enemy camp. Taken by surprise, and without their leaders, the Germans were unable to organize a defense. Writes Caesar: ". . . those Germans able to arm themselves fast enough resisted our men for a short time, fighting among their carts and baggage wagons. But because the Germans had brought everything they had with them when they left their homes and crossed the Rhine, there was also a great crowd of women and children and these now began to flee in all directions. I sent the cavalry to hunt them down" (IV, 14).

With these chilling words, Caesar reported a massacre that stunned even an admiring Rome. To this he added the incredible statistic that the Germans numbered 430,000, no doubt including women and children. On top of that, he claimed that he lost not a single soldier. When his supporters in the Senate proposed the usual thanksgiving celebration, Cato the Younger countered that to atone for the Roman butchery Caesar should himself be handed over to the Germans. His strenuous arguments against the celebration persuaded the Senate that Caesar had gone too far, and the decree for a thanksgiving was defeated. The failure of the bill may have moved Caesar to a feat he was sure would capture the public's fancy: the bridge across the Rhine.

After disposing of the Usipetes and the Tencteri, Caesar found himself somewhat north of the confluence of the Rhine and the Mosel. The Rhine had for centuries been the traditional boundary between the Germanic tribes and the Celts of Gaul. No Roman general had penetrated as deeply into Gaul as Caesar, and now, on the banks of the Rhine, to be the first to cross it was more than he could resist.

His pretexts were the familiar ones. German tribes had repeatedly crossed the Rhine to maraud in Gaul, which he had taken upon himself to protect, and they must be taught that even their river could not protect them from Roman might. Also, one tribe in Germany, the Ubii, had declared their friendship with Rome and petitioned Caesar to protect them from their enemies. Last, a troop of German cavalry that had eluded the Romans in the battle just concluded had fled across the river and taken refuge with another tribe hostile to Rome. Caesar's demand that the cavalry be handed over to him drew a haughty refusal.

When the Ubii offered to supply him with boats, Caesar disdained to use them, saying that it would be too risky and "would not be fitting for my own prestige and that of Rome" (IV, 17). Instead, he set his men to work cutting trees, shaping timbers and driving piles into the riverbed for a bridge across the Rhine. The completed structure consisted simply of several layers of planks laid on crossbeams that had been placed between two rows of piles reaching from bank to bank. The downstream row of piles was buttressed against the current, and scattered piles were placed upstream of the bridge to deflect large floating objects. The precise location of the bridge has never been determined, but a careful analysis of Caesar's text by the French scholar Michel Rambaud concludes that it was built in the vicinity of another famous bridge—at Remagen—between modern Coblenz and Bonn.[11]

Although Caesar's claim that only ten days later his army marched across the first bridge on the Rhine may be exaggerated, the feat itself—a bridge 500 yards long and 40 feet wide across a major river—

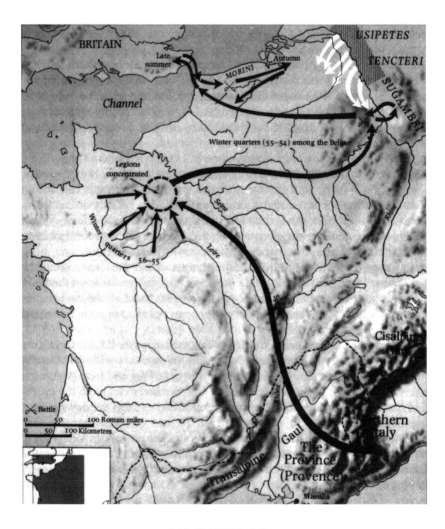

CAMPAIGN OF 55 BC

Responding to a threat from German tribes, Caesar traveled across Gaul from Italy early in 55 BC to his legions' winter quarters in the lower Seine Valley, and then marched with them to the edge of eastern Gaul. After defeating two large German tribes, the Romans built—and then destroyed—the first bridge over the Rhine. Caesar afterward hurried back to the coast, where his fleet was waiting, and sailed up the Channel to Britain with two legions—the first Roman assault on the island.

is evidence of the remarkable organization and engineering skill of a Roman army in the field. Once over the Rhine, however, the Roman incursion into German territory was a distinct anticlimax. After spending only eighteen days burning nearby villages and grain fields, they recrossed into Gaul and tore down the bridge behind them. Caesar writes that he considered that he had "done all that honor or interest required," but with the fighting season dwindling away, it is obvious that he was eager to get to Britain.

Hurrying back across the north of Gaul, he stopped in the region of modern-day Arras and prevailed on Commius the Atrebate, whom he had come to trust and admire, to accompany him to the coast. Once there, he ordered the triremes that had been fitted out as warships and the Gallic freighters to be used as troop transports to be brought to his port of embarkation. This he fails to name, saying only that there the crossing to Britain was the shortest, and that it was in "the territory of the Morini," today the northern French département of Pas de Calais. English and French historians conclude that this spot was most likely at the village now called Wissant, a few miles south of modern Calais.[12] Caesar then summoned to his camp a number of Gaulish traders who regularly crossed the Channel to exchange goods with the British Celts. He questioned them about the names and sizes of the tribes on the island and about the coastline opposite Gaul, especially any harbors that might accommodate a large fleet. They were unable, or unwilling, to tell him what he wanted to know.

As a further precaution he sent a trusted officer, Gaius Volusenus, in a fast warship to reconnoiter the British coast. In his account Caesar is again careful to indicate that Volusenus did not land, saying that to do so would have meant certain capture—thus preserving the notion that Caesar was the first Roman in Britain. Volusenus spent four or five days exploring the shoreline of Kent, perhaps sailing as far as the Isle of Sheppey opposite the Thames estuary. What he reported Caesar does not tell us, but archaeologist Christopher Hawkes judges that Volusenus recommended a landing at Dover and occupation of the hillfort overlooking the Straits.[13] From there, depending on how the Celts reacted, Caesar could enter Kent by marching up the valley of the Dour River.

By now, news of the impending invasion had reached the island, and envoys from several tribes in Britain appeared in Caesar's camp offering to give hostages and submit to the authority of Rome. Caesar gave them "generous promises" and urged them to keep their word. To help them persuade their leaders not to oppose him he sent back with them his own emissary, Commius, accompanied by thirty cavalrymen. His instructions to him were to "visit as many tribes as he could, to encourage them to seek the protection of Rome, and to tell them that I should soon be arriving in Britain" (IV, 21).

When all the preparations for sailing had been completed, Caesar received word that eighteen of his transports had been prevented by bad weather from reaching the port of departure, and were forced to return to their harbor about eight miles to the south. But the end of the sailing season was approaching and he could afford to wait no longer. In a move that was to have severe repercussions on his success in Britain, he sent his three hundred cavalry to the more southern port and instructed them to embark promptly on the eighteen transports there and follow him to Britain.

Because the mainland coastal area was still not secure, Caesar left six legions in Gaul under his commanders Sabinus, Cotta and Rufus to attack the Morini and Menapii and to guard the port. It was about midnight on the 25th or the 26th of August by the modern calendar that the eighty transports and a dozen or so warships drifted out of the harbor on an ebbing tide. On board were two legions of infantry—the VIIth and the Xth—and perhaps two thousand auxiliary troops, including hired slingers and archers. Under a nearly full moon the crossing was calm, and by 9:00 A.M. the lead warships were off the Dover cliffs.

CHAPTER V

EXPEDITION TO BRITAIN

The site of Caesar's first landfall in Britain is no longer in serious dispute. His inquiries and preparations, the length of his trip and his description of the great chalk cliffs all indicate that his first sight of the British Celts was near what was later the Roman seaport of Portus Dubris, modern Dover. At the time of his expedition and for many centuries afterward, a natural harbor at Dover extended as much as two miles inland from the present-day shoreline. Caesar had specifically sought information about a harbor for his ships, and C.F.C. Hawkes' speculation that he intended to attack the Britons' hillfort at Dover is likely to be correct. His opinion is supported by the confirmation in 1959 that the remains of pre-Roman earthworks lay under the site of Dover Castle.[1]

As Caesar's triremes approached the cliffs, one glance at the hostile army ranged along their edge was enough to convince him that his envoy, Commius, had failed in his mission. The Britons apparently had changed their minds and would not accommodate ten thousand Roman soldiers. He was forced to change his plans and find a beach where his men could land and have a better chance to hold a beachhead. But where he did so—which way he turned from the Dover cliffs—is still not known today.

The answer depends on the direction of the tide and wind when he abandoned the landing near Dover and ordered his fleet to proceed along the coast. While waiting for the rest of his fleet to arrive, he summoned his officers to his flagship and warned them that because of the uncertainty of seagoing operations they were to carry out his orders instantly and without question. After dismissing them, he waited until mid-afternoon for the eighty wind-driven troop transports to reach the coast. Then, he writes, "Both the wind and the tide were now in our favor, so I gave the signal for the anchors to be weighed. We moved on about seven miles and ran the ships ashore on a flat and open beach" (V, 23).

Since the mid-nineteenth century, historians and archaeologists have argued about the direction of the tide and wind that Caesar found favorable on that summer afternoon in 55 BC. They have pored over almanacs and tide tables, and consulted astronomers, meteorologists, hydrographers and veteran Channel sailors. Because the offshore winds and Channel currents can vary so dramatically from hour to hour, it is necessary to know the precise day and time that he found himself off the cliffs of Dover.

It was the astronomer Edmond Halley, identifier of the comet that bears his name, who made the first calculation of the date. Caesar writes that his cavalry transports at last set out from Gaul on the fourth day after his own arrival in Britain, and that there was a full moon on the night the Romans sighted them from their camp on the beach. In a paper read before the Royal Society in 1691, Halley announced that the full moon observed by Caesar's army occurred some hours before dawn on the morning of August 31, 55 BC, by the modern calendar.[2] This would have put Caesar at Dover on the morning of the 27th. However, even this date is disputed because it is not clear from Caesar's narrative how he counted the days, or at what time the cavalry transports were eventually seen. To complicate the issue, the direction of the current varies at different distances from the shore, and it is not known how far offshore Caesar's fleet was anchored.

The results of these inquiries are mixed, but the prevalent opinion today is that the tide and wind carried Caesar's fleet northward around the cliffs along the jutting edge of Kent, called the South Foreland. From there it was only a few miles to a gently sloping beach of shingle between what is now the site of Walmer Castle and the town of Deal. Supporting this conclusion is the fact that the coastline seven miles southwest of Dover is mostly marshy land, unsuitable for landing boats. Further, the geography in northeastern Kent is more easily reconciled with Caesar's later recorded movements.

Between Kingsdown at the northern edge of the Dover cliffs and

Sandown Castle to the north of Deal there is today a five-mile stretch of flat and open beach. It is composed of shingle—stones the size of small eggs worn smooth by the action of the waves. The rolling hills behind this stretch of coast are now the sites of several of the country's finest golf courses. In the sixteenth century, Henry VIII built castles at Walmer, Deal and Sandown to protect his coast against the same sort of invasion that Caesar mounted more than fifteen hundred years earlier. After being undermined by the sea, Sandown Castle was demolished in 1859; the other two are presently museums.

In recent centuries Deal's reputation has rested on fishing and smuggling, but today it is a pretty seaside resort catering to the tourist and retirement trade. The townspeople are satisfied that it was here that the first ferocious battle took place between Roman and Briton. In 1946, an even two thousand years after the event, they erected a plaque on the beach to commemorate it.

It was early in the evening, but still light, and eighteen hours since they had set sail, when the men of Caesar's VIIth and Xth Legions reached their landing-place on the open shore of Kent. Using only the single sail and a steering rudder, the Gallic crews maneuvered the clumsy troop carriers, each at least two hundred tons' burden, into a line facing the beach. From there, under a barrage of arrows, javelins and stones from the slingers and archers on the war galleys spread out behind them, they edged forward. Caesar was well aware of the hazards of bringing such heavy vessels to the beach with the tide running out. He writes:

> We were now faced with very grave difficulties, for the following reasons. Because of their size, our ships could not be run ashore except where the water was deep; the soldiers were unfamiliar with the terrain, their hands were full and the heavy weapons they carried weighed them down; they had to jump down from their ships, get a footing in the waves and fight the enemy all at the same time (V, 24).

Each Roman infantryman wore chest armor and a bronze helmet, and carried a sword, shield, dagger and one or two javelins. The

Britons used the same weapons, but wore a minimum of covering; they stained their shaven bodies with an intense blue pigment that gave them a savage appearance. As each Roman transport touched bottom and the first legionaries jumped down into chin-high water, a mob of screaming Britons, brandishing their spears and swords, raced across the shallow surf and attacked them. Those Britons in chariots drove them right into the water, hurling their spears, slashing with their swords and then dashing away out of reach. Others stood sure-footed in the shallows, shooting their arrows or heaving their spears at point-blank range at the Romans struggling to advance through the swirling waves.

Caesar's comment is blunt: "Our men were terrified at this." His explanation is diplomatic: "They were completely unfamiliar with this kind of fighting and did not show the same spirit and keenness as they usually did in battles on land" (V, 24).

Leaping into the waves from their bobbing vessels, the Romans would surely have been routed had this been ordinary combat between soldiers using only their individual weapons. But they had more than swords and spears to use against the Britons. As a result of their wars with the Macedonians, the Romans had learned to construct several types of throwing devices, called *tormenti* because they made use of torsion produced by twisted ropes. On the decks of the war galleys was one type, the *catapulta*, a portable wooden frame holding a bow-like assemblage. A thick rope of hair or sinew several feet in length was attached at either end to vertical poles that could be turned so that the rope was twisted tightly. The thrust of energy created when the thick, twisted rope was released could send a javelin or a one-pound stone several hundred yards with tremendous force. A careful reading of ancient accounts and testing of modern full-scale models confirm that the *catapulta* was accurate enough to bring down a horse or even a single individual from a distance of 250 yards.[3]

Caesar now moved his warships a short distance from the transports, and then ordered them rowed hard and run ashore. From there the archers, slingers and *catapultae* unleashed a stream of missiles into the enemy's exposed right flank with devastating effect. The Britons, their shields on their left arms, were forced to turn away from the water to protect themselves. More than that, they were terrified by the strange *catapultae*, the unusual shape of the high-decked war galleys and the triple rows of fluttering oars they had never seen before. They halted their rush into the water and moved back a short distance.

But still the legionaries hesitated. Those few who had jumped into the water had been struck down by multiple spears and swords, and even though the way was now clear, the water was just as deep.

In each Roman legion was an *aquilifer*, a soldier chosen for his experience and bravery, who carried the legion's standard, the *aquila*, a sculpted wooden eagle painted silver and mounted on a long pole. The *aquila* identified the legion and symbolized its pride and honor. The man who carried the eagle of the Xth Legion now did his duty, Caesar tells us:

> . . . after praying to the gods that his act would bring good luck to the legion, he shouted out loudly, "Jump down men, unless you want to betray your eagle to the enemy. I at any rate shall have done my duty to my country and my general."
>
> With these words he flung himself from the ship and began to carry the eagle toward the enemy. Then the soldiers jumped down from the ship all together, urging each other not to allow a disgrace like that to happen. When the men from the next ships saw what these soldiers did, they followed them and advanced toward the enemy (V, 25).

A more timely act Caesar could not have wished for, nor could he have found a more vivid anecdote to prove the loyalty of his men. The truth of it we will never know.

The Britons now surged back into the water against the Romans, and all along the shore the battle was reduced to the most brutal form of hand-to-hand fighting: thrusting swords and daggers, rearing horses, shouts and screams, and flying spears. The Romans could not get firm footing in the deep, swirling water, so there was no chance for the usual orderly advance of the infantry. Some were separated from their units and fell in with others, and those who found themselves alone were quickly surrounded and cut down by enemy horsemen racing back and forth along the beach. Both attackers and defenders had to clamber over their dead and drowning comrades to get at each other, and the water was soon red with blood.

"The result," Caesar writes, "was great disorder." He now made another tactical move: "When I realized what was happening, I ordered the boats from the warships and also the scouting vessels to be filled with troops, and then sent these to help where I had seen my men in difficulties" (V, 26).

The thousands of legionaries advancing out of the water and the barrage of deadly missiles hurtling into the ranks of their unprotected warriors was a fearsome military assault the Britons could not withstand for long, however. Their cavalry and speedy two-wheel chariots were better suited to open-country fighting and they could not match the Romans' firepower. Caesar records the Britons' plight: "As soon as our men had a footing on dry land and all their comrades had joined them, they charged the enemy and put them to flight. But they were unable to pursue very far because our cavalry had not been able to hold their course and reach the island. This was the one thing that prevented me enjoying my usual good luck" (V, 26).

The landing of Caesar's fleet on the coast of Kent must be classed as one of the most daring and dangerous feats in Roman military history. Neither he nor any of his soldiers had ever taken part in a seaborne invasion of this magnitude, and no Roman warships had ever attempted a landing in the hazardous tides of the Atlantic. That Caesar even considered it is evidence of an enormous, even foolhardy, ambition that drove him to take the most extraordinary risks. A hundred years earlier, the Roman playwright Terence had used the phrase "Fortune favors the brave." Caesar and his men were certainly brave, and it was their good fortune that the Britons could not muster enough men to keep them off the beach. They would never again oppose a Roman landing.

After a midnight sailing and a full day on the Channel, followed by a fierce battle to land and gain control of the beach, Caesar's exhausted legionaries had still to secure their camp. It was several hours after sunset by the time the ten thousand cold and wet soldiers regrouped themselves, posted their guards and began unloading their ships. The eighteen cavalry transports had not yet arrived, and one warship was sent back to Gaul to guide them to the landing-place. The legionaries hauled the warships onto the beach, and left the eighty barge transports at anchor. Some men attended to the wounded and buried the dead, and most of the rest set about with shovels and picks to construct their camp.

Wherever Roman armies stopped for even one night, they set up an elaborate camp in a standard design that varied little over the course of several centuries. Caesar's army needed a well-fortified one because he was in hostile country and had no way to retreat except by boat. And the camp would have to be substantial enough to protect his fleet and serve as his supply depot for the duration of his stay in Britain. Although he is silent throughout *The Gallic War* on the nature of his camps, other writers have recorded the pattern habitually used by armies in the field.[4]

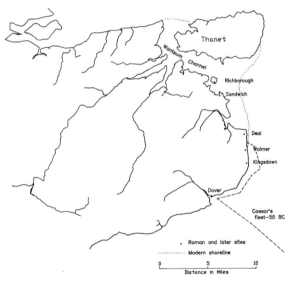

EASTERN KENT IN THE 1ST CENTURY BC

The ancient coastline is inferred from the line distinguishing the relatively modern deposits of alluvium and beach material from the older chalk formation. By medieval times the Wantsum Channel was filled with mud and marshes, leaving Richborough more than two miles inland. By the 17th century, Sandwich was no longer usable as a seaport.

The first requirement of the campsite was that it be on raised ground, preferably sloping downward toward the enemy, and near a safely accessible supply of freshwater. A nearby source of wood, preferably a sapling forest, was also helpful because of the need for fencing and firewood. Once Caesar had picked the location, the *mensuri*, the measurers or surveyors, selected a vantage point from which the whole camp could be easily seen, and planted a white flag on it to mark the location of the *praetorium*, the commander's tent. Because the Romans believed that favorable omens came from the east, his tent faced eastward. After measuring a one-hundred-foot square around the *praetorium*, the *mensuri* marked a much larger square area around this: the outer perimeter of the camp. For the army of two legions in Britain this square was fully seven hundred yards to a side. Then hundreds of legionaries arranged themselves along the outside perimeter of the square and dug a continuous ditch along it about a yard deep, piling the earth in a bank just inside it. If the enemy was near, the depth of the ditch was tripled. On top of the earth bank they constructed a palisade of sharpened stakes interwoven with lateral branches and also sharpened at their ends. The result was a barrier that could be breached only with the most determined effort, even if there were no armed defenders.

In the center of each of the four sides was left a level bridgeway across the ditch and bank, and at those entrances a gate in the palisade fence was constructed. The entire enclosed square of the camp was then divided into two unequal rectangles separated by a roadway a hundred feet wide called the *via principalis*; this was marked out with spears and extended from one side of the camp to the other. In the smaller rectangle in the rear, in a line in front of the *praetorium*, were set up the tents of Caesar's staff, the paymaster, the legionary commanders and tribunes, and the hospital. The select force of cavalry and infantry who made up Caesar's bodyguard, and any guests he had with him, as well as the camp meeting-place—the forum—were also in this area.

In the larger rectangle at the front of the camp, arranged in squares with roadways fifty feet wide between them, went the leather tents of the legionaries, eight men to a tent, making a *contubernium*, a tent-party, the smallest unit in the army. Because a fourth of the men were on duty elsewhere at any given time, tent space was provided for only three-quarters of each unit. Around the entire camp, between the tents and the protective bank and fence, a space about two hundred feet wide was kept clear for a variety of uses: storing supplies, keeping horses, mules and wagons, and housing prisoners. Another wide roadway lined with spears, the *via praetoria,* divided the camp from front to back.

The Roman custom of preparing such a camp each night in the field was already several centuries old when Caesar first took command of a legion, and he was wise to adhere to it. In his memoirs, Napoleon Bonaparte attributed the Romans' military success to this habit, saying, "During ten or twelve centuries of Roman history, there is no case where one of their camps was overrun."[5]

Although Caesar's camp extended over more than a hundred acres, its remains have never been found. Even assuming that the beach between Deal and Walmer was the landing-place, its location would remain a difficult question because the coasts of Kent have changed considerably since Roman times. The town of Sandwich, for instance, was a thriving port until the seventeenth century, but is now land-locked more than two miles inland. Just to the north of Sandwich, the fortress of Richborough overlooked the leading port of Roman Britain, but lies today surrounded by low-lying meadows and meandering streams. The flat chalk peninsula of Thanet was until medieval times an island separated from the mainland by the Wantsum Channel, through which ships regularly made their way to the Thames estuary.

In the area of Deal the accumulation of silt and tidal deposits has pushed the shoreline eastward into the Channel, and it is certain that if Caesar's camp is ever found it will be much farther from the water than when it was built. In 55 BC it cannot have been far inland because Caesar says that his warships were hauled up on the beach and the eighty transports left at anchor. After a difficult landing at the end of the day, he would have camped only a short distance from his ships, and it would have been prudent to stay near them until he knew more about what lay ahead.

Napoleon III, who published a biography of Caesar in the 1860s, asserted that the camp was indicated by the conformation of the ground "on the height where the village of Walmer rises," now some thirteen hundred yards from the beach, and modern archaeologists have come to the same conclusion.[6] In the 1930s, excavations in this area revealed cremation urns from the Bronze and Iron ages, as well as food bones and potsherds, but nothing to indicate a Roman military camp. For the time being its location remains an archaeological puzzle.

Camped on a desolate beach on an island at the very edge of the known world, Caesar's men had little or no idea of where they were, or why they had come there. Caesar kept his plans to himself until it was necessary to reveal them, and it is likely that not even his officers knew the purpose of the expedition or where they were going next. Caesar may have had no clear reason for the expedition. He did not plan it well, and he set out so late in the year that unless he stayed the winter in Britain he had only a few weeks before the return crossing would become too dangerous.

Historians have ascribed political, economic and military motives to Caesar for his first British adventure. By the spring of 55 BC, Gaul appeared to have been conquered, and three years of campaigning had produced not only repeated victories but enormous amounts of booty. It was said that when Caesar's plundered Celtic treasure arrived in Rome the price of gold bullion dropped by one third. No one knew what Britain would produce, but silver, gold and precious stones were possibilities. Suetonius speculates that it was pearls that took Caesar to Britain, citing his love of costly gems and his habit of weighing them in the palm of his hand.[7] Another commodity, however, was far more likely to be found, and it was one that all the Mediterranean societies continued to seek even in the farthest corners of the known world: tin.

For centuries the Phoenicians, Carthaginians and then the Romans had carried on an extensive trade with the Celts for tin, a scarce element needed in the manufacture of bronze. The tribes in control of tin mines kept the locations of these a secret, but many ancient writers allude to the Cassiterides, or "Tin Islands," somewhere off the coast of northern Gaul. The Cassiterides have never been definitely identified, but are thought to refer to the Cornish peninsula, where tin was abundant. After obtaining tin from the Britons, Gaulish merchants then transported it on pack animals along several land routes to Massilia, where they sold it to the Romans.

Now that Rome controlled the coast of Gaul, a direct connection with a source of tin was certainly on Caesar's mind when he contemplated an expedition to Britain, but he never mentions it. Historian Stephen Mitchell has speculated that this was because an economic motive for the invasion of a foreign land would be demeaning to the *dignitas* of a Roman general.[8] Caesar may indeed have been reluctant to appear too mercenary because a tradition of the Roman governing class prevented its members from engaging in moneylending or commercial activities. A specific law prohibited senators from owning seagoing ships, and commercial motives were rarely used as justification for foreign policy. Nevertheless, ready access to British tin mines would have been a welcome result of the expedition.

The most valuable commodity of all, however, was slaves—the backbone of Roman society and a major source of income for Caesar. A vigorous slave trade flourished all over the Mediterranean world, and thousands of captives were transported to Rome every year to satisfy a growing demand by newly wealthy and even middle-class households. Estimates are that slaves made up 35 to 40 percent of the population of Republican Rome, a higher percentage than in the American South before the Civil War.[9] Slaves acquired from Britain might ensure the profitable outcome of a Roman move across the Channel.

For Caesar, however, far more important than booty was his reputation with the Roman voters and his legal status as the Governor of Gaul. So long as he remained in office, he could retain his legions and his legal immunity from prosecution on whatever charges that might be brought by his enemies. But the regular calls in the Senate and elsewhere for his removal had become especially pointed when Gaulish resistance came to a standstill. The year before, the Triumvirate had applied enough muscle to deny the consulship to the dangerous Domitius Ahenobarbus, and then pressured the Senate to extend Caesar's command; but each new election brought another chance for the opposition to remove him. Caesar's political fortune depended in large part on the public reaction to the success of his army. For the past three years all Rome had been attentive to his campaigns against the barbarians, and a daring thrust into an unknown land—something to rival the campaigns of Pompey in the previous decade—would enhance his standing as a popular hero.

The military situation in Gaul was clearer. The Celts had received reinforcements of men and arms from Britain, and several of their tribal leaders had fled to the island when Caesar destroyed their armies. There was always the possibility that they might recruit new forces and attack across the Channel. Despite this danger, a military justification for the British invasion was weak. But in terms of politics it was the most acceptable, and Caesar emphasized it in *The Gallic War*. In the law-conscious Roman world he was mindful of the need for a legal pretext for his actions. Writing after the fact, however, he was careful not to declare a plan beyond what he actually accomplished.

He describes his first invasion as a type of reconnaissance:

Not much of the summer was left, and winter sets in early in these regions because the whole of this part of Gaul faces north. Nevertheless I went ahead with plans for an expedition to Britain because I knew that in almost all of our campaigns in Gaul our enemies had received reinforcements from the Britons.

Even if we should not have enough time for conducting a campaign that season, I thought it would be very useful merely to have visited the island, to have seen what sort of people lived there, and to get some idea of the terrain and the harbours and landing places (IV, 20).

The Britons' overtures to him in Gaul and their escort of his emissary, Commius, and his cavalry back across the Channel with them may have led Caesar to think that he and his two legions would be welcome visitors to Britain. But the battle to land dispelled that notion, and showed that the Britons were not only hostile but extremely dangerous. And though Caesar had cause to feel fortunate, he might have wondered how long his luck would last. At great cost, the Romans had gained a beachhead and secured themselves for the night; but the army had brought a minimum of supplies and food, and unless they returned quickly they would have to find provisions in the countryside around them. Furthermore, without cavalry they could not advance far against the Britons and their nimble chariots.

The sight of these quaint vehicles must have startled Caesar's legionaries. The Romans had never used chariots in warfare, although Roman troops had faced enemy chariots in Gaul in the previous century. But by the first century BC they were a distinct anomaly on the battlefield—reminiscent, as one historian has said, of a scene in *The Iliad*.[10] A few years later, Caesar would reproduce a Celtic chariot on one of his coins, perhaps to remind the public of his deeds in Britain. Indeed, the Roman public was always charmed by the customs of the barbarians beyond their borders. A letter of Cicero's has been preserved in which he facetiously asks one of Caesar's officers to capture a chariot and bring it back to Rome. British chariots later became objects of fashionable interest in Rome, being displayed in gladiatorial fights, sometimes with female charioteers.

As for the defenders, the ferocious conflict on the beach and the size of the Roman army apparently convinced them that further resistance was useless. Many classical observers noted that Celtic armies tended to be impulsive and emotional, and therefore easily discouraged by even temporary setbacks. The Britons came the next day to surrender and offer hostages. With them they brought Commius and his thirty horsemen, whom they had held in chains for more than a week. Caesar presents himself as magnanimous and statesmanlike:

> When he [Commius] had disembarked and was delivering my instructions to the Britons in the role of an envoy, they had seized him and thrown him into chains; now, after the battle, they sent him back to me. In asking for peace they put the blame for Commius's treatment on the common people, begging me to pardon what had been done through their ignorance. I reproached them for having started hostilities without provocation when they had of their own accord sent envoys to me on the continent asking for peace. But I said I would forgive their ignorance and told them to send me their hostages.
>
> . . . [T]he chiefs began to come from all parts of the island to put themselves and their communities under my protection. With this the peace was established (IV, 27).

Caesar was undoubtedly aware that what he had was no more than a truce, and even after the return of Commius and his horsemen he was still unwilling to advance inland without his cavalry. The eighteen cavalry transports that had not come with him were nowhere to be seen. As it happened, they were still in Gaul because when they were ready to sail the wind was in the wrong direction, delaying them even further. The army waited anxiously for their arrival, and finally on the fourth day after landing they saw the transports approaching the coast. What happened next not only denied Caesar the use of his cavalry, but put the entire expedition in jeopardy and removed any hope he had of advancing inland.

A sudden storm blew up in the Channel—so violent that it stopped the transports in their course and drove them away from the shore. Some were pushed back toward Gaul, and others driven down the coast, where they attempted to anchor. This they were unable to do, and before the night was over all eighteen cavalry transports were forced back to the continent.

The same storm, accompanied by the highest tide of the month, roared across Caesar's beached and anchored ships, ripping away their cables, anchors and tackle, and breaking a dozen of them into pieces. The entire fleet was rendered useless, and ten thousand soldiers stranded. Faced with the loss of their ships, no cavalry support and a minimal supply of food and provisions, Caesar's troops were close to panic. The sullen mob of savages in front of them, though subdued at the moment, might be easily reinforced and massacre them on the beach.

Caesar smoothes over this incident as another misfortune, saying "we did not realize" that the highest tides occurred at this time of the month. But there is no question that it was a major blunder, and he was surely more culpable than he admits. Although the Romans had little or no experience with tidal movements, Caesar was familiar with the writings of Greek navigators, who had described the high tides and sudden storms of the Atlantic. His fleet had fought a naval battle with the Veneti off the coast of Gaul the year before, and he had many times seen the Atlantic tides himself. Last, the Gaulish seamen who manned his ships could have warned him that the highest tides of the month came with the full moon, and that it was folly to leave his ships exposed at that time of year. Perhaps they did, and were ignored.

In describing their predicament, Caesar admits an oversight in a way that diffuses his own responsibility: "No arrangements had been made about grain supplies for spending the winter in Britain because it had been generally assumed that we should winter in Gaul" (IV, 29). As the situation never became critical, and the army would return safely to Gaul, he could safely paint the darkest picture of the circumstances.

A key fact is that Caesar had failed to find the great natural harbor at Richborough, which at this time was an island a few miles north of his landing spot. This island lay in the Wantsum Channel, behind and protected by the island of Thanet. In the next century, the armada sent by Claudius found it and used it as the principal port for the successful invasion of Britain, but some scholars question whether it was suitable for a landing in Caesar's time. Nevertheless, it is highly likely that there was a site on Richborough island or elsewhere in the Wantsum Channel that would have offered more protection for Caesar's fleet.

Realizing that the Britons might change their minds at any moment and attack his camp, Caesar took the only course he could, and as soon as the weather cleared he set his men to repairing the ships. The Romans salvaged timber and bronze from the twelve that were destroyed to repair the others, and Caesar sent the first seaworthy galley back to the continent with an order for more materials and equipment. He assigned one legion to work on the ships and guard the camp; the other he sent each day into the nearby farmlands to cut wheat.

For several days the Britons remained at a distance while the Romans laboriously dismantled their wrecked ships and repaired and refitted the others. But before long, just as the Romans suspected, the Britons realized how vulnerable the invaders were, and that the camp on the beach could be overwhelmed if enough men could be found. Caesar wrote: "They were confident that if we were defeated or prevented from returning, no one in the future would cross to invade Britain" (IV, 30). The Britons now ceased sending hostages and quietly began calling back the troops they had sent home.

The first incident occurred on a day when Caesar had sent the VIIth Legion out to strip the nearby fields of grain. Guards on duty at the camp gates reported that they saw a large cloud of dust in the direction the legion had taken. Caesar mobilized two cohorts—nearly a thousand men—and led them quickly out of the camp, ordering all but two cohorts of the remaining legion to arm themselves and follow him. They found the men of the VIIth surrounded by enemy chariots and cavalry, and struggling to hold their ground, spears and stones flying at them from every side. Scattered about the fields, disarmed and busy cutting wheat, they had been surprised by the Britons, who had hidden in the woods near the only area that had not yet been harvested.

At the sight of the reinforcements, however, the Britons quickly abandoned their attack and withdrew. Caesar did not pursue them; he was not yet ready for a full-scale battle. In his account of this episode, he describes the unusual tactics of chariot warfare:

> First they drive in all directions hurling spears. Generally they succeed in throwing the ranks of their opponents into confusion just with the terror caused by their galloping horses and the din of the wheels. They make their way through the squadrons of their own cavalry, then jump down from their chariots and fight on foot. Meanwhile the chariot-drivers withdraw a little way from the fighting and position the chariots in such a way that if their masters are hard pressed by the enemy's numbers, they have an easy means of retreat to their own lines.
>
> Thus when they fight they have the mobility of cavalry and the staying power of infantry; and with daily training and practice they have become so efficient that even on steep slopes they can control their horses at full gallop, check and turn them in a moment, run along the pole, stand on the yoke and get back into the chariot with incredible speed (IV, 33).

Metal finds and coin and literary evidence suggest that a typical British chariot consisted of a small platform, open at front and back, mounted on a wooden axle. Fastened to the axle with bronze fittings were two wooden spoked wheels, about two and a half to three feet in diameter, and almost five feet apart. A strip of iron or, in some cases, double-shear steel about one and a half inches wide was shrunk onto the outer edge of the wheels without the use of nails. The charioteer, or driver, sat at the front of the platform between two sideboards of wood or wickerwork, holding a whip and the reins of both horses. The warrior stood or sat behind the driver, armed with a shield, sword and one or more javelins.[11]

Caesar does not say whether there were scythes attached to the chariots' axles, a practice that was widely believed to be used by the Britons at the time. Both the Persians and Greeks had use scythed chariots in battle, the latter against Sulla's army in Greece just three decades earlier. But they had fallen out of favor in the Mediterranean world because, like elephants, they usually caused as much damage to their own armies as to the enemy. Just as the Britons continued to use chariots after they had been abandoned elsewhere, there is ample literary evidence that they fitted them with scythes to cut down enemy infantry. However, there is so far no archaeological evidence for scythed chariots in Britain.[12]

Caesar was more than a little concerned about the Britons' chariots because his men had not seen them before. Their opponents on the continent used their horses for conventional cavalry. But in Britain most horses were the size of modern ponies, ten to twelve hands, too small to easily carry a man into battle, and more effectively used to pull chariots. The continental Gauls and Germans had imported and learned to breed a larger horse that was capable of carrying a warrior and his weapons, and a single horseman was cheaper and far more mobile than a two-man chariot. The Romans themselves were generally poor horsemen, and in the army of Caesar's time citizens were drafted only into the infantry. Roman generals recruited their cavalry from subject peoples, such as Gauls, Germans and Numidians, who were much more adept at fighting from the saddle.

Bad weather over the next several days kept both armies in their camps, and the Romans continued repairing their transports and warships. After much effort, they were able to restore enough of them to carry the army back to Gaul. But then came another battle.

The Britons, by then, had assembled a large number of warriors, and when the weather lifted they mounted another attack. When the signal came, a horde of spearmen, cavalry and chariots rushed at the Roman camp, each warrior shouting over the noise of drums and the screech of the Celtic *carnyx*, a primitive trumpet. The Britons, however, had picked the wrong way to fight a Roman army, which was most effective at the set-piece battle. Caesar's men formed up in front of the camp and raised an impenetrable line of shields. From behind them their catapults and slingers sent javelins and stones flying into the oncoming mass of horses and men. The infantry held firm against wave after wave of charging warriors, and methodically hacked and thrust its way forward. In spite of their mobility and superior numbers, the Britons could not break the Roman front, and before long they lost heart and fled.

Aided by the thirty cavalrymen of Commius, the Romans pursued them, writes Caesar, "as far as our speed and strength would allow," setting fire to all the buildings in a wide area (IV, 35). Before the day was over, the Britons again sent envoys to ask for peace. This time Caesar demanded twice the number of hostages, and ordered that the Britons themselves transport them to the continent. He had no room in his ships for more prisoners, and was anxious to leave the island before the Channel became too dangerous for sailing.

The Romans hurriedly loaded their transports and warships and weighed anchor soon after midnight. With a favorable wind and tidal stream they reached the continent shortly after sunrise.

Caesar later wrote that only two of the British tribes sent the required hostages to him in Gaul. Indeed, the Celtic warriors, once the crisis had passed, might well have believed that their fierce resistance and martial prowess had discouraged the sophisticated invaders. By any rational standard, in fact, the expedition had not only failed, but come very near disaster. Caesar had spent less then three weeks in Britain and never left the beach. He had not even left behind a garrison, and had returned to Gaul with nothing of value except a modest number of captives to be sold as slaves. Even such an admiring observer as Napoleon Bonaparte, who in his memoirs compared himself to Caesar, called it a failure.[13]

But the expedition had accomplished what had probably been Caesar's chief objective: it put his name and the tale of his daring exploit on the lips of every Roman, and dissipated the talk of depriving him of his Gallic command. And, most important, it introduced the idea that Caesar wanted in every Roman's mind: that the island was there to be conquered, and that there should be a second campaign the following year—this time a full-scale assault.

CHAPTER VI

⟨⊱ · ⊰⟩

INVASION

I n Rome, the news of Caesar's expedition to Britain caused a sensation. Of all the Romans' wars abroad, this was their first venture into what they called simply "*Oceanus*"—the swiftly flowing river that was thought to circle the known world. Although Caesar had brought back no riches from Britain, the news that a Roman army had landed on an unknown island, and returned safely from the edge of the earth, was the talk of the capital. With only a single dissenting voice, not surprisingly that of Cato, the Senate voted another record-breaking thanksgiving period—this time for twenty days.

The oldest name for the mysterious island outside the *orbis terrarum* was "Albion," first used by an explorer from the Greek colony of Massilia in the sixth century BC.[1] About three hundred years later, Pytheas, a Greek from the same city, made a remarkable voyage around Spain, up the Atlantic coast and around the British islands, landing in several places. He called them "The Pretanic Isles," and the inhabitants "Pretani," a name possibly derived from a Celtic word meaning "people who paint themselves." Several ancient historians, including Caesar, noted that the Celts colored or marked their bodies with various substances, especially before a battle, and they may have used the word to describe themselves. Caesar and other Roman writers of his time converted "Pretani" to "Britanni," possibly because of an error in hearing, and thenceforth the island was called "Britannia."[2]

To those who heard them read out in the Senate and elsewhere, Caesar's dispatches to Rome, with descriptions of the skin-clad "*horridi Britanni*" and their strange country, were nothing less than riveting. There had been no firsthand reports from Britain since the time of Pytheas, nearly three centuries earlier. A wave of curiosity, even titillation, swept across the city. References to Britannia appeared in letters, essays, plays and poems. And the notoriety and glory of it all focused on one man, who was all the more intriguing because he could not appear in Rome. Even Catullus, in the last year of his short life, and after a decade of deriding Caesar and ridiculing his pretensions to descent from kings and gods, was moved to call him the one great general of Rome and refer to his recent exploits as

> . . . *the new-won triumphs of mighty Caesar,*
> *Rhine, the Gauls' frontier, and the terrifying*
> *outermost British.*[3]

For Caesar, the British expedition capped a year of personal triumph. By the spring of 55 BC, he had to all appearances conquered "Long-Haired Gaul" and established Roman hegemony from the Alps to the Channel. During the summer he had driven the Germans back across the Rhine and, to the astonishment of Germans and Romans alike, built and then destroyed the first bridge across this ancient frontier. Finally, in the fall he had invaded an island even beyond the border of his latest conquest, defeated the barbarian tribes he found there and returned safely to Gaul. Only a cynic—or a political enemy—would have disputed these accomplishments. But with the advantage of hindsight, it is clear that 55 BC was a triumph of Caesar's public relations more than anything else.

In truth, Gaul was not conquered, only dormant, and Caesar's climactic struggle with his most dangerous opponent, the Gaulish overlord Vercingetorix, was still three years away. The bridge across the Rhine, which Caesar describes in affectionate detail, even alluding to the laws of physics that held the timbers in place, was nothing more than a spectacular, and unnecessary, engineering stunt. The expedition to Britain was poorly conceived from the beginning, and had achieved nothing substantial. And the combination of errors—Caesar's ill-timed landing on a falling tide, the failure of his cavalry to reach Britain and his negligent handling of the ships—could easily have cost Rome two legions. That it did not owed less to Caesar's generalship than to his luck.

Regardless of this, the reaction of the Senate and of the Roman public was all that Caesar could desire, and much of it was due to his own exertions. A skillful manipulator of public opinion, his propaganda was as effective in the capital as his tactics on the battlefield. Wherever he was camped, in Germany, Gaul, Britain or Spain, his couriers were never more than three or four weeks from Rome. He is said to have spent every spare hour, including time on the march, dictating to his secretaries, sometimes two or even three at once. Under the direction of a Roman citizen born in Gaul who was an expert on Celtic affairs, Caesar's headquarters was a fountain of publicity, pouring out proclamations, letters and dispatches to Rome about his exploits. In an age when written words were scarce, and commanded utmost attention, even a small amount went a long way.

Following his brief expedition across the Channel, Caesar remained in northern Gaul for several months to supervise preparations for his invasion of Britain the following summer. He ordered his shipbuilders to repair the boats on hand and to build hundreds more, specifying that the new transports were to be equipped with oars as well as sails so they could be maneuvered more easily. And they were to be built lower and wider than before so they could be beached and unloaded quickly, as well as accommodate the heavy cargo and large number of animals to be carried. In addition to horses and pack animals, the fleet would have to transport cattle to provide meat for the army. He gave instructions that the materials needed for fitting them out were to be brought from Spain, and ordered each of the maritime Celtic tribes to supply a contingent of ships according to its capacity.

This arranged, Caesar returned to Nearer Gaul in January of 54 BC to attend to his civil duties as provincial governor. By then his partners in the Triumvirate had assumed command of their own provinces. Crassus had left for Syria the previous November and was on the verge of leading an invasion of neighboring Parthia; Pompey had chosen to remain in Italy and govern Spain from there. During the winter, Caesar was obliged to travel to his province of Illyricum, where the neighboring Pirustae tribe had been making raids into Roman territory. When he ordered troops raised to defend the province, the Pirustae denied any warlike intentions, and agreed to provide hostages and make reparations. By early spring, Caesar was on his way back to northern Gaul.

It was on one of these trips across the Alps—scholars speculate that it was this one, in 54 BC—that Caesar composed, most likely by dictation, what has been called a serious treatise on grammar, *De Analogia*.[4] They believe that the book advocated the principles of the simple and direct style he used in the *Commentaries*. But only a few sentences of the work survive, including one that characteristically admonishes the reader to "avoid the unusual and extravagant word as the sailor does the rock."[5] Caesar dedicated the book to Cicero, with whom he was corresponding at the time, and praised him in a flattering preface as the creator and master of Latin prose style.

The personal relationship between Caesar and Cicero was now at its warmest—stimulated by the general's need for Cicero's influence and support in Rome, and by Cicero's ambitions for himself and his brother, Quintus. Also, regardless of politics, the two aristocrats, one a born patrician, the other a *novus homo*, admired and appreciated each other's civilized tastes and literary efforts. Marcus Tullius sent Caesar his poem about the recent events in his life, and Caesar praised parts of it as comparable to the best of Greek poetry.

Although they were both senators, the brothers Cicero were in financial straits at the time, and Caesar had made a large loan to Marcus at the beginning of the year. As Quintus also had ambitions for a consulship, Marcus suggested, and Caesar agreed, that the younger Cicero join him in Gaul as one of his *legati*.[6] Each such legionary commander was literally a political appointee, as were the six military tribunes assigned to each of them. The tribunes were noblemen, and the *legati* men of senatorial rank. The expectation was that Quintus would not only enrich himself from military booty, but also benefit politically by accompanying the acclaimed invader of Britain on his next assault across the Channel.

The Ciceros were not the only Romans to see an advantage in fraternizing with Caesar. When he arrived at the Atlantic coast to inspect his fleet, he discovered that word of the planned invasion had prompted hundreds of traders, merchants, politicians and adventurers, as well as common soldiers, to flock to his headquarters to attach themselves in some way to the enterprise. They were lured by the prospect of trade, plunder or simply the association with a victorious army. Caesar welcomed additions to his infantry and cavalry, but the old requirement of military experience for officers was no longer in force, and a successful general was often besieged by callow young noblemen seeking commissions. Caesar had already encountered, at Vesontio four years before, officers who lost interest in the campaign at the first sign of battle. However, two of the young noblemen he took with him to Gaul early in 54 BC had already served abroad under other commanders. One was his *quaestor* Marcus Crassus, the elder son of his partner in the Triumvirate. The other was the twenty-nine-year-old Mark Antony, scion of the prominent Antonii family, who had commanded cavalry in Syria and Egypt.

Over the winter, the Romans and the Celtic tribes under their control had constructed or refurbished six hundred transports and twenty-eight warships in several ports and estuaries along the northwestern coast of Gaul. Caesar now ordered all of them to assemble at the harbor he called "Portus Itius," evidently not the same one he had used the year before. The precise location of this port was long a matter of speculation among historians because all that Caesar says about it is that, from there, the crossing to Britain was about thirty miles, and would be the "most convenient." It was certainly along the same stretch of coastline between Dunkerque and the mouth of the Canche, now in the French département of Pas de Calais. As this made for a greater distance than the previous year's trip, he apparently chose the location because it more easily accommodated his much-enlarged army, its followers and supplies, and a fleet ten times the size of the earlier. The consensus among current writers is that Portus Itius lay alongside the village the Romans later named Gesoriacum, the site of modern Boulogne.[7]

In addition to the military craft, some two hundred private vessels gathered in the same port to follow the invasion fleet to Britain. They were financed by Roman merchants and landowners who hoped to profit by doing business with Caesar's army. Traders and merchants commonly trailed behind Roman armies in the field, purchasing booty from the soldiers and selling them clothing and other items the army did not provide.

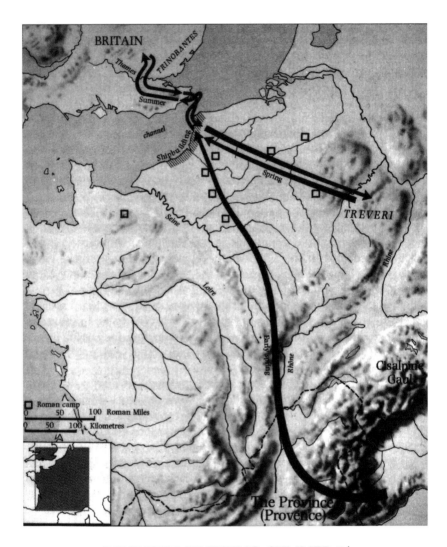

CAMPAIGN OF SPRING–SUMMER 54 BC

Aside from a brief campaign near the Rhine to put down the Treveri, Caesar and his legions spent the first half of 54 BC preparing their fleet for a full-scale invasion of Britain. At the end of July, five legions in six hundred vessels, accompanied by two hundred private merchant ships, landed on the coast of Kent. After marching inland more than a hundred miles and defeating the Britons in several hard-fought battles, Caesar returned to Gaul, having spent less than two months in Britain.

Before setting out, Caesar learned of a threatened revolt of the
Treveri, a large Celtic tribe whose name is preserved in modern Trier in
western Germany. They were also known to have the most powerful
cavalry in Gaul and, from the Romans' point of view, "never did as
they were ordered unless forced to by an army" (VIII, 25). According
to Caesar, their chieftain, Indutiomarus, had failed to acknowledge
Roman authority and "was making overtures to the Germans" (V, 2).
But when Caesar made a rapid march across northern Gaul and confronted the Treveri with four legions and eight hundred cavalry, they
quickly agreed to supply two hundred hostages, including the chieftain's son, to guarantee that they would not attack the Roman camps in
Gaul. Caesar and his troops were back on the coast by early June.

Of the eight legions he commanded in Gaul, Caesar picked five to
take to Britain, along with half the four thousand cavalry he had conscripted from the Gallic tribes. The remaining three legions and cavalry
he left with Titus Labienus, his most trusted officer, who was to see
about grain supplies for the winter and keep the ports secure for the
army's return.

The way was now clear for a military adventure unprecedented in
Roman history. Nevertheless, Caesar makes no attempt to justify it.
Despite the lengthy celebration after his short foray the previous summer, there is no record that the Senate voted to invade Britain, nor is
there any suggestion by Caesar that the undertaking was in any way
legally sanctioned by the Roman government. He apparently considered his reasons for the previous year's reconnaissance enough justification to set out with the largest army the Romans had ever sent from
their territory.

Although the nominal size of a legion was five thousand men, its
actual strength in the field was sometimes as low as three thousand,
and there is no good evidence of the size of Caesar's legions at this
time. Estimates of the invasion force, including cavalry and auxiliaries,
such as slingers and archers, range from seventeen to thirty thousand
men.[8] Even at the lower figure, Caesar's army and fleet were the largest
to cross the Channel in either direction until the First World War, two
thousand years later.

With the ships and troops ready to sail, only the lack of favorable weather delayed the departure. For more than three weeks an impatient Caesar waited for a southerly wind to carry his fleet up the coast and across the Channel. The delay must have been all the more frustrating after the furious pace he had set since the beginning of the year. In January he had left his troops on the Channel coast and traveled to his headquarters in northern Italy, and from there to Illyricum and back. After returning to the Gaulish coast, he had led an army across the territory nearly to the Rhine and back. By July, he had covered more than two thousand miles, either on horseback or in a horse-drawn carriage, and had crossed the Alps twice. For the major portion of his journeys there were no graveled Roman roads (paving was still a rarity) but only rough tracks through heavily forested hostile country, always with the risk of capture. After all this, the prospect of a risky Channel trip and a seaborne invasion of a hostile island might have dismayed an ordinary general. But after nearly a year of planning and preparing, Caesar was not to be put off. At length, at the end of the Roman month of *Quintilis*, later named *Julius* in Caesar's honor, the wind changed, and he gave the order to sail. But there was now a further delay.

A common custom in the ancient world was the giving and taking of hostages to guarantee the future behavior of one or both parties. As insurance against a Gaulish rebellion while he was away, Caesar had taken the extreme step of ordering all the tribal chieftains he distrusted to accompany him to Britain as hostages. Among them was Dumnorix, the powerful and ambitious chief of the Aedui, who was also a Druid and the leader of a strongly anti-Roman faction. While the fleet lay in the harbor awaiting a favorable wind, Dumnorix vigorously protested his enforced trip to Britain, and attempted to persuade the other chieftains to refuse to go. He complained to Caesar that his religious duties required that he stay in Gaul, that he was not used to sailing and was afraid of the sea. Caesar declined to excuse him; but when the day came to sail, and the infantry and cavalry were boarding their transports, Dumnorix and his horsemen bolted from the camp.

Caesar halted the departure and sent a troop of cavalry to bring him back. Within a few hours they caught him, and, when he continued to resist, killed him and then forced his troops back to the port.

This incident was only one of several in which Caesar showed the Celts that he could be ruthless if they resisted him. He was not to be so cruel when he fought his own countrymen in the later Civil War, and he was known all his life as an unwavering supporter of his friends and allies.

It was at sunset on the last day of the month that the great fleet rode out of the harbor on an ebbing tide and moved up the Channel toward Britain, a lantern on Caesar's flagship pointing the way. His plan was to sail directly to the beach where he had landed the year before; but when dawn broke between 3:00 and 4:00 A.M. the wind had died and he found his fleet drifting into the North Sea, the British coast receding on his left. Using flags to signal his instructions, Caesar ordered the ships to be turned toward the sloping shore of Kent between the North and South Forelands.

Within an hour the tide shifted, and with hard rowing the Romans passed south of the treacherous Goodwin Sands and brought the hundreds of ships close to the beach by midday. The landing-place is not definitely known, but the best evidence puts it between Deal and Sandwich, several miles north of the previous year's, and probably along the line where the North Stream today crosses the Lydden Valley. This time the landing was not only unopposed but, as Caesar wrote: "Not one of the Britons was to be seen. I discovered later from prisoners that large numbers of them had assembled there, but had left the shore in terror and hidden themselves on the higher ground when they saw so many ships; more than 800 vessels were visible simultaneously, including those that had survived from the previous year and also the privately owned ones built by individuals for their own use" (V, 8).

Indeed, it must have been an extraordinary sight. Even if they landed in two shifts, the line of Roman ships was certainly two to three miles long, and the beach was soon swarming with thousands of infantry and artillerymen, sailors, officers, servants and traders, as well as horses, pack animals, cattle, and possibly an elephant. The unloading of the ships and the construction of an enormous camp took the rest of the day and half the night. The two most authoritative writers on the invasion, T. Rice Holmes and C.F.C. Hawkes, speculate that this gigantic camp—large enough to house perhaps thirty thousand men and thousands of animals —was built on the modest hill just to the south of the present-day village of Worth.[9] During the first century BC this site was near the beach, but the movement of the coastline to the east has left the hill about two miles inland. Excavations in 1926 unearthed evidence of a Roman temple built over a Celtic shrine of some sort, but no trace of a military camp. Today, between it and the Channel lie a tangle of meandering streams and, at the water's edge, the Royal Cinque Ports Golf Links.

By questioning a few natives his soldiers had rounded up, Caesar learned that a great number of Britons had gathered in a stronghold in the woods several miles inland. Leaving a fifth of his army and several hundred cavalry at the beach to guard the ships, he assembled the remaining four legions of infantry and seventeen hundred cavalry and led them out of the camp soon after midnight. By now his army had been on the move for more than a day and a half, with little opportunity to sleep. But if there were complaints in the ranks, it was obvious to all that Caesar was demanding no more of his men than of himself.

In his haste to engage the Britons, and perhaps because of the sheer size of his fleet, he left his ships at anchor "on an open shore of soft sand, with Quintus Atrius responsible for their safety" (V, 9). Another reason for leaving them afloat may have been that he intended using them shortly to enter the estuary of the Thames and make contact with the powerful Trinovantes tribe in modern Essex, who were known to be friendly to the Romans.

Evidence of this is the presence in Caesar's camp of the young Mandubracius, son of the chieftain of the Trinovantes who had been killed in a battle with a neighboring British tribe, the Catuvellauni. After the death of his father, Mandubracius had fled to Gaul and sought Caesar's protection. Hawkes has speculated that Caesar brought him to Britain to help him establish friendly relations with the Trinovantes. As his allies, they could aid Caesar against the other tribes and also provide him with an excuse for an advance into the interior under the guise of protecting them from their enemies. Caesar does not mention such a plan, and the reason will soon be clear. For now, a foray into Kent would protect his flank and allow him to gauge what resistance he faced.

Early the next morning, after a march of twelve miles inland, Caesar and his men sighted a group of British horsemen and chariots emerging from a wooded hill on the far side of a river. Napoleon III and other nineteenth-century writers concluded that this river was the Nail Bourne, or Little Stour, now a small north-running stream passing about three miles east of modern Canterbury. They put the site of this first encounter with the Britons near the present-day villages of Kingston and Littlebourne. Later archaeologists and historians, measuring the twelve miles from the site near Worth, identify the river as the Great Stour, and place the skirmish at Thanington, today a pleasant riverside suburb a mile south of Canterbury.[10]

A skirmish was what it proved to be. The Roman cavalry forded the river easily and rushed at the British horsemen, who retreated into a stronghold that is almost certainly the heavily wooded hill now called Bigberry. There they made a stand, noted by Caesar: ". . . they enjoyed a position with extremely good natural and manmade defenses. It was clear that they had prepared it previously for some war among themselves, because many trees had been cut down and used to block all the entrances to it" (V, 9).

A deep ditch surrounded the hillfort, and from the bank behind it the defenders showered the Romans with a barrage of stones and spears. The attack came to a standstill, and before long the Britons began to emerge in small groups from behind their ditch. When a large number of them had left the hillfort, Caesar renewed the attack and sent the infantry of the VIIth Legion against the stronghold. Hurling their javelins from a distance, and then advancing in a solid front behind their shields, the legionaries forced their way forward and gradually pushed the Britons back into the fort. With the entrances blocked and the ditch and bank too formidable to cross, the Romans resorted to a familiar tactic. All along the line, groups of legionaries locked their shields above their heads and formed a series of *testudos* (tortoises), or protective roofs, while others brought up baskets of earth and debris to fill the ditch.

The defenders could do little to foil this maneuver, and little by little the Romans built up a series of ramps to the height of the bank. The infantry then advanced across the ramps behind a fence of shields and, reaching the top of the bank, swarmed into the fortress. Fighting at close quarters, the lightly protected Britons were no match for the heavily armed legionaries wearing coats of mail, shin guards and metal helmets. Those who were not killed abandoned the hillfort and retreated into the woods to the west. Caesar writes that the engagement cost the Romans only a few wounded, but rather than pursue the fleeing Britons into unknown territory, the Romans took the rest of the daylight hours to construct their second camp in Britain.

Bigberry today is an oblong plateau of twenty-five acres just to the east of Harbledown, a suburb of Canterbury. At more than two hundred feet above sea level, it commands a striking view of the North Downs and the Stour Valley to the south. Among the thick woods of chestnut, birch and oak that cover it, the visitor will find blackberries, thistle and an occasional brilliant red toadstool. On the slopes of the plateau and around its base lie hop gardens and orchards of Cox's Pippins. There are entrances on both the west and east sides, and the massive ditches and banks of two thousand years ago, now smoothed and rounded, still clearly mark the defensive positions of the Iron Age Britons who resisted Caesar. It was obviously a strategic site in prehistoric times, and one of England's ancient tracks, the North Downs Way, here coincident with the Pilgrim's Way of Chaucer's *Canterbury Tales*, passes along its northern edge. Less than a mile away the A2 trunk road has been built on top of Watling Street, the later Roman road to London.

Indiscriminate gravel-digging at Bigberry during the nineteenth century unearthed hundreds of pottery fragments and a variety of iron objects, but as late as 1874 the site was unidentified by historians and archaeologists. It was first excavated in 1902 by W. Boyd Dawkins, who found an andiron, horseshoes, bits, plow colters, sickles, adzes, and iron rims for cartwheels. Later excavations and archaeomagnetic dating have established that Bigberry was a farming settlement occupied for several centuries before Caesar arrived.[11] An additional enclosure of about eight acres on the north side may have been a cattle pen. Dawkins also found fetters, iron collars, and an eighteen-foot "slave chain" with neck rings, one of several recovered in the British Isles.

The morning after the battle, Caesar divided his infantry and cavalry into three sections and sent them in pursuit of the Britons. They were hardly out of sight when a horseman rode into camp with an urgent message from Quintus Atrius at the beach. The previous night another Channel storm had swept across the eight hundred Roman ships anchored off the coast, snapping their chains and lines, battering them into each other and throwing them on the beach. Almost all were damaged, a great many beyond repair. Caesar was forced to halt his advance and call back his pursuing troops. The entire army of perhaps twenty thousand men and nearly two thousand cavalry packed up its gear and marched the twelve miles back across Kent to the beach.

For the second time in less than a year Caesar and his army were stranded in Britain, their march inland interrupted, and forced to take precious time to repair and rebuild their ships. His failure to beach his transports and galleys, especially after his experience of the year before, can only be because of his plan to use them within a matter of days to enter the interior of Britain on the Thames. But the Channel weather had again thwarted him, and the invasion came to a halt.

Surveying the wreckage on the beach, Caesar found that nearly forty ships had been destroyed and most of the rest would require extensive repair. In a hasty message carried by warship to Gaul he ordered Labienus to begin building more ships as fast as possible, and at the same time demanded that additional *fabri*, skilled craftsmen, be sent to Britain. He then put the entire invasion army to work hauling the salvageable ships up from the beach and enlarging the camp to accommodate them. For ten days and nights, according to Caesar, the work proceeded around the clock, shifts of legionaries working all night by lantern light.

By the middle of August all the ships were secure behind ditches and banks, but the repairing and rebuilding would take weeks more and, with only about another month left before the autumn Channel storms, Caesar had no time to wait. With his fleet disabled he had lost his chance for an easy passage up the Thames and would be forced to fight his way across the countryside. He left a legion to finish the repairs and guard the camp, and with the remaining four legions and his cavalry, marched again toward Bigberry.

In the meantime, the Britons had gathered reinforcements "from all parts of the country" and placed themselves under a single commander, the legendary Cassivellaunus, the first Briton to be named in a written history. Apparently chosen for his war-making skill, Cassivellaunus may have been chieftain of the Catuvellauni, a tribe that had probably originated in the Marne region of Gaul and now inhabited a large area north of the Thames centered in what is today Hertfordshire.

The strategy of Cassivellaunus was immediately clear. As the Romans advanced through the woods, the British cavalry and charioteers avoided a direct confrontation, and instead harassed only the Roman flanks, dashing up close to fight in relays and then retreating into the woods. When the Romans pursued them, the Britons turned and attacked isolated units, and Caesar was repeatedly forced to send reinforcements in all directions. Weighed down by their armor and weapons, and accustomed to fighting in close-order formation, the legionaries were confused and unnerved by the Britons' hit-and-run tactics.

The fighting continued intermittently throughout the day in the wooded hills west of Bigberry, but the Romans gradually gained control of enough suitable ground to begin building their camp. C.F.C. Hawkes places this camp near the present-day town of Boughton Street on the road between Canterbury and London.[12] Before they were finished, however, the Britons attacked again, and several thousand infantrymen had to throw down their shovels and go back into battle. One of Caesar's tribunes was killed before the Britons were driven off and the camp made secure.

Surrounded and outnumbered, the Romans spent an anxious night behind their hastily built banks and ditches. A full cohort of nearly five hundred men guarded each of the four gates, and the night sentries posted along the perimeter kept a close watch on the Britons' fires in the nearby woods.

Under battle conditions, Roman sentinels were especially alert because the penalty for falling asleep or leaving a post was unusually severe. Of the six military tribunes assigned to each legion, two were responsible for maintaining the camp, including supervising the watch. If a guard was accused of delinquency, he was tried by a court-martial of all the tribunes, to which he and the duty tribune could bring witnesses. A guilty soldier was condemned to the *fustuarium*, literally a beating by the men of his own unit, the usual result being death. The same penalty could be imposed for a variety of other offenses, such as stealing, cowardice or boasting falsely to win a decoration. If an entire unit was guilty of cowardice or desertion, every tenth (*decimus*) offender, selected by lot, was subject to the *fustuarium*, hence the English verb "decimate." The Greek historian Polybius, who accompanied several Roman armies in the field, concludes a portion of his description by remarking dryly that "the night watches of the Roman army are scrupulously kept."[13]

Caesar does not mention such punishments in *The Gallic War*, but it is likely that they took place in his armies. It appears that he was neither rigid nor lax, but simply pragmatic. According to Suetonius:

> He judged a soldier neither by his morals nor by his background, but simply by his toughness, and he treated his troops with a mixture of severity and indulgence. Except when the enemy was near, he did not enforce rigid discipline. . . . He sometimes turned a blind eye to their delinquencies and did not pursue them seriously, except for desertion or mutiny, every case of which was carefully investigated and relentlessly punished. After a big battle or big victory he often relaxed discipline and allowed his troops extensive license.[14]

Most punishments were administered by the officers closest to the rank and file: the celebrated Roman centurions, each in command of a "century," which by Caesar's time comprised eighty men. The backbone of the army, the centurions rose from the ranks and were required to serve for twenty-five years. They were easily identified by their silvered armor and the transverse crest on their helmets. What also distinguished the centurion was his vine cane, the *vitis*, which he used to administer corporal punishment. Because they were selected for their toughness and experience, stories of courageous centurions fill Roman military history. For the same reason, their casualty rate was the highest of any group. Throughout *The Gallic War* Caesar frequently describes the brave feats of his centurions, and commends at least five by name.

The next morning, the Britons emerged from their camps in small groups to harass the Roman cavalry. At midday, in an attempt to draw the enemy into battle, Caesar sent out three legions and all his cavalry on a foraging expedition under Gaius Trebonius. The impatient Britons suddenly abandoned their hit-and-run tactics and rushed at the Romans, standing and fighting against the main body of infantry. Quickly regrouping into their pitched-battle formations, the legionaries staged a fierce counterattack, driving the Britons ahead of them and slaughtering them by the hundreds. The cavalry surged into the ranks of the chariots, preventing the Britons from dismounting and forcing them to turn and flee. The entire army of Cassivellaunus broke away from the battlefield and retreated to the west.

Remains of Iron Age earthworks suggest that this decisive battle took place near Whitehill, just south of modern-day Faversham, and Hawkes believes that the nearby hillfort at Judd's Hill must have played a part.[15]

Now committed to an advance by land, Caesar took his legions west, probably along the edge of the North Downs on the track that eventually became the route of Watling Street. Within a day he was at the Medway River, and probably turned south to ford it between what would become Halling and Snodland, where it was not so wide and deep.

Caesar's subsequent march to the Thames took nearly a week, and his legions no doubt terrified the inland Britons, who had never seen anything like a Roman army. The abortive landing of two legions the previous year may have warned them of what was to come, and they now fled in the face of an army twice that size. Traveling four abreast, the file of nearly one thousand pack mules each legion required for its baggage was itself more than eight hundred yards long, and the marching line of four legions and their animals would have stretched for several miles.

The conservatism of the Roman approach to war is revealed in the remarkably similar descriptions of army practices by Polybius in about 140 BC and by the Jewish historian Josephus more than two hundred years later. Both writers, for instance, relate that when the army was ready to break camp a trumpet call alerted the troops to strike their tents and prepare their baggage for the march. At the second trumpet call, they loaded their animals and, if they were in enemy territory, set fire to the palisade and any other structures they had built. When the entire army was ready to march, a herald at the commander's side called out three times, asking the troops if they were ready for war. Their response each time was to raise their right arms and shout loudly that they were ready. At the third trumpet call, each unit of cavalry and infantry, as well as the mule train and the special cadres of troops, filed out the camp gate in a prescribed order. With an enormous army deep in enemy territory, it is highly likely that Caesar adhered to the standard marching formation.

To guard against an ambush, a contingent of cavalry rode at the head of the line, followed by a troop of light-armed infantry. They were followed by a single vanguard legion, chosen by lot and led by its *aquilifer*. Behind these were the army surveyors and a pioneer corps that was expected to clear or bridge any natural obstacles. It was followed by Caesar himself, his bodyguard and his baggage. The army's mules, carrying its artillery and any other siege equipment, were next in line, followed by the senior officers and their escort. The remaining legions, marching six abreast if the roadway permitted, with their trumpeters and their baggage trains, accompanied by their servants, made up the bulk of the line. Bringing up the rear were the camp followers, merchants and slave dealers, protected by both infantry and cavalry.[16] Wings of hundreds of cavalry spread out from the clogged trackway, destroying farms and settlements and sweeping over everything in their path.

The problem of providing food and water for thousands of troops and animals is a constant challenge to a large army in the field. In *The Gallic War*, Caesar frequently refers to the need for water and grain and his various efforts to find them while on the march. It is likely that in southern Britain, even during the summer, there was sufficient water in rivers and streams to keep the army supplied. The availability of grain was another matter. A common tactic of both Roman and Celtic armies was to burn grain fields in order to deny them to the enemy. We do not know if Cassivellaunus resorted to this, but it is certain that in Britain Caesar's army of twenty to thirty thousand men and more than five thousand horses and mules required enormous amounts of food and fodder. The Romans' need for wheat alone has been estimated at one hundred tons each week, more than the annual yield from 125 acres. They had brought grain and cattle with them to Britain, as well as olives and olive oil, salt, and vinegar, which they drank mixed with water. But they could not carry all they needed, and depended for the rest on raiding the Britons' stock pens and foraging in their fields for beans and wheat, as well as hay for the animals.

The main food of the army was *frumentum*, the word used for any type of edible grain, and the legionaries were regularly sent out to harvest what was available, usually wheat. Before it could be eaten it was necessary to grind wheat into flour, either in a portable hand mill or between a pair of millstones that were carried on the march by a pack animal. The legions' cooks mixed the flour with water and then baked it over embers or on hot stones to form a kind of rough bread patty or biscuit. They also used wheat (and barley when wheat was unavailable) as a basis for soup and porridge. The most common vegetables carried on the march were beans and lentils, because of their storage life and ease of transport.[17]

The passage of the Roman legions across Kent and Surrey has left no certain evidence. Caesar disposes of it in a single sentence: "When I discovered what the enemy's plans were, I led the army to the river Thames and the territory of Cassivellaunus" (V, 18). Although his precise route is not known, excavations of Iron Age hillforts in western Kent and Surrey have yielded evidence, if not of Caesar's presence, at least of the Britons' reactions to his movements. The large hillfort at Oldbury Hill near Ightham, for instance, is less than ten miles from the probable site of Caesar's crossing of the Medway. Excavations there in the early 1980s revealed well-preserved Iron Age ramparts, and evidence that it was rapidly fortified on a massive scale in the first century BC, occupied briefly and then abandoned.

At the smaller hillforts at Anstiebury near Dorking, and farther west at Holmbury and Hascombe, all in the County of Surrey, large numbers of smooth, rounded pebbles the size of hens' eggs for use in slings have been found in the trenches. At Hascombe, archaeologists have found sling-bullets of baked clay that were obviously manufactured to defend the site. Although these may have been used by the Britons in wars among themselves, this site also appears to have been occupied for only a short time and abandoned about the middle of the first century BC.[18]

Coin hoards from this period have been found all over southern Britain and on the Channel island of Jersey, and many of them are thought to have been buried for safekeeping at the time of Caesar's invasion. Other finds in the area indicate that Caesar's campaigns in Gaul had made an impact even in the interior of Britain; they consist of large numbers of coins of particular tribes on the continent, and archaeologists believe they were payments made to the Britons by mainland Celts for troops and supplies for their battles against Caesar in Gaul. Recent research has demonstrated that in about 57 BC several tribes of northern Gaul increased their minting of gold coins by factors of ten to twenty, presumably to finance their armies.[19]

The close connections between the British and Gaulish Celts were not only those of proximity and commerce, but also of tribe and kinship. All the Celtic tribes in the British Isles had originally come from the continent, though many had been in Britain for centuries. A few years before he invaded Britain, Caesar was told that Diviciacus of the Suessiones (not to be confused with the Aeduan leader of the same name) had been, within living memory, the most powerful ruler in the whole of Gaul, and had exercised control over large areas of land on both sides of the Channel.

After failing to hold the Romans in Kent, Cassivellaunus appeared to retreat with most of his army beyond the Thames. British resistance was reduced to sporadic guerrilla tactics and brief defenses of hillforts that the Romans either ignored or overran. Caesar concluded that the Britons had given up: "After this rout the additional forces that had assembled from all over the country immediately dispersed, and after that the enemy never fought against us in a general action" (V, 17).

Although this remark is literally correct, Caesar had not yet seen the last of Cassivellaunus. The British commander was certainly Caesar's equal as a strategist, and he must have realized by now that he could not defeat the Romans in a pitched battle. His retreat toward the Thames led the Romans far into the country and away from their ships at the beach, and Caesar, in his tent with his rough map in front of him, must also have realized how vulnerable he was on this island a thousand miles from Rome. He knew that his army, his reputation—and even his life—depended on outwitting Cassivellaunus.

CHAPTER VII

❧ · ❧

THE CELTS IN BRITAIN

The question of when the first Celtic people migrated to the British Isles has occupied archaeologists and linguists for more than a hundred years. That they came from the European continent may be the only generally accepted supposition; but what part of the mainland they came from, what language they spoke, where they settled first and, above all, when they came are still matters for sharp disagreement. There are intriguing indications that the first Celts bypassed Britain entirely and settled in Ireland, perhaps bringing with them Goidelic, an archaic Celtic language unknown in any other part of Europe. Some scholars believe that this may have taken place as early as 2000 BC; but despite the most rigorous analysis of grave artifacts and language development there is still insufficient evidence that there was a Celtic language or culture in Ireland or Britain before about 700 BC.[1]

Whether the migrations were earlier or later, the islands to which the first Celts journeyed had taken their present shape thousands of years earlier. Before the warming climate caused the last glacier to begin retreating from Northern Europe in about 10,000 BC, the British Isles were a single land mass still joined to the mainland from the Channel Islands to the coast of modern Germany. As the northern ice cap melted, the rising Atlantic waters crept up the river valleys and across the lowlands, creating the Irish Sea and flooding the great Anglo-German plain to form the North Sea. Between eight and ten thousand years ago, water finally broke through the last chalk ridge connecting the receding peninsula with the mainland, and Britain was sundered from the continent.

By the time the English Channel first appeared, deciduous woodlands covered nearly the whole of Britain. Over a period of several thousand years, small nomadic tribes roamed the land, feeding themselves by fishing, gathering wild plants and hunting wild ox, deer and pig. During the fourth millennium BC, this culture was gradually replaced by one based on rudimentary farming and stock-raising. In contrast to the circular huts of the nomads, these Neolithic farmers built rectangular wooden structures for themselves, and cleared the land in the river valleys and along the edges of the chalk downs to plant the first crops in the British Isles. They also used a new method of burying their dead: in long barrows of earth and stone.

Excavations of some of their heavily fortified enclosures, such as Hambledon Hill in Dorset and Crickley Hill in Gloucestershire, reveal evidence of arrow and axe warfare and destruction by fire.[2] Among the surviving artifacts are battle-axes made from igneous rock from Cornwall and Wales, and daggers, barbed arrowheads and axes of the flint that was mined in Sussex. It was also during this period that the first pottery was made in Britain and the first plow used. Wheat and barley seed, as well as the first sheep and goats, were brought from the continent; none of them is native to Britain.[3]

Toward the end of the fourth millennium BC, Stone Age tribes began building the first circular enclosures surrounded by a ditch and bank, broken by one or more entrances. More than ninety of these "henges," as they are called, have been identified, from the Orkneys to Cornwall. Neolithic enclosures were common on the continent, but they tended to be rectangular; circular enclosures were unique to the British Isles. They ranged in diameter from thirty to fifteen hundred feet, and some were ringed with stones or pillars of wood. They appear to have been used as ceremonial sites, and many contained graves.

Also toward the end of the fourth millennium the first work was begun on the most famous, and enigmatic, henge monument in Britain: Stonehenge. Because of multiple excavations here over the last four hundred years, many of these the work of careless amateurs, it is likely that a definitive chronology for the building and rebuilding of this structure will never be established. The earliest version, dating from perhaps 3200 BC, was probably a wooden enclosure of some sort, with the so-called Heel and Slaughter stones standing outside and inside the entrance.

In about 2700 BC the inhabitants of the Salisbury Plain built the massive twelve-story mound of earth and chalk rubble now called Silbury Hill—the largest prehistoric structure in Europe. Although archaeologists and prehistorians have excavated and analyzed Silbury Hill and several similar but smaller mounds nearby, the consensus today is that they are inexplicable.

Archaeological evidence from the centuries following 2500 reveals the presence in Britain of the so-called Beaker People—named after the characteristic decorated handleless drinking cups they used. Long believed to have been brought by invaders or immigrants, the Beaker culture is now thought to have developed indigenously in Britain, although elements of it originated in the Low Countries and the Rhineland.[4] The Beaker People kept cattle, sheep and pigs, and planted very little besides barley, which they boiled and ate as porridge, and also used to brew a form of beer. They were also the first inhabitants of Britain with a knowledge of metalworking, notably of copper, which was found in the West Country. Copper daggers from the third millennium BC are the earliest metal objects in Britain. Population estimates for England and Wales in about the year 2000 BC, the beginning of the Bronze Age, range between 50,000 and 200,000 people.[5]

The second millennium BC brought dramatic changes to the British Isles as a result of extended trade routes linking the islands with the European continent and the Mediterranean, and because a few skillful smiths learned to make bronze out of copper and tin. The opportunity to trade, and the new ability to make bronze objects, useful or beautiful or both, created new wealth and, inevitably, greater disparities in wealth among the population. Excavations in Wessex of numerous circular mounds from this period, evidently the tombs of chieftains, have revealed a variety of rich grave goods, including finely crafted gold and bronze artifacts of all types, especially jewelry, daggers and axes. The graves also contained beads and cups carved from amber imported from the continent. Archaeologists agree that these rich burials simply reflected the desire among the newly wealthy to display their status through exotic interments.

It was during the six-hundred-year period beginning about 2100

arly Stonehenge, then more than a thousand years old,
rmed from a nondescript circular bank and ditch into a
and unique megalithic monument. The addition of multiple
massive stones, some capped with lintels of sarsen sandstone,
brought to the site over two hundred miles of land and water,
re uired the labor of thousands of people over many generations.
Indeed, the astounding work of transporting and erecting the many
monuments on the Salisbury Plain is evidence of a highly organized
society with a sufficient surplus of wealth to engage in labor-intensive
public works. In about 1350 BC, the ditched roadway known as the
"Avenue" was extended two miles to the east and south to the River
Avon. Since that time, only the elements have altered it. Although
unfinished in several respects, the Stonehenge we see today is the same
mysterious assemblage the Celts found when they entered Britain.

There is no clear indication of a new culture in southern Britain
during the Late Bronze Age, though there is ample evidence that
metalworking techniques became increasingly sophisticated. Two-piece
casting molds for objects of gold and bronze gave way to multiple-
piece molds, and use of the lost-wax method allowed finer details to be
shown on swords, daggers and ornamental pieces. Another technique
widely used was the forging of bronze or gold sheets from cast bars to
make armor, helmets, bowls and jewelry. Although fortified enclosures
existed as early as the Neolithic Age, the first true hillforts in Britain
were built between 1200 and 1000 BC. The most recent research has
dramatically revised upward the population estimate for this period,
and it may have reached one million by 1000 BC.[6]

It was most likely during the first millennium before Christ that Celtic
tribes from the continent began a massive migration into the British
Isles. They spread quickly into every part of the country, overwhelming
the indigenous culture and establishing the language and society the
Romans found. Within the next five hundred years the first domesticated horses and spoked-wheel vehicles reached Britain, as well as the
first knowledge of the technology that was to give the age its name: the
use of iron.

Of all the countries they inhabited, it is in the British Isles that the

Celts have left their most enduring legacy. Remains of their hillforts and outlines of their fields can be seen today in every part of the country. Stone for tresses survive in Scotland and Ireland, and many Celtic trackways across England can not only be traced, but are still in use as footpaths, roads and highways. The modern names of dozens of rivers, forests, islands and mountain ranges are the descendants of Celtic words. In England, as in Gaul, the Celts would absorb and survive the Romans. The remaining Gallo-Roman culture was later overcome in England by the Angles and Saxons, and in Gaul by the Franks from Germany.

In Scotland, Ireland and parts of Wales, which neither the Romans nor the Anglo-Saxons conquered, Celtic customs and languages have evolved independently for more than twenty-five hundred years, and those in use today are the direct successors of those brought by the first Celtic settlers. There they were preserved for centuries when the rest of Europe forgot the Celts. The ancient Irish law system, for example, the oldest such system in Europe, survived in parts of Ireland until the seventeenth century. Its roots were in Indo-European custom rather than in Roman law, and it retained many Indo-European institutions long after they disappeared from other legal systems.

After the Roman period, the words "Celt" and "Celtic" fell into disuse until the sixteenth century, when the Scottish scholar George Buchanan used "Celtic" to describe the speech of the inhabitants of Ancient Gaul.[7] The idea of an ancient Celtic culture became popular late in the eighteenth century with the beginnings of the Romantic Movement. Physical evidence of the Celtic culture was not recognized until the nineteenth century, when excavations in Switzerland and Austria revealed the details of a prehistoric society that had until then been hidden from modern archaeology.

Ironically, the words "Celt" and "Celtic" were never applied to the peoples of Britain or Ireland by any ancient writer, and there is no evidence that they used the words to describe themselves. How they referred to themselves we do not know. The best guess is that they used the old Celtic word "Pretani," a name that survives, slightly altered, in "Prydein," the Welsh word for Britain. The Irish Celts, in their own dialect, may have pronounced the same word "Qreteni," which has become "Cruithni," a modern Gaelic word denoting an ancient people in Ireland and Scotland.[8]

The principal sources of information about Celtic society in Iron Age Britain are artifacts and other remains found during the last century and a half at dozens of sites throughout the country, but primarily in southern England. During the 1970s and 1980s, intensive excavations by Clive Partridge at Skeleton Green in East Hertfordshire, Geoffrey Wainwright at Gussage All Saints in Dorset, and Barry Cunliffe at Danebury in Hampshire added immeasurably to our understanding of the daily life of the British Celts in the period just before Caesar's invasion.

Another source of information is a unique research experiment begun in 1972 by archaeologist Peter Reynolds at the Butser Ancient Farm near Petersfield in Hampshire. On the site of an actual Celtic settlement, Dr. Reynolds and his associates have constructed and maintained an Iron Age farmstead as it might have existed in about 300 BC. Using only materials and techniques known to the Celts, they have built circular dwellings, stock pens, grain pits and an iron smelter. They have also planted and harvested typical Celtic crops of wheat, vegetables and herbs, and bred varieties of goats and sheep similar to those raised by the Celts.

The culture of the Iron Age Celts was centered on farming and stock-raising. Common household crafts included pottery-making, woodworking and weaving. There was also extensive mining of iron ore and precious metals, as well as smelting and metalworking. The Celts extracted salt from seawater by evaporation or boiling, and probably used it to preserve meat, also giving it to domesticated animals. Fishing and hunting continued to supply a portion of the diet. Besides trading among themselves, the Celts shipped such local products as hides, tin, copper, grain and hunting dogs to the continent in exchange for wine, amber, fine pottery and other luxury goods.

The typical Celtic family lived on an isolated farm, and sometimes as part of a settlement or village. By this time the British Celts were building one-room circular houses in contrast to the rectangular dwellings of their cousins on the continent. The main timbers and rafters were usually of ash, with branches of hazel interwoven among them. Pieces of worked and jointed ash planks with mortise holes for tenons have been found in Somerset in a settlement dating from about 700 BC. A mixture of clay, soil, straw, animal hair and chalk was plastered on the interwoven or basketwork walls, and wheat straw was used for thatching the roof. Reconstructed Iron Age dwellings at the Butser Ancient Farm have successfully withstood winds of hurricane force and winter rains of more than forty inches without leaks or damage.

The Celts were surprisingly sophisticated farmers. Evidence exists that they practiced crop rotation, used manure, and fenced their crops to protect them from wild animals. The remains of their small square fields of a fifth acre to an acre and a half are still visible in many parts of Britain, some on steep slopes that no modern farmer would attempt. To prepare the land for planting, Celtic farmers used cattle to pull an ard, an early form of the plow that was simply a spike that scored a furrow in the ground. Metal tips or "socks" have been found in Britain that are thought to have been fitted over the ends of the wooden spikes. Because it had no mold board, the device did not invert the soil as does a modern plow.[9]

The principal grain of the ancient world was the einkorn, or one-grain, variety of wheat. An accidental crossing of einkorn with a wild goat grass resulted in a wheat called emmer—the traditional bread wheat of the Roman army. Both emmer wheat and another variety, spelt, were common in Iron Age Britain. These three types of ancient wheat had a protein value of between 17 and 20 percent per gram, more than twice the protein content of modern bread wheat. After it was parched to loosen the hull, the wheat was ground by hand in hollowed-out stones. The later rotary quern, in which two stones fitted to each other were turned around an axle, was probably a Celtic innovation, adopted by the Romans only in the second century BC. Cultivation of these wheats at the Butser Ancient Farm has resulted in remarkable yields of over sixteen hundred pounds per acre, a better harvest than the average of fourteen hundred pounds per acre achieved in Britain as recently as 1910.

Excavations at Iron Age farm sites indicate that the Celts stored their wheat in rectangular structures raised above the ground, and also in pits cut into the surface chalk. The pits were sealed with a plug of clay laid directly on the surface of the grain. On top of the clay seal a cap of wet earth was placed and allowed to harden, preventing oxygen and rain from seeping into the pit. Once the pit was sealed, the grain at the top absorbed the remaining oxygen and produced carbon dioxide, which, being heavier than the granular atmosphere, filtered down through the pit and prevented the wheat from rotting. Modern experiments with this method have shown that grain will keep in this way for up to a year and remain usable for seed or consumption. A typical pit a yard across and five feet deep would hold more than a ton of grain, and was probably also used to store salted meats and silage.[10]

Archaeologists have calculated that the total area of land farmed in the Late Iron Age and early Roman period was greatly in excess of that farmed in medieval times, and was not equaled until the seventeenth century. The crop yield was sufficient to support a population that has been estimated at one and a half million in 500 BC and three and a half to four million by the beginning of the Christian Era—far in excess of the one and a half million recorded in the Domesday Book of 1086.[11] Caesar himself mentions that "The population is extremely large, there are very many farm buildings . . . and the cattle are very numerous" (V, 12).

Pollen grains and carbonized seeds are important sources of information about plant life in the Iron Age and about the crops cultivated by the Celts. Seeds that were burned and turned into charcoal reveal that they planted both barley and wheat, and a variety of greens and other vegetables, including lentils, horse beans and smooth tare (a grain-field wheat). The most widespread was the Celtic bean, Vicia faba minor, a nutritious vegetable about the size of a pea that may have been planted in rotation with wheat. Another plant cultivated in the Iron Age was melde, later called "fat hen," which yielded edible seeds and leaves. Today it is regarded as a weed, but it was a staple green vegetable in Britain until the introduction of cabbage and spinach, and has a higher food value than either.[12] The Celts also grew flax, using the leaves for fodder, extracting oil from the seeds and making linen thread from the fiber of the stalks.

The mainstay of the Celtic farmer was his cattle, which produced both milk and meat, and also pulled his plows and wagons. The cattle bones of the Iron Age have been identified as those of an extinct short-horn variety, Bos longifrons, a small, undeveloped rangy animal that resembled a goat. It was the progenitor of the modern Welsh Black cattle and the Kerry cattle of Ireland. The domestic sheep of the Iron Age were small short-tailed animals with coats of brown wool that they shed annually, the yield being more than two pounds per animal. This prehistoric variety has survived virtually unaltered in the Soay breed that subsists today on the islands of St. Kilda and Soay off the northwest coast of Scotland.[13] Farmers also kept goats, which were easier to feed and domesticate than sheep, and were used as a source of milk.

The Celts also kept pigs, geese and ducks on their farmsteads. Caesar remarks that most of the inland tribes lived on meat and milk, but adds that "They think it wrong to eat hares, chickens or geese, keeping these creatures only for pleasure and amusement" (V, 12). There is evidence, however, that they ate both horses and dogs. Their horses were small, with large heads, shaggy manes and spreading tails that hung to the ground, similar to the Exmoor and Shetland ponies of today. The British Celts did not breed horses, but rounded them up in the wild and trained them. They also hunted wild pigs and deer, and probably badger, fox and wild cats. Wolves, lynx, beaver and bears were all plentiful in Britain in the Iron Age, but are now extinct there.

Besides vegetables and meat, the Celtic diet included eels, fish, shellfish, nuts (especially hazelnuts) and a variety of wild berries. The people were noted for their appetite for butter, and were adept at making it, even using sheep's and goat's milk. They baked bread and roasted meat and fish in cone-shaped clay ovens that stood in the center of their houses, where they were also the source of heat. Once they learned the techniques of metalworking, they were able to make cauldrons of bronze or iron that took the place of pottery for boiling and stewing.

The British Celts imported what wine they had, but used barley, wheat and hops to make their own beer, and fermented honey to make mead. They collected honey in the wild or produced it themselves by keeping bees in simple hives called "skeps," which they wove from straw or wicker.

The Celts made cloth garments from wool that they combed,

probably with bone or antler combs, and then spun into yarn on a simple hand-spindle weighted with a whorl of stone or baked clay. At some point in the process the wool was washed to remove the oils and then often colored with vegetable dyes obtained from a variety of plants. Celtic woolen cloaks were prized in Rome, and the Celts were generally known for their brightly colored clothing, often patterned with stripes or squares. Scottish plaid and the Spanish cloak are their modern survivals.

From its beginnings in the third millennium BC, metalworking supplies us with the most vivid evidence of ancient society in Britain. The first metals mined were lead, gold, silver, copper and tin, the latter two being combined to make bronze. The first objects made were undoubtedly trinkets of gold and silver—rings, beads, and torques of various kinds—and small weapons of copper. During the second millennium BC, bronze weapons were widely manufactured in Britain, and by the tenth century BC the first bronze harness fittings appear in the archaeological record.

The use of iron had a long history among prehistoric peoples, beginning with the discovery of smelting techniques in the Near East about 2500 BC. Ironworking spread across the Mediterranean into Europe and reached Britain in the first millennium BC. Iron-bearing ore is much more plentiful than tin, copper and lead ores, and the superior attributes of finished iron soon became obvious. By the seventh century BC, British smiths were smelting iron ore and forging iron weapons and implements of all kinds, including saws and files, and even razors.[14]

To achieve the high temperatures needed to make bronze and to break down iron ore, the Celts learned to make charcoal, a process demanding great skill and weeks of patient work. Charcoal is produced when wood is burned in an atmosphere that is poor in oxygen. To achieve this they ignited a vertical stack of small logs, usually oak, by placing hot embers in the middle, and then covered them with leaves and dirt, leaving a hole at the top for the smoke. After a long period of smoldering, the fire consumed the wood's natural gases and reduced it to charcoal, a porous form of carbon that burns at a much higher temperature than wood.

The hot charcoal was then laid on a bed of iron-bearing rocks that had been broken up and roasted and put in a smelting furnace: a shallow pit lined with clay. A primitive bellows was used to force air into the mixture to heat it sufficiently—a temperature of 1,400°F (800°C) would have been necessary—to cause the rocks to soften. The result was a "bloom," or spongy mass of metal and rock, sometimes as large as a common brick, from which most of the impurities could be hammered out. The remaining lump of iron could then be forged into the desired shape, or transported for reheating and forging elsewhere. Ingots and bars of iron of standard weights were used as a simple medium of exchange for hundreds of years until they were gradually replaced by coins. Peter Reynolds has constructed an Iron Age smelter at the Butser Ancient Farm and used it to produce iron ingots in this manner.[15]

There is substantial evidence that the technique for increasing the carbon content of iron, thus making steel, even high-quality steel, was known and used by some British smiths in the early Iron Age. The most notable examples are a collection of strips and segments of steel bands for chariot wheels found in a lake in Wales. These were made of thin strips of wrought iron that had been carburized into steel, and then welded together to make a 1 by 1$^{1}/_{2}$-inch band of the required circumference, as much as nine feet. The circular bands were then applied while red-hot to the outer surfaces of the wooden wheels, in the modern manner, shrinking and compressing them as they cooled.[16]

Although it is primarily the artifacts of metalworking that survive, the British Celts were more commonly occupied with weaving baskets, making fishing nets and tanning leather for use in horse harnesses. Even in the Iron Age, however, the most widespread and useful craft was woodworking. In his excavation of an Iron Age enclosure in Dorset, Geoffrey Wainwright found evidence of a substantial chariot-making factory that included a variety of woodworking tools and the remains of several types of aged wood, as well as copper, tin and iron. This site, which was occupied for five hundred years until the first century of our era, has also brought to light several other interesting features of Celtic life. Analysis of bones indicated a high frequency of osteoarthritis and dental decay among the inhabitants. Wainwright also found the first evidence of the domestication of cats, as well as the bones of the house mouse.[17]

In the final few centuries before the arrival of Caesar, there are signs of gradual societal change in southeastern Britain brought about by increasing food production and population, and the development of hierarchies based on wealth. New varieties of grains that could be planted in the winter increased the annual yield per acre and provided a dependable year-round supply of food. Additional lands were brought into cultivation and the resulting economic surpluses led to the rise of a modest warrior aristocracy. Grave goods from the period reveal a larger number of implements for the warrior, such as swords, daggers, shields, helmets, war trumpets and pony armor. Warfare became more common and many settlements gave way to hillforts defended by earthworks and ditches.

During the second and first centuries BC, increasing contacts were made between the British Celts and those in northern Gaul, especially the tribes between the Seine and the Rhine—the region the Romans called Gallia Belgica. It is not definitely known, however, whether these contacts involved settlers, invaders, traders, or some combination of the three. Caesar interrupts his narrative of the invasion to describe the people he found on the island: "The interior of Britain is inhabited by people who claim, on the strength of their own tradition, to be indigenous. The coastal areas are inhabited by invaders who crossed over from Belgium for the sake of plunder and then, when the fighting was over, settled there and began to work the land; these people have almost all kept the names of the tribes from which they originated" (V, 12).

Until the discovery of the Iron Age cemetery at Aylesford in Kent in 1886 by Sir Arthur Evans, evidence of an invasion from Gallia Belgica was confined to this passage in *The Gallic War*. In 1921 the excavation of a similar cemetery at nearby Swarling confirmed the presence of a continental mainland culture in Kent in the first century BC. The graves in these cemeteries contained weapons, pottery and coins common in northern Gaul and Gallia Belgica. And the most striking discovery was evidence of burial by cremation—a radical departure from the centuries-old method of inhumation used by the British Celts. It was Evans, the later discoverer of Cnossos (of ancient Crete), who connected what came to be known as the Aylesford-Swarling Culture with the Belgae of the continent and seemed to provide the archaeological proof of Caesar's statement.[18]

Based on this evidence, most twentieth-century archaeologists agree that in the one hundred years or so before Caesar's invasion large contingents of settlers left their homelands in the region between the Seine and the Rhine and entered the southeastern part of Britain. Some of these Belgae intermixed with the British Celts, and in other cases supplanted them, and before long Belgic tribes such as the Atrebates, Morini and Suessiones were entrenched in what are today Kent, Essex, Hampshire and Sussex. It is likely that all the Britons whom Caesar encountered—the defenders of Bigberry, the Catuvellauni of Hertfordshire, and the Trinovantes of Essex—were Belgic immigrants or their descendants.

The theory of a Belgic incursion, however, does not have unanimous support. Barry Cunliffe of the University of Oxford asserts that the undoubted similarities between the Aylesford-Swarling and the Belgic cultures are more likely the result of "regular and intensive social and economic intercourse between the tribes on either side of the Channel." He suggests that if there were such a Belgic migration, it was directed not into Kent, but toward the Isle of Wight and into Hampshire, where there is more evidence of Belgic settlement. To complicate the matter, a modern reexamination of the Aylesford-Swarling material fails to establish that any of it predates Caesar.[19]

The oldest coins found in Britain were lost in northern Kent in the mid-second century BC. They were struck at an unknown mint in Gallia Belgica, possibly by the Ambiani in the Somme Valley, but it is not clear whether they were brought by raiders, individual settlers or simply in the course of commerce. They picture a bearded head in Celtic-style scrollwork and on the reverse a clearly recognizable horse and chariot. The first Celtic coins on the continent had been struck about a hundred and fifty years earlier by tribes in the Danubian Basin. They were copies of gold coins used by Philip II of Macedon and his son, Alexander, to pay Celtic mercenaries to fight in their armies.

About 100 BC the Britons of northern Kent began copying continental coins by melting bronze with a high tin content into a series of clay molds. Within a few decades tribes to the west were striking their own coins in silver and gold, stamping them with images of human heads, horses, chariots and stalks of wheat. Cassivellaunus is thought to have been the first Briton to mint gold coins.[20]

The distribution of Celtic tribes throughout the rest of Britain has been determined from coin finds and from Caesar's account, as well as from the record of the Claudian invasion a hundred years later. The powerful Belgic kingdom of the Atrebates extended over Hampshire, Berkshire and the western parts of Surrey and Sussex; its capital was at Calleva Atrebatum, modern-day Silchester. The Catuvellauni occupied the area of Hertfordshire, and the Trinovantes, the most powerful tribe in southern Britain, controlled the whole of what today is Essex. Most of the north of England was held by the Brigantes, called by Tacitus in the first century AD the most numerous people in Britain. Other outlying tribes were the Dobunni in the lower Severn valley and the Cotswolds, the Durotriges in Dorset and Wiltshire, and the Dumnonii in Devon and Cornwall.

Archaeologists and linguists agree that at the time of Caesar's invasion, and throughout the Roman occupation, virtually all the tribes of Britain spoke Brythonic, or Brittonic, a later variant of the original Celtic tongue spoken by the descendants of Indo-European migrants into Eastern Europe. Brittonic is sometimes called "P Celtic" because the "qu" sound in the parent language was replaced with a "p" sound.[21]

When the Anglo-Saxons invaded England in the fifth century after Christ, they imposed their own language on the Britons as they gradually overran most of the island. Brittonic endured in the western part of the country, where it evolved into Welsh, which remains in use today in a large part of Wales, and into Cornish, which was spoken in Cornwall and Devon until it died out in the eighteenth century. In the fifth and sixth centuries large numbers of Cornish-speakers and other Britons migrated back across the Channel into Aremorica, which became known as "Little Britain," now called Brittany. Their language has evolved into Breton, the third modern remnant of Brittonic.

The Celtic settlers who eventually prevailed over the other popula-

1. Julius Caesar. His military strength and expertise grew throughout his nine-year war of conquest against the Celtic tribes of Western Europe. When he led his legions back from Gaul, Rome itself could not resist his power.

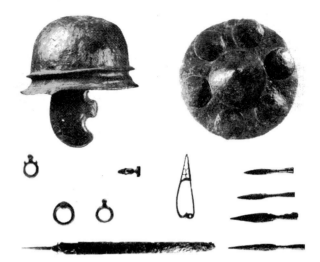

2. A Celtic helmet, shield center and other implements discovered by Napoleon III's archaeologists at the site of one of Caesar's sieges.

3. A scene from a Roman triumphal arch at Carpentras showing Celtic prisoners chained together.

4. Detail from a Roman sarcophagus depicting a battle scene from the Gallic War.

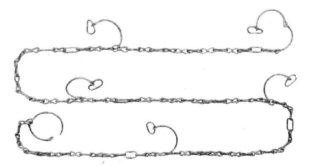

5. Above, a slave chain excavated at Bigbury in Kent, which was once used to link six slaves by the neck. 6. Below, a slinger's missile found in 1968 at the site of Caesar's entrenchment at Alesia.

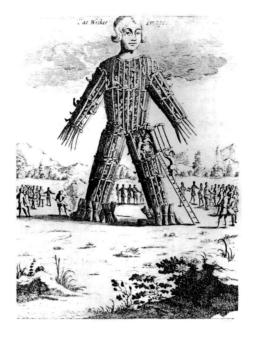

7. Both Caesar and Strabo described a huge Celtic wicker image of a man into which victims were placed for sacrifice. This engraving, from 1676, is perhaps a bit fanciful. 8. Below, the recreation of a Celtic farmhouse at Butser Ancient Farm, Hampshire.

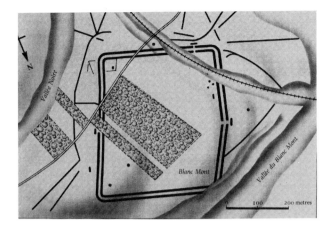

9. Aerial photography has made possible the discovery of several Roman camps, the earthwork outlines of which lie just below the surface in modern France. This camp, found by Roger Agache in the Somme valley, consists of the standard double ditches and entrances, and is large enough to have supported an entire legion. Precise dating is impossible but it may have belonged to the campaigns of Julius Caesar.

10. The Roman onager catapulted large stones high rather than far, and was used not unlike a modern-day mortar in sieges. 11. At the siege of Avaricum Caesar ordered the construction of a massive terrace built of tree trunks, as well as siege towers, in order to surmount the walls. Note the long sheds built to protect the Roman workers and soldiers from missiles fired from above.

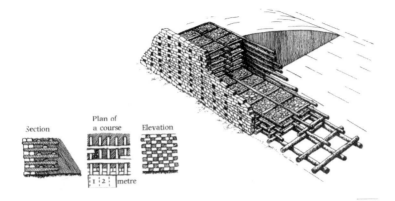

Section   Plan of a course   Elevation

I 2 metre

12. Caesar's description of Celtic defensive works, like the one he encountered at Avaricum, has been borne out by modern excavations like this one in the Côte d'Or. The technique involved horizontal timbering as a basis for a vertical wall of stone.

13. A model of Caesar's bridge across the Rhine. Note the V-shaped palisades placed just upstream to protect the trestles from objects thrown into the river by the enemy.

14. The Romans' battle insignia, identifying legions, cohorts and smaller units, were entrusted only to soldiers who had proven their courage in combat.

15. A remarkable feat of engineering skill, the Romans built their bridge across the Rhine, crossed it briefly and then burnt it behind them when they returned to Gaul. This demonstration of the power of a superior civilization must have had an unnerving effect on the Germans.

16. The pebble covered beach at Deal is commonly accepted as the site of Caesar's first landfall in Britain, notwithstanding some alteration in the coastline over the last 2,000 years.

17. Napoleon III's full-size replica of one of Caesar's triremes (photographed here in 1861) was never tested in the Channel, however the Emperor and his family did sail it on the Seine.

18. The ditch called Devil's Dyke as it appears today at the edge of the plateau at Wheathampstead.

19. Below, the gate and pillars at Devil's Dyke commemorate the last great battle fought by the British Celts against Caesar.

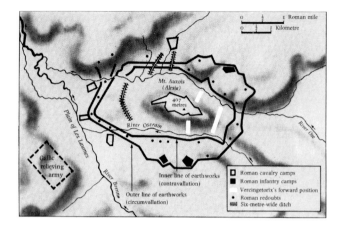

20. The plateau of Alesia, site of the climactic battle of the Gallic War. Caesar's army built a double ring of fortifications: one to encircle the plateau and the other to defend against attacking relief forces. After a desperate series of battles against the largest coalition of tribes ever put together in ancient Gaul, the Romans emerged triumphant.

21. A full-scale reconstruction of Caesar's Alesia fortifications, at the history park near Beaune, Côte d'Or.

22. (cover illus.) Although Caesar's own narrative is typically terse, the surrender of Vercingetorix must have been one of the most dramatic moments in both men's lives, as thousands of warriors looked on.

23. Henri Motte's depiction of Vercingetorix about to surrender his weapons to Caesar at Alesia.

24–25. Cicero, left, knew Caesar well, however he sided with Pompey during the Roman Civil War. Pompey, right, was Rome's other great general during Caesar's time, however he was not able to defeat Caesar and his Gallic War veterans in battle.

26. Vercingetorix has been called the first national hero of France. After surrendering at Alesia, he was kept prisoner for six years and then put to death to celebrate Caesar's ultimate triumph in Rome.

27. This Roman triumphal arch, adorned with fierce battle scenes, was erected in the first century BC to commemorate Caesar's campaigns against the Celts.

tions in Ireland were Goidels, from which the word Gaelic derives, and spoke Goidelic, another variant of the original Celtic tongue. Goidelic is sometimes called "Q Celtic," because of its retention of the "qu" sound of the parent Celtic tongue, subsequently reduced to "k" and written as "c." Goidelic is the ancestor of Irish, Scots Gaelic and Manx. During the Middle Ages the latter two languages evolved among Goidelic-speakers who had invaded and then settled in western Scotland and on the Isle of Man. Although Manx died out in the nineteenth century, the Goidelic culture and its descendant languages were largely unaffected by the Roman, Saxon and, eventually, Norman invasions.[22]

The evolution of the "qu" or hard "c" sound in Goidelic Celtic to the "p" of the Brittonic form can be seen in the modern words remaining in the descendants of the two languages. In Irish, the descendant of Goidelic, the words "head," "son" and "four" are *cenn*, ma*c* and *cethir*. In Welsh, the survivor of Brittonic, the same words are *p*en, ma*p* and *p*edwar.

Among linguists today there is still disagreement about the origins of Goidelic and Brittonic, and how and when they came to the British Isles. One theory is that the two languages diverged from the parent Celtic tongue during an early period, and that Goidelic-speakers migrated separately to Ireland. Speakers of Brittonic later settled throughout what is modern Great Britain. One variation of this theory is that Goidelic-speakers, or some of them (the "Black Irish"), migrated directly from Spain, where Q Celtic inscriptions have been found in the north. Also, several linguists have pointed out that the Sequani in eastern Gaul were Q Celts, and their close association with the Helvetii and their sub-tribe, the Tigurini—Caesar's first victims in the Gallic War—suggests that those tribes were also Q Celts. Although Caesar directed them to return to their homeland, it is conceivable that they later continued their migration and reached the Atlantic coast, as some of the Boii and Tigurini did, and from there sailed to Ireland. It is also significant that many Irish saints and princes derive their names from the Tigurini.[23]

A second theory about the divergence of Brittonic from Goidelic is that it took place after Goidelic-speaking people from the continent had occupied the British Isles for centuries. Emigration of P Celtic speakers into Britain in the latter part of the first millennium BC caused the Brittonic dialect to develop and prevail everywhere but in Ireland, where Goidelic continued to be spoken.

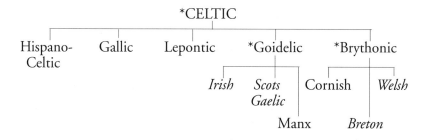

PROBABLE RELATIONSHIPS AMONG THE CELTIC LANGUAGES
The asterisks indicate languages that are inferred or reconstructed, rather than documented by actual texts. Only those in italics are spoken today. Diagram adapted from C. Renfrew, *Archaeology and Language: The Puzzle of Indo-European Origins* (London: Jonathan Cape, 1987).

Beginning with the reports of Pytheas in the fourth century BC, the shape of Britain had been perceived as a triangle, with a perimeter of about 3,900 miles. In his description of the island, Caesar repeats the notion of a triangle, but estimates, on the basis of local opinion, that the length of the three sides was about two thousand miles, somewhat greater than the actual perimeter of sixteen hundred. He correctly places Ireland off the west coast, but thinks that the western side of Britain faces Spain (V, 13). The southeast corner of Britain first appears in the written record as "Kantion," the name used for it by Pytheas, making Kent the oldest surviving place-name in Britain. It is derived from a Celtic word meaning "rim" or "edge," and was thus originally only a geographical term. Caesar tells that there were four kings in the area, but does not mention a tribe, and it appears that the Romans indiscriminately applied the name "Cantiaci" or "Cantii" to all the people in the region.[24]

Although he obtained some of this information from the Britons he questioned, Caesar took his own measurements of the length of the days: "Midway between Ireland and Britain is the Isle of Man, and it is believed that there are several smaller islands too, where, some writers say, there is continual darkness for 30 days in midwinter. We made numerous inquiries about this, but found out nothing. However, from accurate measurements with a water clock, we could tell that the nights were shorter than on the continent" (V, 13).

Caesar's water clock, the *clepsydra*, was a device invented in Egypt that was first used in Rome to measure the time allotted to speakers in court. It was then adapted for use by armies in the field to mark the changing of the watch. In its simplest form it was an earthenware vessel that was filled with a specific amount of water that ran slowly out of a small hole at the bottom. Once the device was tested it could be filled at a known time of day, such as noon or dawn, and the hour determined at any time by the amount of water remaining.

Caesar's other observations about Britain range from those confirmed by modern archaeology to others that are either unlikely or demonstrably false. He remarks that the Britons of the interior did not plant grain, but lived on meat and milk. But paleobotanists have shown without question that cereal crops were cultivated throughout Britain long before Caesar's time. One puzzling comment occurs in a later chapter of *The Gallic War* where he reports that Druidism had originated in Britain, and that those who wished to master it went there to study. Although the Romans indeed later found Druids in Britain, it is unlikely that the practice of Druidism—central to Celtic society—originated in one of the last areas to which they migrated. As it is, Caesar seems not to have encountered any Druids in Britain, because he fails to mention them on either of his campaigns there.

The only other mention of Druids in Britain in classical times appears in the *Annals* of Tacitus, where he describes them cursing and howling at a legionary army approaching the island of Anglesey in the first century AD. Druids in the British Isles are mentioned again in certain old Irish hero-tales in medieval manuscripts that preserve an oral tradition from the fourth century AD, but there are no other contemporary references.

An intriguing possible connection to Druidism was made in 1984 with the discovery of the upper half of an Iron Age body preserved in a peat bog near Lindow in Cheshire. The skull of Lindow Man had been fractured, and he had then been garroted with a knotted cord of animal sinew. At the time he was killed he was no older than thirty, and had a short but full beard; radiocarbon dating put the death at no more than a hundred and fifty years after Caesar left Britain. After a minute analysis of the remains, including the contents of the stomach, archaeobotanists concluded that his last, spare meal had been a deliberately burned portion of a piece of cracker made from unleavened wheat, rye and barley. The man's smooth and manicured fingernails and the remains of a mysterious fox-fur armband, a symbol of the Celtic nobility, suggest that he was an aristocrat, possibly a king or a prince. A single precise stab wound had pierced his jugular vein, perhaps for the purpose of draining his blood, and he had been thrown naked into a shallow pool.

This led the Celtic scholar Anne Ross to speculate that the death was a ritual killing and that "Pete Marsh" (the name the press gave him) may have been an actual Druid priest, sacrificed in the way described by Caesar, Strabo and others. Among other connections with Celtic religious rites, she cites a rural May Day tradition, surviving in some areas until the nineteenth century, in which pieces of biscuit were passed among a group, and the person drawing the charred piece was designated the figurative "victim." In addition, the stomach of Lindow Man was found to contain the pollen of mistletoe, a plant reported by classical writers to be sacred to the Druids. Fantastic as it seems, no other theory accounts for all the evidence.[25]

The discovery of another body in the Lindow Moss three years later has possibly shed light on another ancient subject. The Celts were notable all over the ancient world for tattooing or painting themselves, and the colors mentioned by observers and historians range from gray to blue, green, brown and black. Caesar notes specifically that all the Britons used a blue stain on their bodies, and that it gave their warriors a wild appearance. On the basis of his description in Book V of *The Gallic War*, it has long been thought that the British Celts obtained the blueing agent from woad, a plant that yields an intense blue dye and was cultivated in Britain until the seventeenth century, at which time it was replaced by indigo.

However, X-ray microanalysis of the second body from Lindow, conducted by a team of British scientists in 1991, revealed that the skin tissue contained "massively elevated" levels of copper and aluminum. The skin appeared to have been "at least partly painted with a clay-based pigment, in which the iron and copper provided the basic colorants." After investigating the Latin texts referring to the coloring, they suggested that a possibly mistaken translation of the word "vitrum" in *The Gallic War* has led to the misunderstanding that the Celts used woad to paint themselves. The earliest record in Britain of woad, or *Isatis tinctoria*, is from the Anglo-Saxon period. Their conclusion was that it is likely that the coloring used by the ancient Celts was obtained from clay minerals associated with copper, such as cuprite, malachite and, particularly, azurite, which produces an intense blue color.[26]

Another observation Caesar makes is that by far the most civilized of the Britons—"*humanissimi*" is the word he uses—were those who lived in Kent, and that their customs differed little from those of the Gauls. Obviously the coastal areas would be the first to benefit from innovations brought by immigrants from the more advanced European continent, and modern archaeology confirms that change appeared first in the southeast. It is in Kent that evidence has been found, from about 100 BC, of the first use of the potter's wheel, and also of the use of papyrus to make molds for low-grade coins. Papyrus was available only from Egypt, and its high cost makes it unlikely that it was used only for this purpose. The hypothesis is that simple records and accounts were sometimes written on papyrus, and when they were no longer needed the material was used in mold-making.[27]

It was the defenders of Kent who had the most to fear and to lose from Caesar's invasion. In a few short months his legions cut down thousands of their warriors and destroyed their crops and settlements. He brought them face to face with the most powerful and the most advanced society of the time. Although Britain would not become Britannia for another hundred years, its isolation was at an end. The absorption of the "outermost British" into the history of the ancient world had begun.

CHAPTER VIII

⋘ · ⋙

TO THE THAMES

I t was Mandubracius, the Trinovantian prince accompanying Caesar, who no doubt led him across Kent and Surrey in pursuit of Cassivellaunus and eventually to the southern bank of the Thames. There is some evidence, especially in the British Isles, that the Celts were building their own roads even before Caesar's time, and it is likely that his legions marched along a track cut through the forests by the same tribes that fled in front of him.

Caesar writes that the territory of Cassivellaunus lay "about 80 miles from the sea and [was] separated from the maritime tribes by a river called Tamesis." This phrase, and his laconic remark that "There is only one place where the river can be forded, and even there with difficulty," are the only hints in *The Gallic War* about where he crossed the Thames (V, 11). The question has tantalized archaeologists and historians for hundreds of years, and the proposed locations have ranged from the vicinity of Weybridge, seventeen miles upstream from the center of London, to East Tilbury near the mouth of the river.

Research since the 1920s has demonstrated that in the first century BC the level of the Thames was at least fifteen feet lower than it is today, and it is known that in recent centuries the river was occasionally fordable in several places, especially during unusual weather. In his sixteenth-century *A Survey of London*, John Stow wrote:

We read likewise, that in the year 1114, the 14th of Henry I, the river of Thames was so dried up, and such want of water there, that between the Tower of London and the bridge, and under the bridge, not only with horse, but also a great number of men, women, and children, did wade over on foot.[1]

Discussions of the crossing-place center on the single vivid detail in Caesar's narrative that might identify the place: the famous stakes he found driven into the riverbed to prevent his passage. Caesar writes: "When we reached it, I noticed large enemy forces drawn up on the opposite bank. The bank had also been fortified with sharp stakes fixed along it, and, as I discovered from prisoners and deserters, similar stakes had been driven into the river bed and were concealed beneath the water" (V, 18). He never mentions them again, but, beginning with the first retellings of the invasion and continuing to the present day, there has been endless speculation about what they were, who put them there, and when.

The first elaboration on Caesar's simple statement was made nearly eight centuries later by the founder of English history, Saint Bede of Jarrow, in his *History of the English Church and People*, completed in AD 731. In his short account of Caesar's invasion, he notes: "Traces of these stakes can still be seen; cased in lead and thick as a man's thigh, they stand fixed and immovable in the riverbed."[2] But he does not say where they were.

William Camden, the sixteenth-century antiquarian, was the first to record their location. In his *Britannia*, a compendium of the antiquities of England, published in 1586, he describes a group of stakes at the confluence of the Wey and the Thames:

> . . . At the spot where it falls into the Thames by two channels, stands Oatelands, a beautiful palace in a park, near which Caesar crossed the Thames into Cassivellaun's territories . . . On the other side of this river was drawn up a large army of Britans, and the bank itself defended with sharp stakes driven into it, and some of the same were concealed under water in the bed of the river . . . I cannot be mistaken in this, the river being scarce six feet deep hereabouts, and the place now called from these stakes Coway stakes.[3]

These stakes about a quarter of a mile above the Walton Bridge
have been attested to by many subsequent writers, and several have
been pulled up and placed in the British Museum. The editor of
Manning's *History of Surrey*, published in 1809, wrote that a fisherman
named Simmons had told him that at the place called Coway Stakes he
had weighed up several rounded timbers the size of his thigh, about six
feet long, "shod with iron, the wood very black and so hard as to turn
an axe." He described them as standing in two rows at right angles to
the current.[4] On the basis of Camden's discovery of these stakes,
Caesar's crossing point was fixed at Coway for three centuries.

But late in the nineteenth century, as a result of dredging to
deepen the river, a whole complex of underwater stakes was discovered
farther downstream, extending about four hundred yards along the
river opposite Kew Gardens. These stakes were found in at least two
diagonal lines between the two banks, and others were found along the
south bank. Around the turn of the century, further dredging revealed
hundreds of stakes or piles along a two-mile stretch of the river
between Kew Bridge and Isleworth. Some of these have been put on
exhibit in nearby Syon House, the spectacular ancestral home of the
Dukes of Northumberland. A granite pillar commemorating the crossing was erected at Brentford in 1909, but was later taken down when
the claims for Coway regained precedence.

Pieces of Bronze Age and Iron Age pottery, weapons and other artifacts have been recovered all along this stretch of the Thames, and
wooden piles in association with Iron Age objects have been found
underwater at Hammersmith and Wandsworth. The location and
arrangement of these piles suggest that they may have been the founda-
tions of dwellings on the marshy ground adjacent to the river.

In 1929, Sir Mortimer Wheeler uncovered deeply set timbers and
what appeared to be the flooring of a large wooden pile-dwelling in the
bed of the river just above Brentford. The structure was at least thirty-
five feet long and was situated below the present low-tide level of the
river. The site yielded both Roman and prehistoric pottery fragments,
and Wheeler reported that the farther from the shore he dredged, the
older the objects he found—confirming that the river was lower and
narrower in prehistoric times.[5]

If the stakes at Coway or Brentford were those meant for Caesar, they would be a striking example of artifacts described in ancient history surviving into modern times. The evidence admits of three possibilities: the stakes were put in the river in both places by the Britons to prevent an enemy from crossing at the fords; or, they are the remains of enormous fences, or weirs, placed across the river to trap fish; or, they are the pilings once used for bridges, docks and dwellings that have left no other record.

Throughout the eighteenth and nineteenth centuries antiquarians and historians argued about the stakes and their relevance to Caesar's crossing-place, and the issue is not resolved today. The theory that at least some of the stakes were weirs is plausible—some of those pulled up have been only three to four inches thick—because weirs were common in the Thames and other English rivers until the thirteenth century. On the other hand, the stakes along the bank in the vicinity of Brentford are not likely to have been weirs.

Support for the existence of an ancient ford where the Coway stakes were found comes from the name itself: "Coway," a natural contraction of "cow-way," a cattle track. The river may have been shallow enough there for herdsmen to take their cattle across, and a line of stakes along each side of the crossway was a customary method of marking such fords. Although the name has disappeared from the map, the place was known as "Coway Stakes" until well into the nineteenth century.[6]

The hundreds of stakes found in the vicinity of Kew and Brentford may have once supported prehistoric or even Roman bridges, docks and dwellings. The first recorded bridge across the Thames was built by the Romans about AD 50, a few years after the Claudian conquest. Evidence of it has been uncovered at the foot of Fish Street Hill, a few yards downstream of modern London Bridge.[7] Archaeologists agree that there was no substantial settlement on the site of modern London before the time of Caesar, so a prehistoric bridge elsewhere on the river is not improbable. However, diagonal lines of stakes across the river many yards apart are not likely to be the remains of a bridge.

The theory that they were implanted by the Celts to defend the fords is the most intriguing, and agrees, of course, with Caesar's account. If this is true, it is likely that virtually all the stakes were already in place before Caesar's advance from Bigberry, because the fleeing Britons would have had time to set up no more than a few in the short time before he arrived. They would have already been in use by the Catuvellauni on the north bank to prevent any hostile crossing of the river into their territory. It is significant that ancient trackways from the north, east and west converge on the north bank of the river at Brentford, and two from the south and east meet in the town of Kew on the south bank.

The piles and stakes at Brentford and Coway remain a mystery. Neither their age nor their purpose can be known for certain, much less their connection with Caesar. The strongest likelihood is that most of them are the remains of bridges, docks and dwellings of the Gallo-Roman period, and that some of them may have been used by the Britons for the purpose Caesar describes. The diagonal stakes across the river, the evidence of settlements and the convergence of prehistoric roadways offer the best evidence, flimsy as it is, that Caesar crossed the Thames at Brentford, and this is the view of most modern researchers. Theories about other crossing-points are based on different types of evidence.

Napoleon III asserted that the crossing was at Sunbury, two miles below the Walton Bridge, on the basis of statements by veteran Thames boatmen that the ford there was the most favorable in the area.[8] A crossing at Westminster has been suggested by some on the grounds that the ancient trackway from Kent on which the Roman Watling Street was built appears to reach the Thames at that spot. Some early writers guessed at Kingston, and C.F.C. Hawkes speculated in 1975 that Wandsworth was the place, on the basis of the large number of prehistoric artifacts found in the river there.[9]

In 1977, archaeologist Patrick Thornhill proposed that Caesar may have crossed far downstream between Lower Higham north of Rochester and East Tilbury in Essex. In addition to the evidence of a much lower and narrower Thames in ancient times, he pointed out that prehistoric trackways from the Medway Valley in Kent and from Essex converge at this point. When the ford was made impassable by the rising river, a ferry crossing replaced it, and there is evidence of such a ferry during the medieval period.[10] Against this theory, however, is Caesar's statement that the territory of Cassivellaunus, which he was entering, was "eighty miles from the sea," and thus much farther up the river.

The last hypothesis deserving mention is that Caesar never crossed the Thames at all, and that the river he forded was the Medway, which he mistook for the Thames. This theory suffers in the same way as Thornhill's in that it conflicts with Caesar's plain statement about his general location. Others have suggested that Caesar exaggerated the length of his march into Britain to inflate his achievement. But to pursue this would take us even further into the mists of conjecture than we have already ventured. The problem is by now very likely insoluble, and we will have to be content with the bare words of Caesar's narrative.

Wherever the Romans crossed, the stakes proved to be no barrier to Caesar: "I immediately gave orders for the cavalry to go ahead and the legions to follow them. As the infantry crossed, only their heads were above the water, but they pressed on with such speed and determination that both infantry and cavalry were able to attack together. The enemy, unable to stand up to this combined force, abandoned the river bank and took to flight" (V, 18).

It is here that the story of Caesar in Britain yields its most intriguing question: Did he use an elephant to force his way across the Thames, and if so, why didn't he mention it in *The Gallic War*? The answers to these questions may reveal a little-known example of Caesar's malicious humor at the expense of his political rival, Domitius Ahenobarbus, who two years before had proposed to deprive him of his Gallic command. The only mention of an elephant with Caesar's army at the Thames, or with him anywhere in Britain, is in a collection of accounts of military stratagems made in the second century of the Christian era by Polyaenus, a Greek historian:

> Caesar attempting to pass a large river in Britain, Cassoellaunus, king of the Britons, obstructed him with many horsemen and chariots. Caesar had in his train a very large elephant, an animal hitherto unseen by the Britons. Having armed him with scales

of iron, and put a large tower upon him, and placed therein archers and slingers, he ordered them to enter the stream. The Britons were amazed on beholding a beast till then unseen, and of an extraordinary nature. As to the horses, what need to write of them? Since even among the Greeks, horses fly at seeing an elephant even without harness; but thus towered and armed, and casting darts and slinging, they could not endure even to look upon the sight. The Britons therefore fled with their horses and chariots. Thus the Romans passed the river without molestation, having terrified the enemy by a single animal.[11]

Because this elephant is not mentioned by Caesar, and appears only in this single account two centuries later, most scholars have dismissed it as a confused fiction based on the acknowledged use of an elephant in Britain by the army of Emperor Claudius in the Roman invasion a hundred years later. But C.E. Stevens, an authoritative historian of the Late Roman Republic, has proposed that the incident is correctly reported by Polyaenus. He points out that Pompey had imported twenty African elephants to take part in games to celebrate his gift to Rome of its first stone theater at the end of 55 BC. It would have been an easy matter for Caesar to acquire one and take it with him to Britain. Stevens suggests that the story is based on one of the dispatches sent by Caesar to the Roman Senate after he crossed the river. The report, or a paraphrase of it, may have been included in Livy's *History of Rome,* written at the end of the first century BC and available to Polyaenus, but currently surviving only in fragments.

Stevens' theory is that Caesar deliberately took an elephant with him to Britain to spite Domitius Ahenobarbus, whose grandfather had defeated a Celtic army and brought Further Gaul into Roman hands in 121 BC. According to Suetonius, the grandfather had been so proud of his achievement that he had ridden around the new province on an elephant. Caesar reported his forcing of the Thames with an elephant to emphasize that his conquest surpassed that of his enemy's grandfather. But by the time he published *The Gallic War,* in 50 BC, it was clear that he had neither conquered Britain nor made it a Roman province, and he prudently omitted the incident. Another reason may have been that in 50 BC he was attempting to garner support for an extension of his command, and an unnecessary insult to Domitius Ahenobarbus would not have served his purpose.

Last of all, Stevens points to the first coin issued by Caesar after he entered upon his second consulship in 48 BC. It is stamped "CAESAR" and portrays an African elephant trampling on a dragon—a standard symbol for the remote Oceanus that Caesar crossed to invade Britain. "There is no other connection known between Caesar and elephants," Stevens writes; "they were the badge of another Roman family, the Metelli." By then, both the issue of Caesar's command and Domitius Ahenobarbus himself were dead, and Caesar took the occasion to make the insult permanent.[12]

With or without the elephant, Caesar's successful crossing of the Thames put him and his thousands of soldiers in what is now one of the western boroughs of modern London, most likely Brent, an area then heavily wooded with oak. Those who could not use the narrow trackway would have had to hack their way through a dense undergrowth of hazel, hawthorn and brambles, such as may be seen today in nearby Epping Forest. Caesar writes that Cassivellaunus "had now given up all hope of fighting a pitched battle. He disbanded most of his forces, keeping only some four thousand charioteers," with which he harassed the edges of Caesar's army (V, 19). The route of the Roman legions was probably along the east bank of the River Brent and then northeastward toward the River Lea, the boundary between the Catuvellauni and the Trinovantes. Cassivellaunus' charioteers, unable to stand against the steadily advancing Roman infantry, had to limit themselves to attacking any cavalry that strayed from the main body of troops. Their tactic was to ride ahead of the Romans and drive the inhabitants and their cattle away from the legions and into the woods to prevent their capture.

With Caesar and their exiled prince Mandubracius approaching their territory, the Trinovantes now sent emissaries offering to surrender and provide the Romans with grain. They asked that Caesar protect Mandubracius from Cassivellaunus and allow him to succeed his father as their king. Caesar demanded hostages as well as the grain before returning Mandubracius and, getting both, soon had his right flank secure. Shortly afterward, five other nearby tribes offered their submission to Caesar and told him that an *oppidum* of Cassivellaunus, protected by woods and swamps and filled with a great number of men and cattle, was not far away. With his men rested and his supplies restocked, Caesar turned to the west and the stronghold of the Catuvellauni.

Beginning with the first attempts to locate Caesar's battle-sites in Britain, the location of the headquarters of the fabled Cassivellaunus has stirred the curiosity not only of historians but of the general public as well. It was here that the final and decisive battle of the first foreign invasion of Britain took place, and it rightfully deserves a place with Bosworth, Flodden and Hastings among the storied names of English history. Unfortunately, the perennial obstacles to archaeology—lack of financing and subsequent building upon the sites—have prevented a conclusive solution to the mystery.

Early antiquarians and archaeologists placed the *oppidum* at a variety of ancient sites in Hertfordshire, Buckinghamshire and Essex, and even at London. Among these, Bulstrode Camp in Buckinghamshire has yielded no relevant artifacts, and The Aubreys, at Redbourne, has not been excavated. A few miles south of the town of Tring in the Chilterns lies Cholesbury Camp, a perfectly preserved oval hillfort of eleven acres surrounding the church and grounds of St. Lawrence. But the lack of a nearby swamp renders it an unlikely prospect. At Baldock, on the prehistoric Icknield Way in northern Hertfordshire, there is evidence of a substantial Iron Age settlement, and in 1968 the rich burial of a chieftain of the first century BC was discovered there. But there is nothing that meets the description of the *oppidum* given by Caesar.[13] Gatesbury, near Braughing, and Wallbury, in Essex, are too far east and are likely to have been in, or too near, the territory of the Trinovantes.

Beginning with William Camden in the late sixteenth century, speculation has centered on the complex of prehistoric settlements and ditches in the vicinity of St. Albans. This city on the River Ver has long been known as the successor to Verulamium, one of the largest towns in Roman Britain, and the original terminus of the trackway later known as Watling Street. The remains of the Roman walls and of the cemetery, theater and other structures are among the most impressive in the country. In 1932, Sir Mortimer Wheeler excavated and mapped the original Celtic settlement, just to the southwest at Prae Wood. In articles in *The Times* in the same year he identified the site as the stronghold of Cassivellaunus, but later concluded that the coins, pottery and other physical evidence could not confirm a settlement as early as Caesar's time. Further work enabled him to prove that Prae Wood was the capital of Tasciovanus, son or grandson of Cassivellaunus, and that coins bearing his name were minted there at the end of the first century BC.

Along the northern edge of St. Albans a massive mile-long ditch—Beech Bottom Dyke—thirty feet deep and a hundred feet wide can still be seen. This was evidently part of a pre-Roman boundary or defensework. But extensive excavations throughout the St. Albans area have failed to confirm any settlement as early as the time of Caesar's invasion.

Wheeler's work in the vicinity of St. Albans eventually led him a few miles north to another earthwork just south of the River Lea and the town of Wheathampstead. Here, another enormous man-made ditch, now called Devil's Dyke, extends along the west side of a ninety-acre plateau bounded on its eastern edge by a smaller ditch and a water-filled depression. The circular plateau of the Wheathampstead *oppidum* is among the three or four greatest earthworks in England. Its surrounding ditches and banks suggest a huge enclosure that might have sheltered thousands of men, cattle and chariots. Moreover, Wheeler found pottery fragments in Devil's Dyke that he dated to the middle of the first century BC.

Early in 1933 Wheeler triumphantly announced that he had finally found the last stronghold of the legendary Cassivellaunus, and Wheathampstead took its place among the hallowed place names of Britain's past.[14] Photographs of the deep and curving bottom of Devil's Dyke appeared in the press, and in 1937 a brick-pillared iron gate was built at the head of the ravine to commemorate the coronation of King George VI and Queen Elizabeth. A plaque on one of the pillars reads:

> This Entrenchment
> is part of a
> BRITISH CITY
> built in the
> Ist CENTURY B.C.
> It was probably here that
> JULIUS CAESAR
> defeated the British King
> CASSIVELLAUNUS
> in 54 B.C.

Despite these assertions, Wheeler's claim has repeatedly been questioned on at least three points. The ditch he found at the eastern edge of the plateau, now called The Slad, is thought by many to be a natural formation, and there are no indications of defenseworks on the northern or southern boundaries. Also, the plateau that supposedly housed thousands of men, horses and cattle has yielded none of the evidence that might reasonably be expected from such a place—no remains of horse or chariot gear, weapons, tools or post holes. Although the few bits of pottery found in Devil's Dyke are agreed to be contemporary with Cassivellaunus, the ditch itself appears to be a continuation of Beech Bottom Dyke along the valley bottom, and may not relate to an *oppidum* at all.

The case for a settlement or hillfort at Wheathampstead remains to be proved, and in 1976 archaeologist James Dyer suggested another site in northern Hertfordshire: the remote hill of Ravensburgh just off the Icknield Way. This site has long been known to antiquarians and archaeologists, and is today an imposing tree-covered knoll of sixteen acres surrounded by rolling fields of flax, rape and barley. Its owner has been reluc-tant to allow extensive excavation because it is a haven for his pheasants and other game birds. Dyer obtained permission to excavate a portion of it in 1964, and the work continued into the 1970s. He found evidence that the hill had been occupied and fortified with ditches and ramparts as early as the fourth century BC. In the limited area he examined he found Belgic-style pottery dating to the first century BC, and dozens of ancient post holes that may be the remains of fences for cattle pens. The presence of a marshy area east of the hill, and the obvious destruction of the earthworks after its last occupation led Dyer to suggest that Ravensburgh is a better candidate than Wheathampstead for the last bastion of Cassivellaunus.[15]

A short march of a day or two would have brought Caesar to either Wheathampstead or Ravensburgh, and he writes that he found a well-fortified *oppidum* with excellent natural defenses. The retreating Britons had withdrawn into the enclosure with the cattle and chariots they had not abandoned, and had barricaded themselves against attack. The Romans quickly formed up their cavalry and four legions of infantrymen and stormed the hill on two sides. Outnumbered, and with little time to prepare themselves, the Britons could not withstand the assault of an army of nearly twenty thousand men. Caesar does not report what tactics he used, but simple overwhelming numbers would have been enough. The Romans swarmed through the gates and over the banks, and the defenders fought only briefly before, in Caesar's words, "they rushed out of their oppidum on the other side" (V, 21). The Romans pursued them and slaughtered all they could find, but when the dead were examined the body of Cassivellaunus was not among them.

It was now that Caesar learned that his British opponent had not only escaped unharmed but had ordered a counterattack that threatened to cancel all the Roman victories and turn the entire invasion into a disaster. In Caesar's words: "While these operations were going on there, Cassivellaunus sent messengers to Kent . . . There were four kings in that region, Cingetorix, Carvilius, Taximagulus and Segovax, and Cassivellaunus ordered them to collect all their troops and make a surprise attack on our naval camp" (V, 22).

Far beyond the edge of Rome's frontier, and deep into the interior of Britain with four-fifths of his invasion army, Caesar was dependent for his escape on his ship-camp on the coast of Kent. To lose it would strand him and his troops on a hostile island at the eventual mercy of an overwhelming number of Britons.

The military historian A.H. Burne has suggested that the earlier surprise attack in Kent was a part of Cassivellaunus' strategy from the beginning, and that he deliberately led Caesar's main body of legionaries far inland to prevent their coming to the defense of the camp.[16] When he "disbanded most of his forces," as Caesar writes, "keeping only some four thousand charioteers" in Hertfordshire" (V, 19), he was actually diverting the bulk of his army back to the coast to destroy Caesar's supply base and the Romans' only means of escaping the island.

Other than Caesar's bare paragraph, we know nothing about the attack that Cassivellaunus ordered the four Kentish kings to make on the naval camp. Fortunately for Caesar, the single legion manning the ditches and banks around his ships was able to foil the effort. The Romans apparently advanced out of the camp and attacked first, suggesting that the Britons had either brought up too few troops or, more likely, that the four armies were too disorganized to mount an effective assault. Caesar describes the incident as if it were only a nuisance: "When these forces reached the camp, our men made a sudden sortie, killing many of them and capturing one of their leaders, a nobleman called Lugotorix, before retiring again without loss" (V, 22).

But what he does not say is that as soon as he got word of the attack he took a platoon of horsemen and rushed to the coast himself. The threat to his camp was clearly the gravest situation he had faced in Britain, but he omits any mention of this journey in *The Gallic War*. His reaction, however, reveals that it caused him a great deal more anxiety than he admits, and that he felt he had to see the situation at the camp for himself.

Caesar's hurried trip back to Kent would be lost to history except for the survival of a letter from Cicero to his brother, Quintus, in Caesar's army in Britain. In it he refers to a letter sent to him by Caesar from Kent on September 1—about four weeks before he returned to Gaul—in which he says that Quintus is not with him. This letter reveals Caesar's presence in Kent without his army several weeks before his account in *The Gallic War* has him leading his four legions back to the coast. It suggests that he either made a hasty round trip to his camp on the coast or that he returned there without his army and waited until the four legions joined him. In either case he has concealed from his readers the fact that he left his army in Hertfordshire and made a hurried trip to Kent.[17]

Cicero's letters to his brother also reveal an amusing sidelight on the mix of war, politics and literature among the nobility of the Late Republic. The epic poem was a popular method of expressing patriotic feelings, and was used particularly to curry favor with military heroes. Even before Caesar embarked a second time for Britain, a poet in Provincia had composed an epic celebrating his campaign against Ariovistus in 58 BC. Early in June of 54, when Quintus was with Caesar in Gaul preparing for the invasion, Marcus Tullius brought up to his brother the notion that he would write an epic poem on the British campaign, "*quam pingam coloribus tuis*"—"with colors supplied by you." In subsequent letters it transpired that Quintus, too, was to write a poem, with some verses supplied by his brother—who proved to be dilatory in providing them. At length, Quintus abandoned his poem, possibly after the disappointing outcome of the invasion. Marcus Tullius finished what he called "a very pretty epic," and may have sent it to Caesar after his return to Gaul, but never made it available to the public, possibly for the same reason. Unfortunately, neither Cicero's nor any other poem on the Gallic War has survived.[18]

With the failed attack on the ship-camp, the back of the British defense was broken and Caesar had made himself supreme in Britain. In his own words: "When reports of this battle reached him, Cassivellaunus, alarmed by the many reversals he had suffered, the devastation of his country, and especially the defection of the other tribes, sent envoys to me to ask for terms of surrender, using Commius the Atrebatian as an intermediary" (V, 22).

This is the first mention of Commius in connection with the invasion of 54 BC, and here again the candor of Caesar's account is questionable. If Commius accompanied him on this campaign, as is likely, it is probable that it was Caesar and not Cassivellaunus who enlisted him as an intermediary between them. And if he had not already, Caesar had to decide now, in early September while it was still safe to sail, if he would stay the winter in Britain; the terms of surrender would depend on which course he took. As it was, he had probably made up his mind following the last battle, and now for the record put the best face on his decision: "I had decided to winter on the continent because of the danger that sudden risings might break out in Gaul. There was not much of the summer left and I realized that the Britons could easily hold out for that short time, so I accepted their surrender, ordering hostages to be given and fixing the tribute to be paid annually by Britain to Rome. I gave strict orders to Cassivellaunus not to molest Mandubracius or the Trinobantes" (V, 22).

In this paragraph Caesar comes as close as he ever does to acknowledging that his invasion of Britain, if not an outright failure, fell far short of his own expectations. He had of course been careful not to portray it as an attempt at conquest, but it is clear from the size of his army that he intended nothing less than acquiring a new province for Rome.

The threat of a revolt in Gaul was a real one, but it is also likely that Caesar was disappointed by Britain. He said in another of his letters to Cicero, dispatched from "Shores of Nearer Britain, 25 September," that "Britain is finished off" and he was evidently glad to be rid of it.[19] There had been little or no plunder, and although he had defeated everyone he faced, he had acquired no new permanent territory nor captured anything worthwhile. Despite the surrender terms imposed on Cassivellaunus, Caesar knew he was not to be trusted, and that it was not even safe to leave a garrison on the island. He records: "When the hostages were delivered, I led the army back to the coast, where I found the ships had been repaired. We launched them, and because we had a great many prisoners and had lost some of our ships in the storm, I decided to make the return journey in two trips" (V, 23).

It is entirely possible, as one writer has suggested, that Caesar's engineers bridged the Thames for the army's return journey to Kent. Such a project would have been easier than the Rhine bridge of the previous year, the Thames near modern Brentford, for example, being notably shallow and only half the width of the European river.[20] Admittedly, the legions could have used the ford just as they had before, but a bridge, maintained by the friendly Trinovantes, would have been a definite asset should there be a third campaign in Britain. In any event, Caesar does not mention such a bridge, and no trace of one before the one built in AD 50 has been found.

After half the army had returned to Gaul, the empty ships, along with an additional sixty that Labienus had built on the mainland, were sent back to Britain for a second trip. But another Channel storm drove nearly all of them back to the island, and Caesar waited impatiently for several days before it cleared. Finally the sea became absolutely calm—"*summa tranquillitate*," in his words—and he packed his prisoners and the rest of his army into the ships on hand. Late one evening toward the end of September the dozens of transports cast off for Gaul, and the British Celts were left to themselves again for almost another century.

CHAPTER IX

⤜⋅⤛

TURMOIL IN ROME

E ven though Caesar brought thousands of captives and his entire army safely back to Gaul, the news of the invasion met a cool reception in Rome. This time there was no triumph and no thanksgiving, and for Caesar the news was even worse. As he stepped ashore, he was handed letters from Rome with the news that his twenty-two-year-old daughter, Julia—the wife of Pompey—had died in childbirth several weeks before. Pompey's son, Caesar's grandson, survived his mother by only a few days. That both Caesar and Pompey were devoted to Julia is agreed by every writer about either man, and Caesar's grief was no doubt genuine. But it must also have been tinged with alarm. Julia was the one personal bond between himself and Pompey, and her death could only have a detrimental effect on the strength of their pact.

Earlier in the year, Caesar, through his agents in Rome, had used some of his war booty to begin buying land in the capital to enlarge the Forum and construct several new buildings, including a Basilica Julia. Such projects were used regularly by victorious generals to flaunt their achievements and curry favor with the public, and they usually succeeded. Also, at the time of Julia's death in August the disappointing story of the second British expedition was known only to Caesar's personal correspondents. The result was that his daughter's funeral became the occasion for a noisy demonstration of grief and goodwill toward Caesar. A crowd of mourners interrupted the procession and carried off her corpse to the Campus Martius, where, against the protests of Consul Domitius Ahenobarbus, they cremated and buried

it in sacred ground. From his camp in Gaul Caesar showed his gratitude by ordering gladiatorial games at his own expense and a public
banquet in her honor.[1]

Within a few weeks he was embroiled in another revolt of the
Belgic tribes and their neighbors in northern Gaul. Because of a
drought, the grain harvest was poor, so he had quartered each of his
eight legions in a different location to assure their food supply for the
winter. This dispersion of the Roman troops emboldened the surrounding tribes to organize large armies in each location and attack
everywhere at the same time. In one of the ensuing battles two of
Caesar's commanders, Titurius Sabinus and Aurunculeius Cotta, were
ambushed and killed; an entire Roman legion and half of another were
lost.

Shortly after this, Caesar received a message from a desperate
Quintus Cicero, who had been trapped in his camp with his single
legion for more than a week. He was surrounded and besieged by
thousands of Belgae from seven different tribes, led by the Nervii,
whom Caesar had claimed he annihilated three years before. After
many failed attempts to smuggle out the message, a Nervian named
Vertico, who had deserted to Quintus Cicero at the start of the siege,
persuaded one of his slaves to sneak through the blockade and deliver
it to Caesar. When he received it, Caesar sent word to another legion
to meet him on the way, and then made a rapid march of more than a
hundred miles across Gallia Belgica to the vicinity of Quintus' camp in
what would one day become the province of Hainaut in Belgium.
From there Caesar sent one of his Gallic cavalrymen with a letter of
encouragement to Quintus, taking care to write it in Greek characters
so that it couldn't be read if intercepted by the Belgae.

Within a few days Caesar took a position on high ground and
packed his two legions of seven thousand men into the smallest camp
possible in order to lure the Belgic army, which he estimated at sixty
thousand men, into turning away from Quintus and attacking him.
When their scouts reported his approach, the Belgae abandoned their
siege and brought their entire army several miles' distance to confront
the relieving legions. Caesar ordered his troops to pretend they were
afraid and retreat behind their barricades. The familiar tactic again

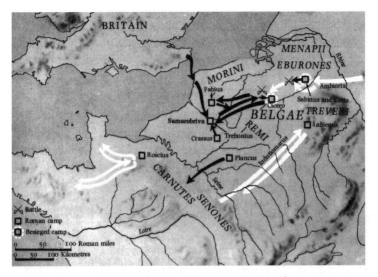

CAMPAIGN OF AUTUMN 54 BC

After their return from Britain the Romans faced a new threat from a coalition of Belgic tribes. In one battle, a full legion and a half, with two generals, Sabinus and Cotta, were ambushed and wiped out by an army led by the Eburone leader Ambiorix. It was the worst Roman defeat of the Gallic War.

bore fruit as the mob of impatient Belgae struggled up the slope and nearly into his camp before the waiting Roman infantry burst out against them, followed by a surge of cavalry. Taken by surprise, the Belgic vanguard fell back, the main body panicked and ran, and the Romans swarmed down the hill in hot pursuit. Within hours Caesar's men relieved a grateful Quintus Cicero and his battered legion.

Caesar writes that he was amazed to see the towers, ramparts and ditches the Nervii had built around Quintus' camp: "They had learned how to do this by watching our methods in previous years, and prisoners taken from our army without our knowing also gave them some instruction. But they were without the proper tools for the work and could be seen cutting the sods with their swords and removing the earth with their hands and in their cloaks" (V, 42).

Caesar's army was having an unexpected influence on the war-making methods of the Belgae; but the impact of the years of war had not fallen only on them. After many seasons of desperate fighting and the deaths of so many of their comrades, Caesar's troops were suffering a loss of morale, and for the first time in the five years since he had brought an army into Gaul he decided to remain with them throughout the winter. Suetonius reports that he swore to neither cut his hair nor trim his beard until Sabinus and Cotta were revenged. Meanwhile, the Belgae and their allies persisted—until Labienus at last cornered their leader, Indutiomarus, the chieftain of the Treveri. Caesar sent his cavalry to hunt him down and they caught Indutiomarus as he tried to escape across a river. In a gesture to the ways of their opponents, the Romans returned to their camp with his head.

At the time of his final return from Britain in the fall of 54 BC, Caesar had been at war for nearly five years. His indelible mark on Roman history had yet to be made, and would require eight more years of fighting, the last four against his own countrymen. What Caesar accomplished in Britain was of minimal benefit to Rome. He opened a potential new market for Roman goods and he halted the Britons' aid to the Gauls, but Roman historians in the next century dismissed the invasion as a pointless act of bravado that, at best, merely pointed the way to another province for Rome. In the face of what was to come, the episode of Britain was eventually relegated to a footnote in the history of Rome and even in Caesar's career.

What he achieved for himself was more substantial. The first expedition had gained him the triumph he craved and the political support he needed. The invasion had deflected for another year the pressure on him to lay down his command, and now added a new dimension to his exploits. He used the scanty tribute that came only briefly and the proceeds from looting and slave sales to finance his campaigns in Gaul and to purchase new allies in Rome. It was perhaps to amaze and reasssure those allies that he concludes Book V of *The Gallic War* with the story of his opponent's head being brought to him, and the remark: "After this success my province of Gaul was somewhat more peaceful" (V, 58).

Even as he wrote this, however, it was clear that he had not yet brought the whole of Gaul under Roman control. When he takes up the story again on the first page of Book VI it is midwinter and the Germans and Belgae are at it again: "I could see that preparations for war were being made on every side. The Nervii, the Aduatuci, and the Menapii were in arms and had been joined by all the German tribes on the west bank of the Rhine; the Senones refused to come at my command and were intriguing with the Carnutes and other neighboring tribes; the Treveri were continually sending deputations to woo the German tribes. I concluded, therefore, that I must make plans for a campaign earlier in the season than usual" (VI, 2).

His first step was to replace his lost troops and add even more. Shortly after the turn of the year, Caesar sent three officers into Nearer Gaul to recruit two new legions, and then persuaded Pompey, now Governor of Spain, to lend him enough troops to bring his army up to ten full legions. Despite the disappointment over Britain, in the eyes of Rome Caesar was still the consummate general, the warrior in the trenches with his troops, the strategist who never lost. Cicero, for instance, for all his toadying, was no doubt genuinely grateful to Caesar for saving his brother's life the previous autumn. He agreed to defend Rabirius, a Caesarian supporter who had been charged with receiving money illegally obtained by another. At the trial he bored the jury with a speech full of legalisms and technicalities, but when he managed to bring up his client's patron his language seemed to soar with genuine feeling and admiration:

> Many are the great and amazing virtues [*virtutes magnas incredibilisque*] which I have found in Gaius Caesar, but the generality of them are designed for display upon an ample theatre and almost before the public gaze: to select a site for a camp, to set an army in array, to storm cities, to rout hostile forces, to endure extremities of cold and stress of weather such as we can scarce support within the shelter of our city houses, to be pursuing the enemy at this very season when even the beasts of the field crouch in the covert of their lairs and when all wars are suspended by general consent of nations—these indeed are great achievements . . .[2]

Although Cicero would later govern a province and lead an army, he never pretended to be a military man, especially one in the inhospitable North, and preferred lawyering and politicking on the home front. It is likely that his amazed esteem for Caesar was because the hardened general was so accomplished in the capital as well as in the field.

In the meantime, Caesar was busy in northern Gaul leading his troops back and forth across Gallia Belgica as one tribe after another threatened his camps. From his headquarters at Samarobriva on the Somme, he took four legions himself against the apparently restored Nervii, and then five into what is today Holland against the Menapii, forcing the submission of both tribes. The Treveri, who had reorganized under the family of the slain Indutiomarus, mounted an attack on Labienus and the single legion that had spent the winter in what would become Luxembourg, at the edge of the tribe's territory. Caesar sent out two more legions to assist and, after feigning a retreat, Labienus turned and attacked with such ferocity that the Treveri surrendered within hours. Caesar and Labienus afterward marched to the Rhine, built a second bridge across it and harried the Germans to prevent them from reinforcing the Belgae.

Once more refusing to pursue the Germans into their country, the Romans crossed back into Gaul and destroyed the eastern half of the bridge, leaving a squad of troops to hold the western end. Caesar moved his headquarters to Atuatuca in the southern part of modern-day Belgium and spent the last few months of the fighting season contending with the Eburones and then the Sugambri, a tribe of invading Germans. At the close of 53 BC, he quartered two of his legions with a friendly tribe, the Lingones, another two at the border of the territory of the Treveri and the remaining six under Labienus at Agedincum, modern Sens in France.

Throughout the same year in Rome, the political struggle between the *optimates* and those aligned with Caesar had brought the normal election process to a standstill. There were calls for a single "strong man," a dictator, to restore order; and the name most often mentioned was that of Pompey. Unwilling to confront Caesar, Pompey refused to allow the *optimates* to name him dictator—a legal procedure reserved for emergencies. But the political turmoil delayed the elections so long that the consuls for 53 BC did not take office until July.

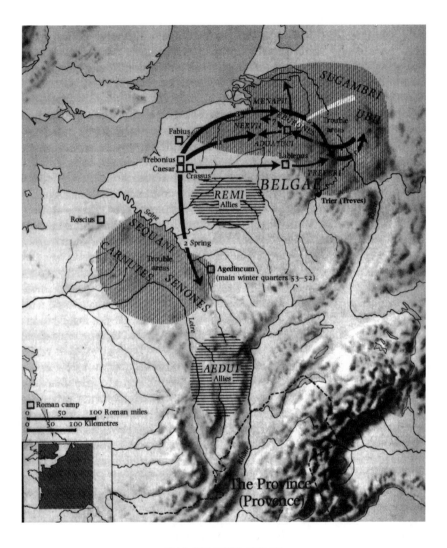

CAMPAIGN OF 53 BC

During 53 BC, Caesar recruited additional legions to deal with rebellions of the Nervii, the Treveri and, in what is now Holland, the Menapii. After building another bridge across the Rhine for a brief raid into Germany, he spent the final months of the fighting season contending with German and Belgic tribes in what is today Belgium. His army of ten legions was by then the most potent military force in the Roman world.

In autumn, word reached the city that at Carrhae, in what is now eastern Turkey, the Parthians had inflicted the worst defeat on a Roman army since the time of Hannibal, and then murdered its commander, Marcus Crassus. With the loss of its third leg, the Triumvirate—and control of the Republic itself—became dependent on the unstable alliance of Caesar and Pompey. Although the war in Gaul was not yet over, and Caesar's worst defeat and most decisive victory were still ahead of him, the questions of his command, his army and his immunity would absorb him and the entire Roman world for the next three years.

When Caesar returned to Italy in January of 52 BC, Rome was in a state of near-anarchy. The elections had once again been delayed and Publius Clodius, a candidate for *praetor* and one of Caesar's most effective supporters, had been murdered in the street by his political opponent. Clodius' angry followers carried his corpse through the city and, when they tried to cremate it on a funeral pyre in the Senate House, burned down the entire building. The public was outraged. The Senate declared a state of emergency and appointed an *interrex*, then passed new laws against violence and bribery. All men of military age were ordered to register for service in the army. Pompey was placed in charge of the newly organized troops and instructed to safeguard the capital. When it became clear that the general disorder in Rome would make the normal selection of consuls impossible, Pompey relented and allowed the Senate to bypass the election process and appoint him sole consul.

Aside from the continuing unrest in Gaul, Caesar's political fortunes, and perhaps more than that, depended on his resolution of two overriding problems. The first was his bond with Pompey.

On the surface the two men maintained their partnership, but beneath the crust of cooperation each was jealous and suspicious of the other. Paraphrasing the poet Lucan in the century to follow, Pompey would tolerate no equal and Caesar no superior.[3] Mindful of the beneficial effect that Julia had had on their relationship, Caesar now suggested that he would divorce Calpurnia, his wife of nearly seven years, and marry Pompey's daughter, Pompeia. At the same time, he made the astounding proposal that Pompey wed Octavia, Caesar's grand-niece and sister of the future Augustus, even though she was at the time married to Gaius Marcellus, a leading *optimate* politician. Pompey rejected both suggestions, and later in the year married Cornelia, daughter of the ardent anti-Caesarian Metellus Scipio. To put a cap on the matter he promptly arranged the election of his new father-in-law to serve with him as co-consul.

Caesar's other problem was his vulnerability to prosecution at the expiration, in the spring of 49 BC, of his second term as Governor of Gaul. The only way he could retain his immunity was to take office as consul before his term was over. His political support was sufficient to elect him again, but by law he could not return to the consulship until January of 48 BC, ten years after he had last held it. This left a period of nine months when he would be without his immunity, and the only solution was a further extension of his governorship. Even if he obtained that, however, another law required that candidates for consul appear in person in Rome, and so long as Caesar was a provincial governor he was prohibited from entering the city (both Pompey and Crassus flouted this law).[4]

Caesar's faction now addressed this issue by pushing through a decree, supported by Pompey, that allowed him to stand for the consulship of 48 BC without presenting himself in Rome. This abrogation of a long-standing law is evidence that Caesar and Pompey had enough influence, between them, to force the passage of any legislation that suited them both. But Pompey wavered between support of his partner and the pleadings of his *optimate* friends to abandon Caesar and take control of the government himself. His reluctance to do so reflected the fact that Caesar still had a strong following in Rome that he regularly rewarded with judicious gifts and well-placed bribes. No less important were Caesar's ten legions in Gaul—the most potent military force in the Republic. Even the least astute politician realized by now that without a compromise between the two factions legislation would only be as effective as the military strength behind it.

To ensure continuing control over his legions in Spain, Pompey persuaded the Senate to extend his governorships of the two Spanish provinces for another five years. Nevertheless, he continued to vacillate, and later in the year the Senate, with his approval, restored the requirement that consular candidates appear in Rome in person. Even though Pompey added an exception to this in Caesar's case, it is certain that had Caesar tried to run without appearing, he would have provoked a storm of protest.

News of the turmoil in Rome quickly reached Gaul, and the tribal leaders surmised that if Caesar were preoccupied with Roman politics they could safely attack his less-talented commanders and drive the Romans out of Gaul for good. Among those organizing this effort was Commius, chieftain of the Atrebates, who had served Caesar in Britain but who now turned against him and joined his fellow Gauls. When Labienus, Caesar's commander at Agedincum, heard of the defection, he sent one of his tribunes, Volusenus, at the head of a party to assassinate Commius. They succeeded only in wounding him, however, and he escaped.

The Gauls made their initial attack on the Roman grain depot at Cenabum, today Orléans, where they overran the garrison, killed a number of Roman traders and seized the storehouses. The success of this venture led the surrounding tribes to unite their forces under the command of a young nobleman of the Arverni—Vercingetorix—who for the rest of the year directed what was to be the most formidable revolt of the Gallic War.

CHAPTER X

⋇ · ⋇

REVOLT IN GAUL

Linguists familiar with the background of Celtic languages have translated the syllables of Vercingetorix's name into the phrase "Great Leader of Warriors." This reflects the practice of the Celts to use topical names, what amounted to nicknames, for specific reasons or occasions—their real names remaining a secret.[1] Vercingetorix's tribe later stamped his romanticized profile on its coins, and in the course of time he came to be considered the first national hero of France.

Vercingetorix had served as an officer in a troop of Gaulish cavalry fighting for Caesar, but when he heard the news from Cenabum he decided that now was the time for Gaul to unite against the Roman invaders. Starting out with a small group of followers, he quickly drew thousands to his cause, and before long had organized a majority of the tribes of central Gaul into a massive army. Energetic, fearless and astute, Vercingetorix was cast in the same mold as Caesar, and would prove to be his most dangerous opponent.

The first move of the rebel army was to the south, and its leader sent his most aggressive commander to attack Provincia. It was not until late February that Caesar was able to break away from his political maneuvering in Italy and hurry northward to organize the Roman response. Once in Provincia he recruited additional troops to defend its northern border, and strengthened the garrison at Narbo Martius. His army having spent the winter in northern Gaul, Caesar now found the main Gaulish forces positioned between him and his nearest legions, and he was unwilling to allow his commanders to engage

Vercingetorix by themselves. Having very few troops at hand, he could not himself undertake a battle, and was forced to find a way around the enemy to reach his army—at considerable risk of capture.

Caesar accomplished this by making a difficult march over the snow-clogged passes of the Cévennes Mountains with a small troop of cavalry; then he proceeded eastward to the Rhône. From there, traveling northward day and night, he made his way up the valleys of the Rhône and the Saône to the vicinity of modern Dijon, where two of his legions were camped. Within a few days he had assembled his entire Gallic army of ten legions near Agedincum, about sixty miles southeast of Lutetia (today Paris), the *oppidum* of the Parisii.

Caesar now maneuvered to the south with eight legions to confront Vercingetorix. During the following two weeks the Romans encircled and captured Vellaunodunum, the *oppidum* of the Senones, and then recaptured, sacked and burned enemy-occupied Cenabum on the Loire, taking thousands of prisoners. From there the massive army moved on several miles to attack another nearby *oppidum*, forcing it to surrender after driving off the cavalry of Vercingetorix, who attempted to intervene. Caesar was now in the territory of the Bituriges, who, on the demand of Vercingetorix, had burned more than twenty of their settlements to deny shelter and supplies to the Romans. But they pleaded with him for the chance to defend their capital, Avaricum, modern-day Bourges, which Caesar called "perhaps the most beautiful town in the whole of Gaul" (VII, 15).

Avaricum was almost completely surrounded by a river and impenetrable marshes, and was accessible only along a narrow stretch of land where it was protected by a solid wall of timber and rock. With Vercingetorix and his army camped a few miles away and harassing the flanks of some of the legions, the Romans quickly began erecting a massive terrace of tree trunks fully a hundred yards across and eighty feet high against the wall of the town. At the same time they started building a ramp on each side of the terrace and two movable siege towers in which to bring up their archers and *catapultae*. For more than three weeks in the winter cold and rain the Romans labored around the clock on the ramps, towers and terrace, while the defenders tried by every means to obstruct them. The Gauls of Avaricum built their own towers and threw stones, hot tar and fire down on the legionaries, and even tunneled beneath the wall to undermine the terrace.

Finally, in the middle of one night, when the entire Roman assemblage was nearly complete, the Gauls succeeded in setting the terrace on fire from below. As flames rose to envelop the mass of tree trunks, the defenders swarmed through the city's gates and over the wall and fell on the Romans. Caesar's own words capture the moment:

> Throughout the rest of the night, fighting went on everywhere, and the enemy's hope of victory was being renewed all the time; they could see that the sheds that protected the men moving our towers had been burnt, making it difficult for our troops to advance without cover to help their fellows, whereas in their own ranks fresh men were continually relieving those who were exhausted. They thought the whole fate of Gaul depended on that very moment, and, as we looked on, there was an incident I consider so remarkable I must not leave it out.
>
> One Gaul stood in front of the gate of the *oppidum* taking lumps of tallow and pitch that were handed to him and throwing them into the fire opposite one of our towers. He was pierced in the right side by an arrow from a catapult and fell dead. Another Gaul, standing nearby, stepped across the body and did the same job. When he too was killed in the same way by a catapult shot, a third man took his place and then a fourth. The post was not abandoned by its defenders until the fire on the terrace had been put out, the enemy pushed back at every point, and the fighting brought to an end (VI, 25).

The day after, the Romans took advantage of a heavy rainstorm to move one of their towers up the ramp and mount their own attack on the wall. Within a few hours they penetrated the town and proceeded to massacre its entire population, sparing not even women, children or the aged. Caesar reports that of the forty thousand inhabitants only eight hundred were able to escape and flee to the camp of Vercingetorix.

Allowing his troops several days to plunder the town and replenish their supplies, Caesar then posted two legions to rejoin those at

Agedincum and ordered Labienus to take these all north against the
Parisii. He himself set out with the remaining six into the mountainous
region of extinct volcanoes that is today called the Auvergne, the territory of Vercingetorix and the Arverni, one of the most powerful tribes
in Gaul. Caesar's objective was the Arverni's capital, Gergovia, a fortified mountaintop not far from what is today Clermont-Ferrand, a
hundred miles to the south of him.

For several days the two commanders led their armies along the
Allier River toward Gergovia, Caesar on the east bank and Vercingetorix on the west. To reach Gergovia, Caesar had to cross the river,
but it was too deep to ford, and Vercingetorix destroyed each bridge he
passed, harassing the Romans from the opposite bank so they could
not rebuild it. Caesar writes that he was in danger of being barred by
the river until it subsided at the end of summer, but he soon found a
solution. After camping one night near a dismantled bridge, he concealed two of his legions in the woods and sent on the rest of his army
arranged to look as if it contained all six legions. Vercingetorix took the
bait and proceeded south opposite the main army. At the end of the
day, the hidden legions emerged and rebuilt the bridge; that night, the
main Roman army doubled back and crossed.

With Gergovia in sight and Caesar hard on his heels, Vercingetorix
chose not to barricade himself in what was reputedly his birthplace,[2]
but stationed his troops around its southern perimeter and around his
own camp in the nearby hills. When Caesar reached the vicinity, he
found that the Arvernian stronghold was situated on a mountain
plateau twelve hundred feet above the plain, surrounded by steep
slopes, and nearly impervious to a direct assault. The southern, and
most vulnerable, edge of the plateau was protected by a masssive wall.
Halfway up the slope along this southern side was another six-foot-
high wall of huge stones, and camped between the walls was the front
line of hundreds of Arvernian troops. After some preliminary fighting
for position, Caesar set up his main camp two miles to the east of the
plateau, and created a smaller one a mile south of it—contemplating a
blockade. Within a few days, however, when he observed Vercingetorix
moving most of his men to a hill to the west that controlled the easiest
approach to the plateau, Caesar devised another plan.

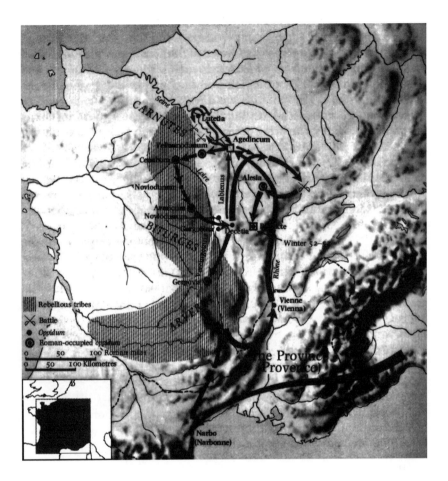

CAMPAIGN OF 52 BC

In the spring of 52 BC, the Carnute tribe attacked the Roman grain depot at Cenabum, modern Orléans, signaling the start of the greatest revolt yet seen in Gaul. Under the leadership of Vercingetorix, the rebel tribes tangled with Caesar in several places in central Gaul, including Avaricum, Gergovia and finally the Burgundian stronghold of Alesia. There the greatest siege of the war pitted ten Roman legions against a gigantic army of dozens of Celtic tribes.

The concentration of Arvernian troops on the hill at the west end of the plateau now left the southern slope in front of the plateau of Gergovia nearly undefended. To create the appearance of a plan to attack the strongly defended hill, Caesar sent several squadrons of cavalry during the night to positions opposite it. In the morning he instructed the drivers of the army's packhorses and mules to put on cavalry helmets and, accompanied by a single legion, ride their animals out in the same direction. After explaining to his commanders that he did not want a battle or an attack on the stronghold, but only a surprise capture of the wall and the Gallic encampments behind it, Caesar sent three of his legions straight up the front of the slope.

The tactic worked only too well. The Romans swarmed over the lightly defended loose-stone wall halfway up the slope and quickly took control of the camps. Finding the way clear, they surged on up the slope and attacked the southern wall of the fortress. Caesar ordered his trumpeter to sound the recall, but in their eagerness to capture the town, or because they did not hear the signal, his troops continued advancing right up to the gates. By then, Vercingetorix had seen the line of attack and sent reinforcements rushing in from the hill on Caesar's flank. A few Romans managed to climb the wall, but when the defenders brought up hundreds of troops on both sides of it, the legionaries at the front were cut to pieces and the rest driven back. Suddenly, the entire Roman front collapsed and the mob of shouting Gauls drove them back down the slope to level ground, where Caesar's two remaining legions rushed to support them—and finally halted the rout.

Although the Romans were able to reach their camps safely, they had missed their best chance to close on the stronghold and had lost almost seven hundred men, including forty-six centurions. Caesar writes that he reprimanded his troops for their rashness and lack of discipline, but it was clearly a failure of command, and his efforts to excuse himself are not convincing. To restore his soldiers' morale he led them out the next day to provoke a battle, but Vercingetorix refused to engage them. A few days later, the Romans struck their camps and Caesar abandoned Gergovia. It was his only personal defeat of the entire war. At the time Napoleon III's archaeologists excavated the site in 1862, the village situated at the base of the plateau was known by the uninspiring name of Merdogne. As a tribute to its single glorious moment, the Emperor ordered it renamed Gergovie.

The Gallic War was now at a turning point. News of the successful stand at Gergovia was passed from tribe to tribe, and those who had held back rushed to take up arms against Caesar. Nearly all the chieftains in central Gaul now joined Vercingetorix at the mountain stronghold of Bibracte—Le Mont-Beuvray in modern Burgundy—where they again pledged their armies in a final effort to rid themselves of the Romans. The most serious defection was that of the powerful Aedui, who had been allies of Rome even before Caesar came to Gaul.

From Gergovia, Caesar took his six legions on a forced march to the north, forded the Loire and set up a camp near present-day Troyes on the Seine River in the territory of the Lingones, one of the few remaining friendly Celtic tribes. Within a week, Labienus and his four legions abandoned the attack on what is today Paris and fought their way back up the river to join Caesar. The Romans remained in camp for several weeks, and their commander-in-chief took the opportunity to recruit additional cavalry and infantry from German tribes who were eager to share in the plunder of Gaul. The entire army then began moving south to relieve Provincia, which was again under attack.

It was about thirty miles north of modern Dijon that Vercingetorix saw a chance to intercept Caesar before he reached Provincia.* After exhorting his men not to be stopped, the Gallic leader sent thousands of his cavalry from three directions in a surprise attack against the Roman column. Caesar deployed his infantry in an enormous hollow square around the baggage train and sent out his own cavalry in three groups. Had Vercingetorix chosen to use his entire army, which by then may have numbered almost 100,000 men, he might have inflicted a severe defeat on the Romans. But, inexplicably, he held back his foot soldiers, and Caesar's cavalry, with the help of the German reinforcements, beat back the Gauls, leaving thousands of them dead on the field.

*Napoleon III's archaeologists determined that the site was at the present-day town of Prauthoy on the E2 highway to Langres.

Unnerved by the defeat of his cavalry, Vercingetorix now made the mistake of withdrawing all his forces into the nearby mountain *oppidum* of Alesia, today called Mont-Auxois, about thirty miles northwest of Dijon in Upper Burgundy. At a height of more than fifteen hundred feet, Alesia was a virtually impregnable plateau no more than a mile in area, and surrounded on three sides by river valleys, behind which rose a ring of craggy hills. On the west side lay a plain three miles across that provided the only easy access to the circle of valleys around the plateau. Vercingetorix positioned most of his men in four camps on the steep slopes of the plateau, and the rest inside the walls of the fortress. When he arrived at the site, Caesar quickly ordered eight infantry and cavalry camps constructed at strategic places on the ring of hills and across the plain, thus surrounding the plateau. The greatest siege of the war now began.

With ten legions of infantry, several thousand cavalry, and numerous servants, drivers and auxiliaries, Caesar had at his disposal more than fifty thousand men. He now set them to work constructing the most elaborate siege fortifications ever seen in Gaul. Around the eleven-mile circumference of the plateau they dug a ditch eight feet deep and fifteen feet wide and piled up a bank of earth behind it; along the top of the bank they put up a wooden barricade and, at intervals, twenty-three small forts. Among the legions assigned to man the forts was one commanded by Mark Antony, now a *quaestor* and one of Caesar's most trusted lieutenants.

While the construction was going on, a brief cavalry battle took place on the plain to the west. When Caesar's Gallic and German horse routed the enemy cavalry, they fled to their camps, and eventually Vercingetorix withdrew all his troops behind the walls of his stronghold. But with supplies and food for only a month, he realized he could not hold out against a lengthy siege. The question of what to do with the horses, at this point, must have posed a dilemma: though difficult to keep fed, they in turn could serve as food if the siege dragged on. In any case, a few nights later, before the ring of fortifications was complete, Vercingetorix sent all his cavalry out through a gap in the line with orders to go to every tribe in Gaul and persuade them to send troops to break the blockade.

When Caesar learned of this plan, he had the opportunity to back away from what was appearing to be a difficult and protracted siege. Indeed, neither his military reputation nor his political career depended on his (re)conquering the Gauls. Avoiding defeat was sufficient. And no objective person would blame him for declining battle in a confined location against the collected armies of the Gallic tribes. But if this line of thought entered his mind, he never mentions it and gives no sign of it. He moved quickly to reinforce parts of his defense line with three additional trenches fifteen and twenty feet wide, and diverted water from the river to fill the inner one where it ran across the plain. In the other trenches, his men covered the bottoms with a variety of barbs, hooks and sharpened stakes to prevent the Gauls from getting across. As for the threat of an army that would soon be approaching from the outside, Caesar decided to stay where he was and face them down. He ordered a second and similar barrier and circle of ditches to be constructed around the rear of the Roman lines, and manned them with troops and artillery facing away from Alesia. The result was that Caesar and all ten of his legions of infantry were barricaded between two rings of defenseworks surrounding the plateau. He placed his cavalry in four camps outside the rings to the north and west of the plateau, adjacent to sources of water.

Meanwhile, the call to battle had reached even the most distant tribes, and from every part of Gaul Caesar's old enemies—the Veneti, Nervii, Helvetii, Morini, Parisii, and dozens of others—sent thousands of men to the Aeduan capital of Bibracte, southwest of Alesia, where they formed an immense relieving army to rescue Vercingetorix. As one of their four leaders they chose the recent defector Commius, who brought with him four thousand of his own Atrebate tribesmen. It was not many days later that the largest collection of fighting men ever seen in Gaul, said to represent forty-three tribes, and reported by Caesar to number a quarter of a million, marched north to Alesia and camped on a hill a mile west of the Romans' outer fortifications. Here again, Caesar's numbers are questionable.[5] An army of a quarter of a million would have been three times the size of the largest ever reliably recorded in the ancient world until then: the army the Romans assembled against Hannibal in 216 BC at Cannae. Also, as military historians have pointed out, the relieving army's tactics and movements were not those of one that greatly outnumbers its opponent. It is likely, as Napoleon Bonaparte surmised, that the total Roman and Gaulish forces at Alesia were about equal in size.

Within a day or two, both the relieving and the Roman armies sent out their cavalries, and a great battle filled the plain with hundreds of horsemen—Roman, Gaulish and German. Shouting and yelling to encourage their men, thousands of soldiers in the two armies and on the plateau watched their cavalry fight in full view for an entire afternoon. In Caesar's words: ". . . it was impossible for any brave deed or act of cowardice to escape notice. Men on both sides were spurred on to acts of valour by their desire for glory and their fear of disgrace" (VII, 80).

At last, Caesar's Germans formed up all their squadrons on one side of the field and charged straight at the Gallic cavalry, driving them back to their camp. Though the Romans held the field, the spectacular afternoon had, in fact, ended with no clear decision for either side.

The following day no fighting took place, but at midnight a large body of Gauls quietly approached the Roman siegeworks with bundles of brush, ladders and grappling hooks. As they made their charge across the ground toward the outward-facing ramparts they shouted to those behind the *oppidum* walls to attack. They threw enough brush into the trenches so that some could get across, and then storm the fences, while the Roman artillery sent a barrage of missiles and spears at them. In the pitch-black of night Vercingetorix led his men out of the fortress, but they were held back by the obstacles in front of the inner circle of ramparts. Throughout the night, the Gauls repeatedly struggled up to the outer barricades, but whenever they threatened to break through, Mark Antony and Gaius Trebonius sent reinforcements to the towers under attack. Just before dawn, those assaulting the outer ring, afraid that the Romans would break out and surround them, began to fall back, and the watchful Vercingetorix also withdrew his men. The second assault on the Romans had failed.

The Gaulish commanders now abandoned the frontal attack and, after consulting the local tribe about the terrain, sent the best quarter of their troops on a night march around the hills to the north. At noon the next day they rushed down on one of Caesar's most vulnerable camps. At the same time, their cavalry and infantry surged across the plain from the western encampment against the outer line of Roman fortifications, and Vercingetorix sent his men out from behind the fortress walls to attack the inner barricades. Within minutes the entire valley surrounding the plateau erupted with the din of battle—the Gauls trying desperately to bridge the trenches and break down the ramparts, the Romans, thinly spread around the line, sending a hail of spears, arrows and boulders against them. Plainly visible in his red cloak, Caesar galloped back and forth between the barricades, exhorting his soldiers to hold fast. Wherever the Gauls broke through and pulled down the barrier or a tower, he sent in fresh cohorts of infantry to plug the gaps.

Late in the afternoon, Caesar and Labienus could see that their trenches and ramparts were not going to hold the enemy back much longer. Caesar then detached a few cavalry squadrons and cohorts of infantry and led them along the slopes directly behind a body of Gauls that was beginning to break through the outer ring of defenseworks, and attacked them from the rear. These Gauls were now caught in a vise with no trenches or barriers to protect them, and, according to Caesar, "There was great slaughter." Confusion among the relieving army due to this unexpected attack gave way to panic, and as more and more Romans turned to exploit the success on the plain, the massive assault against the Roman outer defenses began to disintegrate, with men breaking in every direction. Watching from his central vantage point on the plateau, Vercingetorix saw the rescue effort crumbling, and quickly ordered his men back behind the walls of Alesia.

By now, three attempts by the Gauls had failed to breach Caesar's extraordinary double ring of fortifications and they had not the will to try again. On the plain, the vast army, perhaps too large to be controlled, soon lost all its cohesion and at midnight the Roman cavalry was still chasing stragglers into the forests and surrounding countryside. Inside his fortress, with a dwindling food supply and no hope of rescue, Vercingetorix called his officers together and offered to either let them kill him to appease Caesar or hand him over alive. They could not decide, and sent a messenger to ask what Caesar wanted. He merely ordered that they surrender their weapons and hand over their leaders.

Making the most of the moment, Caesar the next day staged a formal ceremony in which he had the rebel chieftains led before him where he sat on a platform erected in front of the Roman fortifications. The last to appear was Vercingetorix, who, in the words of Plutarch, ". . . put on his most beautiful armor, had his horse carefully groomed, and . . . after riding round him in a circle, leaped down from his horse, stripped off his armor, and sat at Caesar's feet silent and motionless until he was led away under arrest, a prisoner reserved for the triumph."[4] Of the thousands of captured Gauls, Caesar allowed the Aedui and Arverni to return to their homes in exchange for their future cooperation. "The rest I distributed as booty among the entire army, giving one prisoner to each of my men" (VII, 89).

The fall of Alesia marked the end of any large-scale resistance to Caesar in Gaul, and has since assumed its place as the first significant event in the history of France. More than that, one historian has described it as "one of the most extraordinary operations recorded in military history."[7] In the early 1860s, Napoleon III ordered excavations of the great plateau of Mont-Auxois, on the slopes of which perches the tiny village of Alise-Ste-Reine. A great number of bones of humans and horses were uncovered, as well as weapons and coins of the first century BC. In the 1950s further excavations at the base of the plateau revealed the remains of extensive ditches that matched Caesar's description of the trenches dug by his army.[8]

After completion of the excavations in 1865, Napoleon III commissioned a gigantic statue of Vercingetorix by the sculptor Aimé Millet. It was transported from Paris to Alise-Ste-Reine by boat up the Seine and then down the Burgundy Canal, to be placed on a pedestal at the western end of the plateau. The head of the long-haired figure in a loose tunic and full mustache was said to resemble that of the Emperor himself. From this spot the visitor can gaze over the entire plain of Les Laumes, the scene of the largest assemblage of Gaulish might in ancient times. On the base of the statue is engraved a statement that Caesar in *The Gallic War* attributes to Vercingetorix:

"A single and united Gaul, all of the same mind, can defy the universe."[7]

But Gaul was not united, and the greatest Gallic revolt of the war had been extinguished. It would be more than a hundred years before leaders comparable to Vercingetorix would organize the Celts against Rome, and they, a man and a woman named Caratacus and Boudicca (Boadicea), would do so in Britain, fighting a descendant of Caesar. The Celts of Gaul continued to struggle, but their rebellions were scattered and ineffective.

From Alesia, Caesar took his army about fifty miles south and seized the fortress at Bibracte, another Iron Age site that is identifiable today. Even though the stronghold was abandoned just a few decades later, portions of the ditch and bank extending more than three miles around this mountain capital of the Aedui can still be seen among the hazel and beech covering the slopes. Caesar made his winter headquarters here and, perhaps in the final months of the year, completed Book VII of *The Gallic War*, the last one he was to write. In his concluding sentence he refers to the twenty-day thanksgiving (*supplicatio*) declared at Rome in the wake of his victory at Alesia.

Ironically, the *supplicatio* gave Caesar's enemies in the Senate another opportunity to call for an end to his command. They lauded his victory, and then argued that henceforth a Roman army in Gaul was no longer needed. Nothing came of the effort, and the question of when, and in what capacity, Caesar would be able to enter Rome to celebrate his *triumphus* remained hanging in the air. It could only be answered when the larger issues of his governorship, his immunity and his candidacy for consul were settled. In the meantime, he continued to reward his supporters in the capital and to recruit new ones with a stream of gifts, loans and bribes, all financed by his war booty and the fines he imposed on defeated tribes.

In his preface to Book VIII nearly ten years later, and after Caesar's death, Aulus Hirtius protests that although he is not qualified, he has "continued the commentaries our friend Caesar wrote of his achievements in Gaul" (VIII, Preface). He remarks on the elegance and precision of Caesar's style and on the ease and speed with which he wrote. We do not know for certain, but it is likely that Hirtius based Book

VIII on what survived of Caesar's notes as well as on his dispatches to the Senate. He takes up the story of the war in the fall of 52 BC, when Caesar left Bibracte in Mark Antony's charge on two occasions while he led his legions on brief campaigns against the Bituriges and the Carnutes in the Loire Valley. At the end of December he found it necessary to go to the defense of the Suessiones in northern Gaul. After their defeat by the Romans six years earlier, the Suessiones had joined with the Remi in a pro-Roman coalition, and were now under attack by their neighbors, the Bellovaci, a much larger tribe. Although the Bellovaci had, in the second year of the war, surrendered their capital to him without a fight, Caesar has described them as "the toughest tribe in Gaul" (VII, 59).

Marching with four legions from southern Burgundy into their territory some sixty miles north of modern Paris, he was surprised to find that he faced a substantial army of troops from at least six tribes, under the command of the Bellovacian chieftain Correus. From prisoners and other informants he learned that the persistent Commius had not only brought his usual contingent of warriors to the campaign, but was at this time on his way east to recruit help from the Germans. The Gauls were camped on high ground in a wood protected by a marsh that was passable only at a few narrow places. On the opposite side of the marsh the Romans constructed their usual heavily fortified camp, complete with ditches, towers and palisades.

Within a few days, Commius returned with several hundred German cavalry and Caesar, realizing that his army was too small to mount a successful siege, sent word to Gaius Trebonius, who was occupying the site of Cenabum on the Loire, to march north with three more legions as quickly as possible. In the meantime he decided that to prevent the enemy from slipping away and thus dragging out the campaign, he would have to cross the marsh. Hirtius appears to be somewhat less enthusiastic than Caesar about his army's engineering achievements. In a single sentence he writes that Caesar "had causeways laid across the marsh" and marched his legions over them.

It is perhaps fortunate that Hirtius mentioned it at all, because French archaeologists have not only located the marsh near the town of Breuil-le-Sec in the département of Oise, but have excavated it sufficiently to identify the remains of two remarkable bridges more than 650 yards long that the Romans laid across it. They were made up of hundreds of identical sections of planks, each about a hundred feet square, much like a modern bailey bridge. The sections rested on bundles of brushwood piled on top of one another in the bog and held in place by stakes driven into the bottom. Varying in width between ten and sixty feet, the two bridges started near each other and then diverged, probably for tactical reasons, so that they reached the opposite side at different spots. Construction engineers have estimated that they required the labor of thousands of men, and judged them ideally suited for the terrain.[8]

After being reinforced by Trebonius' three legions, Caesar led his army, without opposition, across the bridges to the opposite side of the marsh and occupied a ridge overlooking the Bellovacian camp. According to Hirtius, the Gaulish leaders now found themselves in a highly vulnerable position, but also realized that to retreat in front of such a large Roman army was to invite a murderous pursuit. They resorted to an ingenious trick to cover their withdrawal, one that Caesar apparently never encountered throughout the nine-year war. Hirtius describes it: "They usually had great quantities of sticks and bundles of straw in their camp. These they now passed from hand to hand and put down in front of their battle line. At the end of the day, when the word was given, they set fire to them all at once. A sheet of flame suddenly hid their entire force from the Romans, and as soon as this had happened, the Gauls fled, running away as hard as they could" (VIII, 15).

Suspicious of an ambush, Caesar reacted cautiously and ordered only the cavalry to pursue them. But the cavalry was frightened of the dense barrier of smoke and flame. "Those who were eager enough to advance into it could hardly see the heads of the horses they were riding. Fearing a trap, they did nothing to stop the Bellovaci getting away" (VIII, 16).

Both armies next moved east toward what is today Compiègne, where Correus prepared an elaborate ambush on a meadow near the confluence of the Oise and Aisne rivers. Caesar learned of it, but continued as if he hadn't, after warning his cavalry in the vanguard of what to expect. He also held back part of his army and, when the attack came, rushed them in, easily trapping the Bellovaci in the elbow of the rivers. Those who were not killed or taken prisoner scattered into the woods or the river, but Correus refused to surrender or flee, fighting on with great courage, until he "provoked our victorious troops to such anger that they shot him down" (VIII, 19). The durable Commius slipped away to safety among the Germans. After one more encounter with the Romans, in which he again barely escaped with his life, he made his way to Britain, where he, and then his son, Tincommius, became chiefs of the British Atrebates.

With the Bellovaci under control, Caesar summoned Mark Antony from Bibracte and left him with the equivalent of one and a half legions to keep watch on them and the other Belgae, while he set out to the east in pursuit of Ambiorix, a leader of the Eburones. It was Ambiorix who, two years earlier, had been responsible for the ambush and death of Sabinus and Cotta and the loss of thousands of legionaries. However, after several weeks of pillaging and burning in his territory between the Meuse and the Rhine, Caesar was unable to find him, and abandoned the effort.

With the subjugation of all the major tribes of Gaul, and Roman garrisons quartered at strategic locations throughout the country, Caesar perhaps turned his mind more fully to his political future. Early in 51 BC, through his spokesmen in Rome, he proposed to the Senate that his command in Gaul be extended through the end of 49 BC, allowing him to take office as consul the following year without a break in his immunity. He asserted that his achievements in Gaul in the cause of Rome over the previous seven years entitled him to this, and cited as a precedent the Senate's extension of Pompey's term in Spain the year before.

What he also did at this time, some historians argue, was offer the first seven books of his *Commentaries on The Gallic War* as evidence to support his proposal. Whether he had dictated a book at the end of each year's campaign or had done them all at once over the winter of 52–51 BC is still a matter of scholarly debate.[9] But in either case there is reason to speculate that the author of this classic historical narrative offered it to his peers to save his political life. The plain but detailed

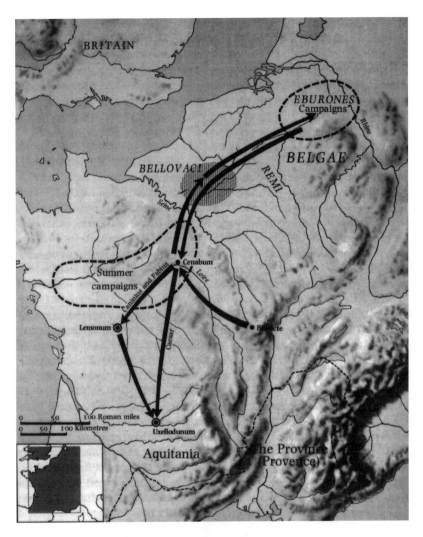

CAMPAIGNS OF 51 AND 50 BC

Even after the fall of Alesia the previous year, rebellious Gallic tribes continued to test Roman control of their territories during 51 BC. After a difficult
campaign against a Belgic coalition just north of what is modern Paris, Caesar
marched nearly to the Rhine in a futile search for the Eburone chieftain
Ambiorix, the killer of Sabinus and Cotta. Caesar's last major campaign in
Gaul was the siege of the southern town of Uxellodunum on a plateau overlooking the Dordogne River.

story of his marches, his battles, his tactics against barbarian enemies, and the persistent heroism of his citizen-soldiers was unlike anything ever seen in Rome. The papyrus rolls that circulated among literate society throughout the capital no doubt made compelling reading. But the Senate was not convinced. His proposal was rejected and the debate continued. In September 51 BC, with Pompey still unwilling to take a stand against Caesar, the Senate postponed discussion of the matter until the following March.

Meanwhile, Caesar was fighting his last battles in Gaul, and at the summer's end he laid siege to a stronghold of the Aquitani at Uxello-dunum, on the plateau of Puy d'Issolu, overlooking the Dordogne River in the south of modern-day France. This time he was faced with not only the usual unassailable fortress, but one with sufficient food supplies to wait out a long blockade. It was vulnerable in only one respect, which Caesar was quick to exploit—it depended for water on what flowed into the stronghold from a single spring rising just outside the wall surrounding it. After putting up a tower of ten stories opposite the wall and a wooden shed to protect themselves from stones thrown down on them, the Romans dug deep enough to divert the under-ground streams away from the spring and leave it dry. In a matter of days the garrison surrendered, and Caesar, in a cruel act to deter fur-ther rebellions, ordered his soldiers to cut off the hands of all those who had used weapons against the Romans.

After a brief tour of Aquitania, Caesar moved north, to retire for the winter at the northern town of Nemetocenna, modern Arras. He was now free to devote his full time to politics, and it was with the contin-uing debate in the Senate that he concerned himself for the entire year of 50 BC. To ensure his soldiers' continued service and allegiance, he doubled their pay, granted them special allowances and distributed to them even more booty. To enhance his public image he gave funds for municipal buildings throughout Italy and Gaul and as far away as Spain and Greece. He paid supporters' debts, gave lavish presents and made gifts of slaves wherever political favor was to be had. Part of this largesse he financed with the enormous wealth he had accumulated in seven years of war; another part he financed by issuing, either that year or the next, a series of silver coins from a mint somewhere in Gaul, a practice of provincial governors that had begun under Sulla thirty years before. The coins pictured Venus, Caesar's favorite goddess, and on the reverse various scenes and objects to celebrate his victories in Gaul—including one of the bound and kneeling figure of Vercingetorix looking upward, the letters "CAE" and "SAR" on either side of him.[12]

The two consuls for 50 BC were both hostile to Caesar, but the silence of one he promptly bought for a large sum; the other, even Caesar had not the nerve to approach. He was Gaius Marcellus, husband of his grand-niece Octavia, the woman whom Caesar had proposed two years earlier be handed over to Pompey in marriage. Caesar's most successful coup was persuading a long-time enemy—Scribonius Curio—to become his supporter. A popular and skillful politician, Curio was a tribune of the Assembly, and thus in a position to veto proposals of the Senate.

The immediate result of these benefactions was a prolonged stalemate in the Senate. Every attempt by the *optimates* to force Caesar to relinquish his provinces or disband his legions was blocked by his allies. There seemed to be no compromise acceptable to both camps, and for the first time in decades the specter of an armed conflict hung over the capital. Far from making any threatening gestures, Caesar left his army in northern Gaul and made a tour during the summer across Nearer Gaul in the manner of a political candidate. According to Aulus Hirtius, the victorious general was received throughout the province with enthusiasm and affection.

Late in the fall the Senate resumed the debate and, following a series of parliamentary maneuvers, passed a resolution that both Caesar and Pompey should lay down their commands and their successors be appointed. Caesar's tribune, Curio, vetoed the resolution, but the Consul Marcellus, on his own initiative, authorized Pompey to take command of two legions stationed at Capua and raise additional troops to defend the Republic.

The position Caesar assumed at the time is reflected in the plaintive tone of the final paragraph of the last book of *The Gallic War*, written nearly a decade later by the loyal Aulus Hirtius: "After that, no one could possibly doubt what plans were being made against Caesar.

But he decided that he must endure it all as long as there was any hope left that he could reach a settlement by constitutional means rather than make war" (VIII, 55). Nevertheless, when Caesar learned that Pompey was gathering an army, he sent word to his two legions in Provincia to begin the march to his headquarters at Ravenna.

Both commanders hesitated, however. Couriers rushed between them and back and forth to the Senate, and in mid-December Caesar made a new proposal: he would relinquish his command of Further Gaul but keep his other two provinces along with two legions, until he was named consul.

This plan, or one very similar to it, was apparently acceptable to Pompey, even though the situation created a curious irony of history. Nearly forty years earlier, when Pompey was in his teens, his father, Gnaeus Pompeius Strabo, after a victorious campaign in one of the civil conflicts of the 80s, had refused to give up his command and his army until the Senate named him consul for the coming year. The effort came to nothing when the man suddenly died in an epidemic.[11] The incident must have crossed Pompey's mind as he maneuvered to avoid a confrontation, but the *optimate* leaders pushed him to stand up to Caesar. It was the prospect of Caesar as consul that they feared, and they persuaded the Senate to respond that a legal issue of this magnitude could not be settled by a private bargain. With this reply in hand, Caesar sent another letter to the Senate—one that took the form of an ultimatum. In it he summarized his services to the state and demanded that either he be allowed to keep his provinces until he was elected consul or that all holders of military commands relinquish them at the same time. Without such an agreement he was prepared to assert what he considered to be his rights and those of the Roman people.

Caesar sent Curio to Rome with the message, which he presented to the two new consuls on the day they took office, the first of January, 49 BC. When the consuls refused to allow Curio to speak, Caesar's lieutenant, Mark Antony, demanded that the letter be read out to the Senate. Confronted with their last opportunity to resolve the conflict, the majority, had they the will, would have approved any option that prevented bloodshed. But the *optimates* would concede nothing. They shouted down the last attempt at compromise and bullied the frightened senators into voting that Caesar, by a date they would choose, must disband his army or be considered an enemy of the state.

Caesar's tribunes tried desperately to veto the measure, but were ruled "out of order." After several more days of debate and meetings with Pompey, the Senate proclaimed a state of emergency and stripped Caesar of his provinces and all his legions. Caesar's spokesmen fled the city and the Senate approved the *senatus consultum ultimum*, a rarely used emergency measure that charged all the officers of the government, including any provincial governors in the vicinity, to "take steps to see that the State suffer no harm." Rome declared war on Caesar.[12]

At Ravenna, when he was given the news, Caesar had a simple choice. He could relinquish his governorships and his legions and submit to prosecution, with the likely result of conviction and exile. Or he could gamble that his popular support and his legions were sufficient to defy the Senate and defeat its army. Even had he not spent a lifetime daring fate and relying on his luck, which course he would take may have been inevitable. It was on the eleventh of January of 49 BC that he assembled the troops of the single legion he had with him, the XIIIth, and exhorted them to "defend my reputation and standing against the assaults of my enemies." He writes that when they "clamored that they were ready to avenge the wrongs done to their general"[13] he led them across the bridge over the small stream that marked the southern boundary between his province and the Roman homeland: the Rubicon.

CHAPTER XI

❦ · ❦

DIVUS JULIUS

Despite the symbolic significance given by history to Caesar's crossing of the Rubicon, this first overt act of arms was no more than his next move in the unfolding chess game with Pompey and the Senate. He was not done with negotiating, and when he had marched down the Adriatic coast and entered several major towns without appreciable opposition, he sent another dispatch to the Senate. In this he offered to disband his army, give up his provinces and his immunity, and appear in Rome as a candidate for consul; in return, the Senate was to lift its decree, and Pompey was to send home his troops and go to his Spanish province. But when the bearers of the message arrived in Rome they found that Pompey, the consuls and the senators had already abandoned the city and fled south to Capua. In their fear and haste they had left the treasury intact behind them.

By the time the demoralized senators reassembled themselves and heard Caesar's offer they were too frightened to believe that he would voluntarily lay down his arms. They offered to disband their army if he would do so first, but he refused. Caesar offered to meet with Pompey, but he declined. And so, in confusion and distrust, the war that would destroy the Republic quickly took its shape.

Despite his legal standing as defender of the state, Pompey had difficulty recruiting troops, and even those who joined him were reluctant to face Caesar's veterans. Every soldier and civilian had to choose between Caesar and Pompey, and many chose Caesar. One who did not was Titus Labienus, Caesar's most talented *legatus*, and his second in command. Although he had supported Caesar for more than a dozen years, and had stood with him from the beginning against the Celts, he now abandoned his legions in Nearer Gaul and defected to

Pompey. As it was, Labienus had an even older allegiance to Pompey (they were from the same district) and apparently they both believed that Caesar's soldiers would not fight against their own countrymen. But Caesar's veterans had very little fighting to do, and many towns simply opened their gates to him.

One exception was Corfinium in the Abruzzi, due east of Rome, then under the command of Domitius Ahenobarbus, the relentless enemy who had been trying for more than five years to topple Caesar and prosecute him for treason. Despite orders from Pompey to abandon the region and follow him to the south, Domitius chose to stay and defend it. But his troops were unable to deflect the assault, and were reduced to barricading themselves behind the town gates. With the arrival of a second legion, and with defecting soldiers swelling his army every day, Caesar ordered two fortified camps built on either side of Corfinium and prepared for a siege. Within a week, however, as the towers began to rise around the walls, Domitius' own soldiers decided they would not fight and sent word to Caesar one evening that they were prepared to surrender and hand over their leader. Caesar sent back the messengers without an answer, and throughout the night the besieged defenders, and Caesar's army as well, waited and wondered what course he would take the next morning.

Caesar understood that this was as much a political as a military campaign, and his main interest was to bring public opinion around to his side. At dawn he had the town's leaders brought before him, as well as Domitius Ahenobarbus, whom he had not seen for eight years. Even though, as one historian has said, Caesar knew what his own fate would have been had their positions been reversed, after a few words of reproach he freed them all, even allowing them to keep a large sum of money Pompey had sent to pay the troops.[1] He broke camp the same morning and set out immediately to the south, after Pompey. Over the coming months he adhered to a policy of *clementia* and forbade any looting, burning or unnecessary killing. Those he captured he forgave and freed, inviting them to join him.

During the following two weeks, Caesar occupied a large area of the country to the east of Rome, while Pompey, the consuls, and those supporting them gradually retreated south to Brundisium (today

Brindisi), on the Adriatic Sea. With his army now grown to six legions, Caesar pursued them down the coast and continued to send messengers offering negotiations, hoping by some method to prevent their escape. But his blockade of the port at Brundisium was too late. Pompey and what was still the legally constituted government of Rome abandoned Italy to Caesar and crossed the Adriatic to safety at Dyrrhachium, a large seaport midway along the coast of what is modern-day Albania.

In the middle of March, Caesar started back to Rome to form a new government and legitimize his success. In just over sixty days, and with a minimum of casualties, he had taken possession of Rome and of all Italy. But the war had only begun. Pompey still controlled substantial armies in Spain and Greece, and to defeat them Caesar knew he needed a secure base in the homeland. To accomplish this, he cajoled, bribed and offered high office to any prominent person, and some not so prominent, who would join him in forming a new Senate. He was especially eager to win the support of Cicero, the influential ex-consul with whom he had been on friendly terms at various times in the past.

The veteran politician was torn between the brilliance of Caesar and the legitimacy of Pompey, between remaining in Italy and fleeing with the *optimate* government. Unable to make up his mind, he decided to retire to his country house at Formiae, and from there wrote to Caesar praising him for his policy of clemency. In a letter to Atticus, his closest friend, he related Caesar's reply: "You divine correctly, from your knowledge of my character, that nothing is further from my nature than cruelty. And while I derive great satisfaction simply from having acted as I did, I am jubilant at your approval of it. Nor am I shaken by the fact that those I set free are said to have gone off to make war on me again. It suits me perfectly that I should be true to my character, and they to theirs."[2]

The charming letter-writer was not so charming in person. Traveling on the Appian Way from Brundisium to Rome, he stopped to meet with Cicero and invited him to join him later in the capital. In his next letter Cicero reported their conversation: "'On my own terms?' I asked. 'Who am I,' he answered, 'to dictate to you?' 'Then,' said I, 'I shall take the line that the Senate objects to your going to

Spain or to transferring forces to Greece; and I shall express deep sympathy for Pompey.'"

The general's answer was short and plain: "I cannot have such things said."[3] He told Cicero to think it over, and continued on to Rome. Two months later Cicero made his choice and, against the pleas of his family, left for the east to join Pompey.

Once in Rome, Caesar wasted no time. Against no effective opposition, he assembled a makeshift Senate, took control of the government and broke open the treasury. He placed Mark Antony in charge of all the troops in Italy and assigned the provincial commands and other important posts to his closest associates. Realizing that Pompey's army in Spain was the most immediate threat to his security, he ordered six of his legions in Gaul to invade across the Pyrenees. It was only now, nearly five years after the death of his daughter, Julia, that Caesar arranged to remove the name of Pompey, his former partner and son-in-law, from his will. Then, after merely eight days in Rome, he set out for Spain via Provincia with three legions and nine hundred cavalry.

At Massilia he found that the city had declared itself neutral and barred its gates against both factions. After a brief attempt at negotiations, Caesar concluded that the city was hostile to him, but he could not afford to leave it available as a base for Pompey. He spent a month trying in vain to break in, and then left Gaius Trebonius to besiege it while he continued toward Spain.

It was late in June when Caesar joined his Gallic army outside the town of Ilerda, modern Lérida in Catalonia, where six of his legions faced the Pompeian general Afranius, who had five of his own. Following several weeks of fighting, during which his troops were nearly trapped on a peninsula between two rivers, Caesar outmaneuvered Afranius and surrounded his camp, cutting off its water and food. Rather than attack the helpless army, Caesar offered a place in his ranks to any who wished it, and freedom to return to their homes to those who did not. When Afranius refused these terms, most of his officers and centurions defected to Caesar and the Pompeian commander was forced to surrender. Caesar offered the same *clementia* throughout both Spanish provinces and by October the peninsula was his. He appointed a governor and hurried back to Provincia.

The siege of Massilia had been in progress for more than six months and the city was on the verge of collapse when Caesar arrived there in late October. With his troops poised for a final assault, he chose not to attack and instead allowed the old metropolis to surrender, stripping it of all its outlying territory and appropriating its navy and treasury. Leaving two legions to occupy it, he returned to Rome, where the flight of the Senate and the wrenching disruptions of the Civil War had meanwhile all but paralyzed the government.

While he was in Spain, Caesar had forwarded instructions to his supporters to use the law-making powers of the Assembly to postpone the consular elections and create a temporary dictatorship with him as the incumbent. His support in the Assembly was sufficient to pass both measures, and he entered Rome as a legally appointed dictator with sweeping authority to rule by decree, without fear of veto. He distributed free grain to the public and issued edicts to ameliorate some of the economic disruptions caused by the war.

But in spite of his successful military coup, Caesar was anxious to be legitimately installed as consul before leaving Rome again. Within a week of returning to the capital he ordered the consular elections and, predictably, he and a compliant colleague were named for the coming year, 48 BC. Having at last achieved the office for which he had maneuvered, negotiated and battled over the last three years, Caesar relinquished the dictatorship and again turned his attention to Pompey.

Although Caesar was now master of Spain, both Nearer and Further Gaul, and the Roman homeland, he could not take effective control of the state without a decisive defeat of Pompey. After fleeing Italy, Pompey had marched deep into Macedonia and assembled a massive army, supplemented by troops sent by his allies throughout the eastern provinces, the scene in the decade past of his greatest military exploits. Caesar was obliged to pursue him, and he gathered his Gallic and newly recruited legions at Brundisium for an expedition across the Adriatic and into Macedonia.

Lacking sufficient ships to take his entire army across in one trip, he was forced to embark with only seven under-strength legions totaling about twenty thousand men. Despite a Pompeian navy of hundreds of ships patrolling the southern Adriatic, the convoy made the difficult winter crossing without incident and reached the mainland about eighty miles south of Dyrrhachium in the first week of the new year. Caesar's army occupied several nearby cities and then began a hurried march to Dyrrhachium, which he hoped to reach before Pompey. Alerted to Caesar's landing, Pompey raced back to the coast and successfully occupied the city and its southern approaches before his opponent could reach it.

For the next three months the two armies maneuvered for position along the coast and in the hilly country south of Dyrrhachium. There was sporadic fighting, but Pompey was reluctant to commit his army to battle in any but the most favorable circumstances, and Caesar was so badly outnumbered that he dared not make a direct attack. It was not until April that the balance of his troops, under Mark Antony, was able to cross the Adriatic and join him.

With these reinforcements, Caesar then positioned his legions in a huge semicircle around Pompey and pinned his army against the coast. Nevertheless, in the middle of July, after both his soldiers and horses had begun to suffer from lack of food, Pompey broke through the blockade at its southern end and inflicted so severe a defeat on Caesar's troops that they were barely able to stagger back to their camps. The commander himself nearly lost his life as he tried to rally his fleeing army. But when Pompey inexplicably withdrew and allowed him to escape, Caesar is said to have remarked, "Today the enemy would have won, if they had a commander who was a winner."[4]

Still, Caesar's prospects were at a low ebb when he regrouped his demoralized army and retreated southeast into the interior of Macedonia. By a long march he joined forces with his general Domitius Calvinus, who had been contending on the plain of Thessaly, in east-central Greece, with Metellus Scipio, Pompey's father-in-law. Pompey hurried after Caesar and joined Scipio. For several weeks the two reinforced armies gradually made their way southward in the fierce summer heat until they reached a broad plain near the town of Pharsalus. There they turned and faced each other for the decisive battle of the war.

In *The Civil War*, Caesar's unfinished narrative of his conflict with

Pompey and the Senate, he writes that his 22,000 legionaries faced 47,000 under Pompey, and that Pompey's 7,000 cavalry outnumbered his own by seven to one. A modern analysis of the various ancient sources by the German scholar Hans Delbrück concludes that although Caesar has exaggerated, he was in fact outnumbered: his infantry by 40,000 to 30,000, and his cavalry by 3,000 to 2,000.[5]

With the numerical advantage at hand, when Pompey set up his camp in a favorable position on a hill overlooking the plain, he was convinced that his moment had come. His generals were in a triumphant mood, and are said to have negotiated and squabbled over the coming rewards and high offices, including the consulships for years to come, and the houses and property of those in Caesar's camp. Caesar wisely refrained from sending his legions up the hill against a larger army, and for several days each commander waited for the other to strike. Finally, with his supply of food dwindling, Caesar gave the order to withdraw, and his troops began to move northward, to where more grain was available. As they were leaving the field, the impatient Pompey decided to attack. Caesar called back his troops, and on a morning in early August of 48 BC the two massive armies positioned themselves for the largest battle ever fought between Romans.

Caesar observed that Pompey had placed himself and all his cavalry and archers on his own left flank. It was there, opposite Caesar's own small troop of cavalry, that he evidently intended to make his main thrust and outflank Caesar's army. After arranging his eight legions across his front in the usual three lines, Caesar resorted to a tactic that he had often used successfully against the Celtic tribes and Germans. He detached a cohort from each legion, a tenth of his infantry, and concealed them behind the cavalry on his right flank. When the front lines of the two armies ran at each other, hurling their javelins and then closing in behind their shields and wielding their swords, Caesar's center, commanded by Domitius Calvinus, and his left, under Mark Antony, held fast. When his right flank began to yield to Pompey's cavalry, he threw in his reserves. The impact of the fresh troops effectively halted the cavalry, then gradually forced them back until they retreated to the hills behind them. Within minutes, Pompey's infantry was outflanked and began withdrawing to its camp. Caesar urged his men on.

They rushed toward the ramparts and stormed into the camp just as Pompey, after discarding his scarlet cloak and all other evidence of his rank, commandeered the nearest horse and galloped out the back gate.

The surrender of the remainder of Pompey's army marked the turning point of the Civil War. Nineteen months after crossing the Rubicon, Caesar had, in a single day, delivered the decisive blow to the *optimate* government and placed himself in a virtually impregnable position. The news from Pharsalus caused a host of foreign kings, independent cities and those who had been neutral to take his side. Nevertheless, as long as Pompey was alive the danger remained that he would rally his scattered supporters and resume the war. With a small legion and a few hundred cavalry, Caesar set out after him.

Pompey had made his way to the eastern coast of Greece and from there to the isle of Cyprus; then, late in September, he appeared off the coast of Egypt near the city of Pelusium (today just east of the Suez Canal). The ten-thousand-year-old Egyptian kingdom was at the time under the nominal control of ten-year-old Ptolemy XIII, a direct descendant of one of Alexander the Great's generals. Before Pharsalus, Egypt had supplied Pompey with troops and ships, but after Caesar's victory Ptolemy and his advisers were loathe to ally themselves with a losing cause. As the sixty-year-old Pompey was being ferried to shore, one of Ptolemy's officers stabbed him to death—an act that deprived the Republic of one of its most illustrious heroes and ended a career second only to Caesar's in brilliance. Arriving in Alexandria three days later, Caesar is said to have turned away and wept when the head of his former son-in-law was offered to him.

Riding the crest of the victory at Pharsalus, Caesar entered Egypt's capital as the indisputable ruler of Rome, a state with vital political and financial interests in the wealthiest kingdom in the eastern Mediterranean. Installing himself in the royal palace at Alexandria, he soon found even more to interest him—in the person of Cleopatra VII, one of the extraordinary women of ancient times, and a factor in the history of Rome for the next two decades. She was not Egyptian at all, of course, her Greek and Macedonian lineage having been preserved by continual intermarriage among her ancestors, the Ptolemys, for three hundred years.

From an early age, Cleopatra was at the center of the intrigues and maneuverings for power that had characterized the ruling family of Egypt since the death of Alexander the Great in 323 BC. When she was fourteen, her father, King Ptolemy XII, ordered the murder of her older sister, Berenice, and elevated Cleopatra to the throne to serve with him as Queen. On his death four years later, she married her ten-year-old brother, as was the custom, and the two children attempted to reign together. But this tandem rule quickly broke down and a civil war between them ensued, the boy-king gaining the upper hand and driving Cleopatra out of the country. During the summer of 48 BC, while Caesar and Pompey were maneuvering across the Greek peninsula, she had raised an army in Syria and brought it to the eastern border of Egypt, where it was now stalled by her brother's troops.

Although for centuries Cleopatra has been a symbol of romantic love, what is more accurate is that she used her sex appeal to superb advantage in her battles for political survival. Shrewd and resourceful beyond her twenty-one years, the Queen made her way secretly to Alexandria and had herself rolled up in a carpet and smuggled into Caesar's quarters. Her emergence from her hiding-place was the beginning of his most notorious love affair (but not, as it turned out, of hers). Although her legendary beauty may be overstated, ancient writers emphasize her intelligence and charm and her seductive voice.[6] She was said to be fluent in seven languages, none of them Latin; presumably, she and Caesar conversed in Greek. She succeeded in persuading the middle-aged general to remain in Egypt in order to enforce her claim to the throne against her brother. In *The Civil War* Caesar mentions none of this, stating only that he was delayed in Egypt by his wish to safeguard the interests of Rome and by contrary trade winds.

Caesar immediately sent to his generals and allies in the eastern Mediterranean for warships and additional soldiers. Cleopatra remained with him in the palace while his few thousand troops held off a siege by Ptolemy's army. Then Caesar's troops broke out of their palace stronghold adjacent to the docks and set fire to the Alexandrian fleet, burning most of it. Using their own ships, they then landed on the island of Pharos, which extended across the harbor's mouth, and captured the thirteen-story marble lighthouse—the most famous tower in the Mediterranean. The fire, meanwhile, had spread to the buildings near the palace that housed the Royal Library, founded by the first Ptolemy nearly three hundrd years before. This immense repository of hundreds of thousands of papyrus scrolls—the largest collection of the written word up to that time—was nearly completely destroyed, depriving posterity of a precious legacy of the ancient world.

The Romans held off the Egyptians for several weeks, until the fleet of Domitius Calvinus arrived with grain, assorted *tormenta* and two additional legions. Although Caesar now controlled both ends of the harbor, the Egyptians still held the Heptastadion, the causeway dividing the harbor and connecting the city with the offshore island. Caesar now led his troops in a naval assault on the Heptastadion, but the Egyptians drove them back and, in the scramble to escape, Caesar was forced to abandon his own overloaded galley and swim through a hail of arrows to another vessel. Although this adventure cost him four hundred legionaries, the result was a standoff that left the Romans temporarily secure in the palace and surrounding area.

Early in March of 47 BC, a full five months after Caesar had entered Egypt, a substantial army of Syrians, Arabians and Jews—under King Mithridates of Pergamum—arrived at the eastern front to relieve the Romans. Within a day, they subdued Pelusium, then marched south to cross the Nile at Memphis, and finally backtracked along one of the river's western arms toward Alexandria. In the meantime, Caesar took his army to sea and landed on the coast west of the city, circling behind the Egyptians to join Mithridates. Together they converged on Ptolemy's army on the banks of the Canopic Nile, its westernmost branch, and a furious battle ensued. When the fighting eventually turned against the Egyptians, they attempted to escape on boats, and, in the haste and confusion of the retreat, the overloaded royal barge sank, drowning the precocious young king. At the end of March of 47 BC, six months after his arrival, Caesar restored Cleopatra to the throne of Egypt.

In the interim, however, the remaining supporters of Pompey had not been idle, and had assembled an army of more than a dozen legions on the coast of Africa, just opposite Sicily. Also, Caesar's general Domitius Calvinus had suffered a severe defeat at the hands of King

Pharnaces in Cappadocia (eastern Turkey), and there were reports of trouble in Italy. Caesar seemed to ignore these potential threats, nevertheless, and lingered in Egypt for two more months with Cleopatra. That he risked what he had just won, as well as his own life, to intervene in a civil war, and then delayed even longer while his enemies rearmed and regrouped is evidence that this seductive and accomplished Egyptian queen was a match for the most attractive women in Rome.

It is also perhaps significant that after nearly fifty thousand words of carefully composed and self-serving narrative about the war he was fighting with the Senate, Caesar laid down his pen and left *The Civil War* unfinished after his meeting with Cleopatra.

Although no contemporary accounts of the affair survive, descriptions in the next century by Suetonius and Lucan of the lovers' extravagant feasts and a lengthy cruise up the Nile on a luxurious barge became the sources of one of the most repeated legends of the ancient world. Most authorities agree that Cleopatra became pregnant about that time and later bore a son whom she claimed to be Caesar's, giving him the name "Ptolemy Caesar." The argument about his parenthood began soon after the boy's death sixteen years later, and continues today.[7] There is no record that Caesar ever denied his fatherhood, and it is undisputed that he later brought Cleopatra and the boy to Rome. On the other hand, he never acknowledged him as his son, even though the Alexandrians called him "Caesarion" ("Little Caesar"). There is also a question whether Caesar was able to produce offspring at all after the birth of Julia, his only certain child, in 83 BC. Over thirty-four years of marriage to three different women and a lifetime of notorious sexual activity in an age when contraception and abortion were, at best, inefficient, it is strange that no other children are attributed to him.

When Caesar finally departed Egypt in June, he left three legions to protect Cleopatra and marched with less than a thousand men to Jerusalem, then to Antioch and into Cappadocia. After waiting for reinforcements, he continued two hundred miles north to Zela, in the Kingdom of Pontus, now northern Turkey, where he easily defeated Pharnaces, the last eastern King to support Pompey. It was about this battle that Caesar later uttered his famous "*Veni, vidi, vici*" ("I came, I saw, I conquered"), a boast he borrowed from the Greek Democritus, who had used it four centuries earlier.

By now, affairs in Rome could wait no longer, and Caesar quickly made his way to the Aegean coast and sailed for Italy. His victory at Pharsalus and Pompey's death had swept away the last doubts about the outcome of the war, and Cicero met him at Tarentum (today Taranto) to offer his enthusiastic support. Caesar remained in Rome for only two months—long enough to order a partial remission of debts and to arrange his election as consul for the following year. Another thing he found time to do was arrange for his sixteen-year-old grand-nephew, Octavius, to be elected to the College of Priests, the same benefaction that had been extended to him at a similar age. However, when a great number of his veteran legionaries became impatient for their rewards, and staged a march on the Capitol, Caesar skillfully admonished them, then threatened them, then promised them even greater returns, and finally mobilized them for the campaign in Africa.

Sailing from Sicily with six legions, Caesar landed on the eastern coast of modern-day Tunisia in early October. At the head of the Pompeian armies in Africa were King Juba of Numidia, Metellus Scipio and Caesar's former lieutenant, Titus Labienus. Caesar and his badly outnumbered army spent several weeks avoiding battle, but were finally cornered by Labienus' cavalry and for a few hours the campaign, the war and Caesar himself were within his enemies' grasp. Nonetheless, nearly surrounded by a larger army, Caesar maneuvered his troops so adroitly that he managed to extract them from the battlefield intact, although they suffered heavy losses.

Two months later, after two fleets of reinforcements had arrived, he marched with ten full legions, four thousand cavalry and two thousand archers and slingers to a position adjacent to the coastal town of Thapsus (today Ras Dimas). By placing his army between the sea and a huge marsh, Caesar forced Scipio and Juba to divide their forces and fight along two narrow fronts. Scipio had brought up sixty-four elephants, and put them at each end of his front line, but the first volley of stones and arrows from Caesar's slingers and archers sent the animals scattering in panic and then stampeding through the men behind them, throwing the entire enemy army into confusion. Caesar's veterans surged after them and into Scipio's camp, where most of the Pompeian leader's men were trapped and killed. Those remaining of Scipio's men retreated around the marsh to Juba's camp, but the other half of Caesar's army had already overrun it in the same way. Thousands in the Pompeian armies were massacred when they tried to surrender, but the three generals managed to escape: Labienus fled to Spain; Scipio and Juba later chose suicide over surrender.

Although a few towns remained to be taken, the battle of Thapsus marked the end of the African campaign and, except for a final confrontation in Spain, the end of the struggle between Caesar and the *optimate* government. Once again, Caesar's generalship had enabled him to escape a larger army and then lure it into battle on his own ground and defeat it. No one in his time, and perhaps no general of the ancient world, equaled his brilliance on the battlefield. What he lacked he concealed; what he had he used superbly. His acute sense of timing, and the startling speed of his movements, repeatedly surprised his opponents and turned a likely defeat into a crushing victory. But it was this same *celeritas*—swiftness—and the lack of adequate planning that were his weaknesses. The desperate situations in which he frequently found himself were often the result of impulsive attacks, poor preparation or insufficient attention to supply lines. That he escaped so many of them was due as much to *fortuna* than to his genius for improvisation.

On his return to Rome by way of Sardinia in the spring of 46 BC, the Senate, voting him numerous honors and titles, proceeded to proclaim him *dictator* for ten years, and declared a thanksgiving period of forty days. In the fall, after more than a decade of military successes, and months of elaborate preparations, Caesar celebrated his first *triumphus*. To make up for those denied him in the past, he staged four triumphal parades, each on a separate day, for each of the campaigns he had fought and won on foreign soil: Gaul, Egypt, Pontus and Africa. In each procession marched the senators and magistrates; Caesar's soldiers and their prisoners; musicians, animals, wagons filled with booty; and enormous painted pictures of victories and statues of vanquished enemies. Wearing a wreath and holding a scepter in one hand and a laurel branch in the other, Caesar, his face painted red, rode in a magnificent chariot drawn by four white horses wearing crowns. Among the many prisoners herded in chains along the route was the unfortunate Vercingetorix who, after surviving six years in prison, was then strangled for the occasion. (The Celtic hero was, it is believed, by then only about twenty-six years old.)

At the conclusion of the final parade, an enormous banquet was prepared and 200,000 citizens sat down to feast and drink at 22,000 tables. In the following days they were treated to the most lavish games and entertainments ever seen in the capital. Throughout the city Caesar staged gladiator fights, wild-animal hunts, athletic contests, dramatic performances, chariot races—and even a mock naval battle on an artificial lake. At a time when the *denarius* was nearly a day's pay, every surviving soldier was given a bonus of five thousand *denarii*, every centurion twice as much and every tribune twenty thousand. Each Roman citizen received one hundred *denarii* and a free ration of grain and olive oil.

Shortly after Caesar's celebratory extravaganza, Cleopatra journeyed to Rome with her year-old son, and the Dictator installed her and her royal household in a villa outside the city limits on the far side of the Tiber. There she presided over a foreign court under the eyes of a disapproving Roman nobility. Married to Calpurnia, what Caesar had in mind for himself and Cleopatra is not clear. Suetonius relates that one of Caesar's henchmen later claimed that he had, "under instructions," drafted a law to be passed by the Assembly when Caesar was absent from the capital. It would have allowed him to marry as many women as he wished, and would legitimize any offspring.[8]

The Egyptian queen's presence in the capital offended many Romans, not so much because of the impropriety of the married Caesar openly keeping a foreign mistress, but because of the pernicious influence this female Eastern potentate might have on the politics of Republican Rome. Their fears were not allayed when Caesar formally opened his new Forum Julium, at one end of which stood a Temple of Venus. Beside the marble statue of his divine ancestress Caesar ordered a gilt-bronze statue of Cleopatra erected.

Despite these distractions, Caesar busied himself for the next several months with repairing the administrative breakdowns of the past three years and introducing his own reforms. Issuing personal edicts or simply instructing the Senate to pass decrees, he ordered a new census of the population of Rome and reduced the number of its citizens receiving free grain. To encourage foreign doctors and teachers to remain in the capital he granted them Roman citizenship, and at the same time placed limits on the time that citizens might live abroad. He increased the penalties for murder, required jurors to be senators or wealthy businessmen, and placed curbs on luxurious living. He also limited the terms of provincial governors and increased the size of the Senate to nine hundred, filling it with his supporters, including provincials, centurions and even sons of freed slaves.

Among the few reforms that survived his regime, and the only one that remains, is the Julian Calendar. The old Roman year of 355 days required regular adjustments by the Collegium Pontificum (College of Priests) to keep it in line with the solar year. But because of the political turmoil of the previous decade they had neglected this duty to the extent that, by 46 BC, the calendar was eight weeks ahead of where it should have been. After consulting with the Alexandrian astronomer Sosigenes, Caesar ordered a one-time addition of sixty-seven days between November and December, and decreed that the year thenceforth would contain $365\frac{1}{4}$ days, an additional day being added every four years. This intercalation, combined with one of twenty-three days made by the priests earlier in the year, extended the Roman year of 708 *ab urbe condita* (since the founding of the city) to 445 days. Arbitrary and confusing as it was, the change brought the Roman calendar, beginning with what we call 45 BC, into agreement with the solar year. With a minor correction in the sixteenth century to omit certain leap-year adjustments, the Julian Calendar remains in use today.

After only eight months in Rome, Caesar once more found it necessary to return to Spain, and to the battlefield. In the three years since he had defeated Afranius at Ilerda, the inept governor there, Quintus Cassius, had so alienated the population that the province was ripe for revolt. In addition, Pompey's two sons, Sextus and Gnaeus, had fled to

Spain after Thapsus and organized thirteen legions of troops to resume the war. On the twenty-seven day trip to Spain, Caesar is said to have spent his time composing a poem titled *Iter* (Journey) that no longer survives.

Arriving in the southern part of the province in the middle of winter, Caesar took command of eight legions and eight thousand cavalry, and for the next few months maneuvered among the Andalusian hills in pursuit of the sons of Pompey. By mid-March the brothers had split their forces, the younger son, Sextus, holding the provincial capital, modern Córdoba, with two legions. His brother, Gnaeus, after yielding two towns to sieges by Caesar, retreated with the rest of his army to high ground near the town of Munda, about seventy miles south of the capital.

Although the armies at Munda were more evenly matched, the battle between Caesar and Gnaeus Pompey—the last for each of them—had an eerie similarity to the one between Caesar and the elder Pompey nearly three years before. Just as his father had done, the younger Pompey deployed his cavalry and eleven legions of infantry across a wide hillside and awaited Caesar's attack. At the head of his horsemen rode the persistent Labienus, who was on the field for the fourth time against his former general. From a distance of four or five miles, Caesar's troops advanced slowly to the base of the hill, where he stopped them, not wanting to fight uphill. Then young Pompey's troops started moving down the hill, Caesar's moving up it, until the air rang with a gigantic collision of tens of thousands of horses and men.

Despite the larger number of Caesar's cavalry, Gnaeus Pompey's infantry, fighting downhill, had a clear advantage, and as the battle wore on they gradually began pushing back their opponents. Seeing his veterans falter, and the battle slipping out of control, Caesar leaped off his horse and ran out into the ranks, shouting at them that this would be his last day, and theirs, if they did not hold.

Startled at the sight of their distraught commander, exposed to enemy missiles, they rushed to protect him and shored up the line, halting the retreat. Caesar then ordered a troop of cavalry to make a renewed assault on Gnaeus' right flank. To counter this, Labienus detached a legion from the opposite wing and sent it across the hill behind the center of Pompey's army to support the right. But the movement of troops behind them led Pompey's soldiers on the battle-front to think that a retreat was under way, and they began to with-draw. Seeing the effect, Caesar reinforced the illusion by urging his men to attack again. The spark of panic among Gnaeus' troops ignited a general retreat that soon became a confused and headlong rush to escape. Caesar's infantry broke through the line and the cavalry closed on both flanks, slaughtering thousands in the crumbling Pompeian army—Labienus among them. The last battle of the Civil War was over.

Caesar nevertheless remained in Spain for another three months, traveling to several cities to receive renewed assurances of loyalty from the inhabitants. At the end of April he was in Hispalis, today Seville, where he found time to send a letter of consolation to Cicero, whose wife, Tullia, had died two months before. In the meantime Caesar's sol-diers had chased down Gnaeus Pompey and inflicted on him the same grisly decapitation suffered by his father; Sextus Pompey managed to escape.

In May, Caesar was joined by his seventeen-year-old grand-nephew, Octavius, to whom he had taken a liking, and who would be his heir in less than a year. In the next month they returned to Rome and Caesar celebrated another *triumphus*. A fawning Senate declared a thanksgiving period of fifty days, and the Roman nobility scurried to find new ways to flatter the Dictator. Among the numerous statues of Caesar placed about the capital was one inscribed "To the invincible god," and his portrait, the first in Roman history of a living person, appeared on a coin issued by the government. His birthday was declared a public festival day and his birth month, *Quintilis*, renamed *Julius*.

Beneath the surface of these gestures, however, ran a current of resentment and mockery. The traditional Roman aversion to anything resembling a king, together with Caesar's seizure of every shred of authority and privilege, was arousing widespread bitterness among the noble families accustomed to sharing the government among them-selves. Although there were none of the mass killings and banishments that had marked Sulla's dictatorship, Caesar's trappings of monarchy were conspicuous—among these, the luxurious litter on which he was borne about the city and the purple toga and golden wreath adorned with jewels he wore while sitting on a throne of gold before the Senate. In another letter to Atticus, an indignant, aging Cicero wrote from his seaside villa that when Caesar came to visit his neighbor he was accompanied by a retinue of two thousand soldiers, assistants, bodyguards and hangers-on.

With this patent megalomania came an ultimate change in Caesar's attitude and demeanor that antagonized even his strongest supporters. After a lifetime of strenuous activity, the man was physically weary and his temper flared often. The all-too-realistic coin portraits displayed, in fact, a gaunt face, sunken cheeks and a much-furrowed neck. He was bothered, further, by dizzy spells and stomach upsets, and had difficulty sleeping. The charming manipulator became imperious; the clever conciliator became impatient. Caesar heard the jibes and knew the truth, but public opinion was something that no longer seemed to matter.

Despite this friction with those who were now his subjects, Caesar proceeded with a series of reforms to streamline the functions of government and projects to further the glory of Rome. If he was careless of republican institutions, he was intent on preserving the place of Rome as the world's foremost civilization. Among his schemes to change the face of the capital was a diversion of the Tiber River to make room for new buildings: a new theater, a new Senate house and an enormous temple dedicated to Mars. He also gave instructions to have the unwieldy mass of Roman statutes codified and reduced to usable proportions, and directed the scholar Terentius Varro to collect the works of Greek and Roman writers and establish Rome's first public library. In addition, he ordered the cities of Carthage and Corinth rebuilt and resettled thousands of Roman citizens in new colonies in Gaul, Spain, Africa, Asia and Macedonia. He commissioned four Greek geographers to produce a map of the entire world, a task that was not completed for another generation.

In February of 44 BC, the year of Caesar's fifth consecutive consulship, the Senate conferred upon him the title of *dictator perpetuo*, removing the last pretense that he was to be anything but the sole and permanent ruler of Rome. But for a man of Caesar's restless temperament, even absolute authority over what had become in everything but name an empire was not enough. He craved the excitement and glory of military conquest. On occasion he had alluded to the achievements of Alexander the Great, the shadow of whose exploits hung over the ambitions of every Roman general. It was to the East that Alexander had marched, and Caesar now made preparations to take an army into Syria and beyond Rome's easternmost frontier. It was perhaps there that he saw his destiny—to match the feats of the greatest general of all and, at the same time, avenge the humiliating defeat of Crassus and the Roman army nine years before at the hands of the Parthians.

At the time that Caesar was planning the eastern campaign, a group of nobles—as many as sixty—was plotting to commit murder. From the letters and histories of the period, at least three of their motives are evident: personal ambition, bitterness about Caesar's arrogance and a genuine belief in the Roman tradition of representative government. Among his peers, only those he favored supported him; and, even among these, many were disgusted by his conduct.

Of the four leaders of the conspiracy, Marcus Brutus, Gaius Cassius, Decimus Brutus and Gaius Trebonius, the latter two had served for years as Caesar's legionary commanders; the two others had stood with Pompey at Pharsalus, but had been pardoned by Caesar. At the time they were plotting his death they all held important posts to which he had appointed them. Despite their high offices, however, they preferred to take their chances with the rough-and-tumble of partisan politics rather than swallow what was thrown them by a dictator.

On the morning of the fifteenth of March—the so-called Ides— Caesar was carried on his litter to the hall adjoining Pompey's theater to meet with the Senate. As he seated himself on his golden throne before the assembled senators, a group gathered around him, and Tillius Cimber began to speak to him about releasing his brother from exile. As he drew closer he pulled Caesar's toga away from his shoulder, signaling the moment for the assault. The daggers came from every side and, after one shout of indignation, Caesar, struck twenty-three times, silently pulled his toga over his head and fell at the foot of a statue of Pompey.

Abruptly and completely, the most dazzling career in the history of the Roman Republic was ended. The scoffer at omens, the gambler whose skill and luck had enabled him to cheat death a dozen times on the battlefield, was finally struck down by those who were his peers and colleagues until he had forcibly raised himself above them. Caesar's fifteen-year domination of Roman politics and his five years of absolute authority were transformed, within minutes, into near-anarchy, and then a ruinous civil conflict between his partisans and enemies.

That the legends of Caesar's last hours are so believable is because they typify his persistent and careless bravado. At dinner the previous night, he expressed a preference for a sudden and unexpected death; on his way through the capital on his final day, he brushed away the warnings of a soothsayer; and he had in his hand at the end, unread, a letter revealing the conspiracy.

If Caesar's assassins thought they would be hailed as liberators, and republican government restored to Rome, they were deluded in the extreme. Within hours of the deed, they were forced to barricade themselves in the public buildings on the Capitoline Hill and call on what loyal soldiers they could find to protect themselves from the angry mobs that now roamed the city. The general feeling among the nobility was one of relief, but they were afraid of Caesar's troops. At the same time, Caesar's supporters feared a general purge, and cowered in their houses. Every man was suspect. The truth was that no one knew what to do or what would happen next.

In the chaotic days following the assassination, Mark Antony, who had shared the nominal consulship with Caesar for the year, wisely chose to make peace with the conspirators. He then persuaded the Senate to ratify all of Caesar's acts and appointments with the simple argument that to do otherwise would deprive many of them of their new positions. Cicero, too, supported a general amnesty, and within a few days a procession escorted Caesar's body to the Forum for a traditional Roman funeral.

Surrounded by Caesar's most emotional partisans, as well as by the murderers themselves, and with the fallen general's soldiers in the background, Antony attempted to conduct a subdued and decorous ceremony. But he was soon caught up in the moment and, in the words of Plutarch:

> . . . picking up Caesar's robe, stiff with blood as it was, he unfolded it for all to see, pointing out each gash where the daggers had stabbed through . . . [A]t this his audience lost all control of their emotions. Some shouted aloud to kill the murderers, others . . . dragged out benches and tables from the neighboring shops and piled them on top of one another to make an enormous pyre. On this they laid Caesar's corpse and set fire to it. . . . Then, as the flames began to mount, people rushed from all sides, seized burning brands, and ran through the city to the murderers' houses to set them alight.[9]

Although the assassins escaped for the moment, their stunning act reverberated throughout the country and into every province. Caesar's charisma was such that for a decade and a half after his death men still fought for him or against him. And those who believed in his divinity had only to point to the skies for confirmation. According to Plutarch, a "great comet . . . shown very brightly for seven nights after Caesar's murder and then disappeared," as if to underline the enormity of the event.[10]

A coincidental eruption of major proportions shook Mt. Etna in Sicily and threw so much debris into the atmosphere that for the remainder of the year the sun grew dim over all of Italy. The loss of light and warmth devastated crops throughout the Mediterranean and produced unseasonable snowstorms and severe winters for the next several years. The twenty-five-year-old poet Virgil observed the same phenomenon, and in his first *Georgic* said of the sun:

> . . . *he had pity on Rome at Caesar's death,*
> *and veiled his shining face in dim and rusty red.*[11]

From his conduct during the Civil War, the Romans had had reason to believe that Caesar would restore their traditional form of government, and that his *clementia* would heal the wounds that had torn apart the Republic. In the end, however, his moderation had given way to grossness and his *dignitas* to vulgarity. His arrogance became so hateful that after the assassination Cicero wrote: "So great was his passion for wrong-doing that the very doing of wrong was a joy to him for its own sake even when there was no motive for it."[12] There is little known justification for such a judgment, but opinions of this sort were widely held.

Caesar was the classic opportunist whose brilliant gifts served only himself. Utterly pragmatic, he took whatever circumstances he found and turned them to his own purposes. He was not the first to assemble a personal army, but he used it so skillfully that he was able to keep it intact and loyal to him for the last fifteen years of his life. He capitalized on Rome's natural urge to expand, and turned the centuries-old threats from the Celts into urgent national causes. And he has a claim to being the first public relations man—the first to bombard the public with the written and spoken word, inflating even his genuine accomplishments and continually appealing to the curiosity, fears and patriotism of his audience.

Although his successor arranged for him to be termed "*Divus Julius*"—Julius the God—Roman historians of Caesar's time and for centuries afterward, condemned him, to a man. But after the Renaissance, and until the middle of this century, judgments of him ranged from hero-worship to a grudging acknowledgment that his rough politics were nothing new in Rome. (One notable exception was France's Jean-Jacques Rousseau, in the eighteenth century.) Most historians saw Caesar as a brilliant reformer hemmed in and then goaded to battle by Pompey and the *optimates*. But beginning after the Second World War, perhaps because of the shocking atrocities of the Axis dictators, several scholars condemned Caesar and Caesarism as evil and corrupt. New studies of his writings found them riddled with self-serving propaganda, evasions and outright lies.[13] His defenders answered that by the standards of the ancient world he was a candid writer and a humane general, no more corrupt than any other politician, and far more effective.[14]

Even in Caesar's day, gifted men with moral flaws were no novelty.

Since then, both art and history have added many examples. But Caesar's breadth of accomplishment, his many-sided genius may have no parallel. His combination of skill as an orator and politican, repeated success on the battlefield and literary excellence may never be equaled. But he never demonstrated the generosity of purpose that marks great human beings. What he achieved makes one of the most remarkable stories of the ancient world—but he achieved it for himself.

CHAPTER XII

❧ · ❧

AFTERMATH

The death of Caesar not only failed to restore the elective process to Roman government, but actually opened the way for one-man rule by his descendants for the next century and a quarter. In his will Caesar had named his grand-nephew, Octavius, heir to three-quarters of his fortune and adopted him as his grandson, thereby convincing the nineteen-year-old to assert that he was also heir to Caesar's political power. Octavius was immediately opposed by Caesar's two most powerful partisans, Mark Antony and Marcus Lepidus; but after contending briefly among themselves the three formed the Second Triumvirate, each seizing absolute authority in a third of all Roman possessions. They pursued the conspirators and their armies into Macedonia, and when Cassius and Marcus Brutus took their own lives at Philippi in 42 BC, the triumvirate's revenge on Caesar's murderers was complete.

They then turned on each other. In 36 BC, Lepidus made an attack on Octavius, but his legions deserted him and Octavius seized his province in Africa, stripped him of his triumviral powers and forced him into private life. In the meantime, Antony had contracted a fateful marriage with Cleopatra, and he and Octavius maintained an unstable political alliance similar to that between Caesar and Pompey a decade earlier. Within a few years, however, just as before, it erupted into armed conflict, and again the scene was the Greek peninsula.

In September of 31 BC, Octavius' and Antony's gigantic navies joined battle in the harbor off the Greek city of Actium. Marcus Vipsanius Agrippa, Octavius' admiral, attacked from the sea and in the course of a few hours captured or destroyed the bulk of both Antony's and Cleopatra's fleets. The lovers fled to Egypt, but there was no escape from the relentless Octavius, and their subsequent suicides left him the undisputed master of the Roman state. Taking care to leave alive no possible successor to his great-uncle, he ordered the murder of the sixteen-year-old Ptolemy Caesar, and of Antony's oldest son, Antullus, as well.[1]

Returning to the capital in 29 BC, Octavius ceremoniously closed the doors of the Temple of Janus, signifying that the nation was finally at peace—the first time in more than eight decades. In fact, Rome had been at war in all but seven of the previous 211 years.

Far more sensitive to Roman traditions than his great-uncle, Octavius retained the trappings of the Republic while gradually consolidating his authority until he was Emperor in all but name. He adopted the name Augustus, and then added to it his predecessor's cognomen—Caesar—thus transforming this family name into a title borne by Roman rulers for a century, and later by numerous others (e.g. Kaiser, Czar) for the next two thousand years. As part of his posture of modesty he took the unassuming title *princeps*, or First Citizen. Among the provinces for which he chose to retain direct responsibility was the one that Caesar had taken the momentous decision to defend: Provincia.

The Celtic tribes that had surrendered to Caesar had not only been beaten on the battlefield, but had also suffered enormous losses of population and destruction of property. So much gold had been taken from their territories that almost none was left for the minting of coins. For more than thirty years after the battle at Alesia, Gaul remained in an unruly state of military occupation, as Roman troops in one region after another turned back repeated uprisings of the Aquitani, Morini, Treveri and others. It was primarily for the use of the legions during this period that the Romans constructed the four great trunk roads emanating from Lugdunum—modern Lyons—that were the core of the remarkable road system completed in the following century.

Augustus visited Gaul as early as 38 BC, and over the next several decades imposed an administrative system on the region based on *civitas*, or capitals, in each of the tribal areas. At the same time he founded many new colonies throughout the region, notably Augustodunum, modern Autun, in east-central France, and Durocortorum, today Rheims, in what would become the region of Champagne. In 27 BC the three parts of Gaul roughly equivalent to those identified by Caesar were formally declared the Roman provinces of Aquitania, Lugdunensis and Belgica.

Even before the time of Caesar, Gaul had been a producer of hides and woolen goods, iron and precious metals, and in the century after his death it continued to supply such commodities to the Roman homeland. Eventually, Gaul became the source of a variety of foodstuffs and manufactured goods as well, especially iron tools. In fact, the technology for making tools of every kind—for artisans in wood and metal, farmers, cooks, potters, etc.—was so advanced that it changed very little between Caesar's time and the Industrial Revolution.[2]

In 12 BC the Romans advanced across the Rhine into Germany, and within three years reached as far east as the Elbe. But two decades later three legions under Quinctilius Varus were wiped out in the vicinity of the Harz Mountains in north-central Germany, and Roman attempts to subdue the region ended. The Rhine thereafter was, generally, the eastern frontier of the province of Belgica until the collapse of the Roman Empire in the fifth century.

In Britain the revolution that convulsed the Roman state after Caesar's return from Gaul passed almost unnoticed. The news of Caesar's murder would have reached Cassivellaunus within a few months but, aside from the satisfaction he no doubt felt at the demise of his conqueror, it would have had no impact. In the ten years since his surrender, Cassivellaunus had not only failed to pay the annual tribute imposed on him, but had probably also ignored Caesar's stricture that he refrain from attacking the Trinovantes. In fact, it appears that Cassivellaunus actually consolidated his power and founded Britain's first recorded dynasty, one that was to rule most of southern Britain for the next century. Coins minted in the second decade BC at Camulodonum, the Trinovantian capital (modern Colchester), bear the name of Tasciovanus, the son or grandson of Cassivellaunus. Colchester is also the site of one of Britain's most stunning Iron Age burials—the Lexden Tumulus—dated to the same period and possibly that of Tasciovanus himself.[3]

Coin evidence suggests that for the two decades following Caesar's departure southeastern England was torn with conflict among a series of tribal chieftains based in Hertfordshire, Essex and Kent. In about AD 10, the territory of the Catuvellauni and the Trinovantes, extending from Essex as far west as the River Cherwell in central Oxfordshire, was united under the leadership of Cunobelinus, son of Tasciovanus— and the traditional first King of Britain. In the course of the next decade, Cunobelinus organized the largest kingdom yet seen on the island, one that rivaled the enormous tribes that had dominated Gaul. By about AD 25 he had also overrun the area of modern-day Kent and may later have extended his domain into Surrey and Wiltshire.

Farther west, Commius, another survivor of the wars with Caesar, had established himself as chieftain of the British branch of the Belgic Atrebates. His coins, minted at his capital, today's Silchester, and bearing his name and the distinctive three-tailed horse of the Atrebates, are the first in Britain inscribed with the name of a ruler.[4]

In the 30s and 20s BC, Augustus made at least three tentative moves to invade Britain, apparently with the intention of surpassing the exploits of his divine ancestor, but was forced to abandon the campaigns because of uprisings in Gaul or Dalmatia or Spain. Throughout Augustus' reign and that of his stepson, Tiberius, a period of more than eighty years, a number of British chieftains who had been defeated in tribal wars fled to the continent and to Rome, where they asked for help against their enemies. In AD 7, for instance, Tincommius, the son of Commius, Caesar's ally and then adversary of nearly sixty years before, sought the protection of Caesar's successor in Rome.

In AD 40, Cunobelinus expelled one of his sons, Adminius, from Britain and the young man made his way to Rome to surrender and ask for aid. The Emperor Caligula, the grandson of another of Augustus' stepsons, responded by bringing an army to the coast of Gaul opposite Britain, ostensibly for the purpose of invading the island. What followed was one of the more ludicrous incidents of his bizarre reign. According to Suetonius, he positioned his *catapultae* and other *tormenti* along the shore pointed at Britain, then turned to his troops and gave the order: "Gather seashells!" He declared the shells "plunder," ordered that a lighthouse be built to commemorate the victory—and then abandoned the campaign.[5]

Not long after, following four years of cruel and erratic tyranny, officers of the Praetorian Guard assassinated Caligula (in AD 41) and proclaimed his uncle, the fifty-year-old Claudius—a Roman born in Gaul—as the new Emperor. At about the same time, the death of Cunobelinus ended both his forty-year reign and his neutral policy toward Rome. The suspicions of his two successor sons about their brother Adminius and his alliance with Rome strengthened the anti-Roman faction among the Britons and induced the Roman rulers of Gaul to wonder about the security of their northern territories. Emperor Claudius saw an opportunity to both solidify his standing with the public and remove a potential threat to a prosperous province by emulating, and perhaps surpassing, the first Caesar. Thus the eyes of Rome turned once again to Britain.

On a fall morning in AD 43, a band of Celtic tribesmen stood on the chalk-cliff coast of southeastern England overlooking the narrowest part of the English Channel. Through the cool mist they could see a group of long warships, each with a triple bank of oars and loaded with soldiers, steadily approaching the shore. The ships had high, curved prows and flew a strange flag. Among those watching, no doubt, were those whose great-grandfathers had seen an identical sight nearly a hundred years before. The tales of the first invasions from the mainland and of the valiant deeds of their ancestors had been told again and again around their evening fires. The stories of marching columns and armored horsemen, pillage, fire and massacre had thrilled and frightened the young, and soon became bitterly familiar. With trembling pride the storytellers had celebrated the brave men who fell, and their battles that pushed the enemy into the sea. But this time brave men would not be enough. This time the invaders had come to stay.

⊰⊱ · ⊰⊱

THE ENGLISH SEARCH
FOR CAESAR

Julius Caesar's campaigns in Gaul, Germany and Britain were one of the great military adventures of the ancient world, and unquestionably the best documented. Caesar's account is unique in Roman history in that it was written on the spot by the commander himself, who was both a stylist and narrator of the first order. As Cicero said, he supplied the material for those who would write history, and the story has been told and retold by ancient, medieval and modern historians for more than twenty centuries.

Aside from Caesar's own dispatches to the Senate and a few tales told by his veterans, there is no other primary source for the details of his campaigns. Roman historians in the centuries after his death—Livy, Strabo, Cassius Dio and others—all mined the *Commentaries* for material, as did the biographers Suetonius and Plutarch. One intriguing detail comes from Tacitus, who reports that in about AD 75 he heard Marcus Aper say that he had met an old man in Britain who claimed that he had taken part in a battle on the beach against Caesar. Although this is not an impossible tale, it is clear that the process of myth-making was underway.[1]

The story of Caesar in Britain and of every other aspect of British history remained in the hands of Roman writers throughout the four hundred years that Britain was a Roman province. Early in the fourth century of our era the Emperor Constantine imposed Christianity throughout the Empire, and the first histories written in Britain were in Latin by Christian monks. Although the Romans abandoned Britain only a hundred years later, it has been resolutely Christian ever since.

During the fifth century, Anglo-Saxon invaders overran the greater part of southern Britain and pushed the surviving Celts into the western and northern regions of the country. The Germanic-speaking conquerors called the Britons *wealas*, a disparaging word for foreigners subject to Rome, from which the word "Welsh" derives. The Welsh called themselves *Cymry*, "fellow countrymen," and it remained to the *Cymry* to preserve the native version of the British resistance to Caesar.

The earliest-surviving mention of Caesar's invasions by a writer in Britain is by Saint Bede, an eighth-century Benedictine monk in the abbey of Jarrow, in what was then the Kingdom of Northumbria. His *History of the English Church and People*, completed in about AD 731, is the most respected of the early English histories. His brief account of Caesar's invasions is taken nearly word for word from the first world history by a Christian—*History Against the Pagans*—whose author, the Spanish theologian and historian Paulus Orosius, undertook the work at the urging of St. Augustine in about 416.

Caesar is next mentioned in the *Historia Brittonum*, a collection of myths and semi-historical tales that was gathered together and transcribed in Latin in about 830. The work has traditionally been ascribed to a Welsh monk named Nennius, but his authorship has come into question. Just as the Romans claimed descent from the Trojan Aeneas, so also did Nennius identify the first Britons as followers of Aeneas' grandson, Brutus, who led his people in a conquest of the island of Albion. The *Historia Brittonum* is the oldest-remaining record in the literature of the British Isles of the legend of the "Brut"—the story of the people who founded Britain and named themselves and their country after their leader. The notion of the Trojan origin of the Britons is no longer credible, but the authenticity of the Brut was to be argued for centuries by medieval and Renaissance historians.

As to the events of 55 BC, Nennius wrote that, after the Britons spurned his overtures for a peaceful occupation, ". . . Julius Caesar . . . was extremely angry, and came to Britain with 60 keels, and made land in the Thames estuary, where his ships suffered shipwreck . . . and Julius returned without victory, his soldiers killed and his ships wrecked."[2] According to Nennius, Caesar then led a second expedition up the Thames, this time with a fleet of three hundred ships, but was foiled by the "iron stakes" in the river. The last attempt by Caesar ended with a battle at "Trinovantum," where the Romans were victorious and "Julius acquired dominion over the British race . . ." Even though he depended on the same source as Bede, Nennius garbled nearly every detail, omitted any mention of Cassivellaunus and invented a third invasion.

Several manuscripts of the so-called Anglo-Saxon Chronicle, begun during the reign of King Alfred in the ninth century, contain the first description of Caesar's invasions in the earliest version of the English language: Old English, or Anglo-Saxon. By then Caesar's name had evolved into a noun denoting "emperor," and it was in that sense that the Old English word *casere* was used, as was *keiser*, the same word in Middle English. As comparative newcomers to Britain, the Anglo-Saxons had little interest in its early history, and the Chronicle's account of Caesar is only a clumsy paraphrase of what Bede had written in the previous century.

Early in the twelfth century, an obscure cleric from Wales, Geoffrey of Monmouth, living at Oxford and writing in Latin, produced a book that became famous all over Europe after its appearance in about 1136: *Historia Regum Britanniae*, or *History of the Kings of Britain*. It had a broad and lasting influence on medieval literature in England and on the continent, and was the source of numerous characters and legends, such as the story of King Lear and his daughters, that remain a part of Britain's cultural heritage.

Geoffrey's origins are not clear, but it is likely that he was born in or near Monmouth in Wales, and that his family was Welsh or Breton. The *Historia* is a sweeping panorama of the history of Britain from its earliest settlement through the end of the seventh century of the Christian era. Its theme is the loss of Britain or, as one historian puts it, the "passage of dominion" from the Britons, now called the Welsh, to the invading Saxons.[3] It is filled with the glorious exploits of demigods and warrior kings, among them an obscure Celtic chieftain named Arthur—whom Geoffrey elevated to the level of myth, and who eventually became Britain's most popular hero.

Geoffrey repeats the story from Nennius about Aeneas the Trojan, Brutus and the founding of Britain, and adds many new details. His account of Caesar's contemplation of Britain from the seacoast of Gaul is a good example of his style:

> From there he gazed across at the island of Britain and enquired of those standing about him what land it was and what folk inhabited it. When he had been told the name of the kingdom and of the inhabitants, he went on gazing out to sea. "By Hercules!" he exclaimed. "Those Britons come from the same race as we do. . . . All the same, unless I am mistaken, they have become very degenerate when compared with us, and they can know nothing at all about modern warfare, living as they do beyond the deep sea and quite cut off from the world. It will be a simple matter to force them to pay tribute and to swear perpetual obedience to the majesty of Rome. First of all I must send a message to them, to order them to pay tax, just as other peoples do homage to the Senate without their having been approached or attacked by the people of Rome, for we must not shed the blood of our kinsmen, nor offend the ancient dignity of our common ancestor Priam."[4]

Caesar sends his message to "King Cassivellaunus," whose reply is offered verbatim by Geoffrey:

> Cassivellaunus, the King of the Britons, sends his greetings to Gaius Julius Caesar. The cupidity of the Roman people, my dear Caesar, is really quite beyond belief. They have an insatiable thirst for anything made of gold or silver, to the point that they cannot leave even us alone, although we live over the edge of the world and far beyond the perilous seas . . . We have become so accustomed to the concept of liberty that we are completely ignorant of what is meant by submitting to slavery. . . . If you start attacking the island of Britain, as you have threatened, you must clearly understand, Caesar, that we shall fight for our liberty and for our kingdom.[5]

Geoffrey puts Cassivellaunus at the head of the Celtic army defending Britain against Caesar's first landing. During the battle,

Cassivellaunus' brother squares off against Caesar himself, and is severely wounded. He manages to stagger off with Caesar's sword and, throwing his own away, uses it to slay every Roman who comes near him. Caesar is eventually forced to retreat to Gaul, but returns two years later "with so many troops that no one could count them." This time he sails up the Thames, but his ships are stopped by the sharp stakes clad in lead that Cassivellaunus has placed there. "Thousands of soldiers were drowned as the river-water flowed into the holed ships and sucked them down."[6] In the subsequent battle the Romans are again defeated, Caesar returns to Gaul and the Britons celebrate a great victory.

Obviously depending on Nennius for his information, Geoffrey has Caesar invade the island a third time, on this occasion at the invitation of a relative of Cassivellaunus' who has quarreled with him. Caesar lands at what is now Richborough in the northeastern corner of Kent and eventually surrounds the Britons on a hilltop, attempting to starve them out. "Two days now passed without Cassivellaunus' having anything to eat. He began to fear that hunger would beat him and that he would be captured by Caesar." Cassivellaunus surrenders and agrees to pay a yearly tribute to Rome of three thousand pounds of silver. "Julius and Cassivellaunus then became friends and gave each other presents." Caesar spends the winter in Britain with his new friend, and later marches to Rome "to attack Pompey."[7]

Modern scholars consider much of *History of the Kings of Britain* to be romanticized history—a clever elaboration of the factual, the fictional and the vaguely traditional into a stirring tale that the English public was reluctant to doubt. Most of it can be found in Bede, Nennius and the later Roman historians, although Geoffrey seems not to have made use of Caesar's own precise account of his expeditions. But the sources of many of the characters and incidents are obscure. Geoffrey himself claimed that his work was simply a translation of "a certain very ancient book written in the British language" that his friend, Walter, Archdeacon of Oxford, brought from Wales and gave to him. This book has never been found, and it is generally thought to have never existed, being merely a device Geoffrey used to give credence to his story. But it is clear that he made use of traditional legends and stories, and that he had access to Welsh manuscripts that are unknown to us. His sources may also have been unknown to his contemporaries. The respected twelfth-century historian Henry of Huntingdon said that he was "stupefied" when he read the account of pre-Caesarian Britain in the *Historia,* because his own investigation of the period had turned up nothing at all, either written or oral.

Some scholars believe that Geoffrey's "ancient book" or something like it was entirely possible. The respected medievalist R.W. Southern wrote in 1970: "Personally I am convinced that the source which he claimed to have received from Walter, archdeacon of Oxford, really existed."[8] The question of Geoffrey's sources, and the possibility that indigenous accounts of events in pre-Roman Britain survived into the Middle Ages have bedeviled literary historians for centuries.

The controversy centers on a number of medieval Welsh prose works that were transcribed about the time that Geoffrey composed his *Historia,* and that survive today in museums and libraries in Britain and Wales. The three most important of these are *The Mabinogion, The Triads of the Island of Britain,* and a group of several dozen manuscripts known as the "British Histories." Each of them is in a different form, but they are all collections of myths and tales from the distant past, some of which appear to have been preserved only in oral form by the descendants of the Celts and then written down during the Middle Ages.

The many manuscripts of the "British Histories," all written in Middle Welsh, contain differing versions of events in ancient Britain, beginning with the legend of the "Brut." Some of them include accounts of Caesar's invasions, the Roman occupation, the wars with the Anglo-Saxons, and of events in Wales as late as the twelfth century. Those that have been examined and dated were produced after the appearance of Geoffrey's *Historia* in 1136.

It was Sir W.M. Flinders Petrie, the eminent archaeologist and Egyptologist, who first called attention to one manuscript titled *Brut Tysilio,* or "Tysilio's Chronicle," which he believed to be a genuine native account of the earliest history of Britain. His assertion was that the *Brut Tysilio* was one of Geoffrey's sources, and that it may have been the "certain very ancient book" that he claims to have used.

However, it has since been shown that the earliest-known manuscript of the *Brut Tysilio* was produced after Geoffrey's *Historia*. Thus it appears that the borrowing was in the opposite direction and that the *Brut Tysilio*, as well as the other manuscripts of the "British Histories" that have been securely dated, were translations, some with modest additions, of Geoffrey's book into Middle Welsh. However, it is well known that many ancient manuscripts we possess are copies of others that may have been transcribed centuries earlier. In addition, many of the "British Histories" have not been translated or examined closely, and there are some intriguing arguments against the orthodox theory that they are entirely dependent upon Geoffrey's *Historia*.

In his edition of the *Historia Regum Britanniae*, the American scholar Acton Griscom included a long essay analyzing the evidence of the use of British sources by Geoffrey of Monmouth. He found striking examples of the dependence of Geoffrey on a source "written from a native point of view," with a knowledge of British affairs and incidents totally absent from any other history to that time. Griscom wrote: "I cannot escape the conviction that when scholars return to these primary sources, early British history will be found by them to have survived in legendary or story form . . ."[9]

Griscom cites one example of this kind of survival in the incident of the skulls in the Walbrook, the small stream that flowed into the Thames along the western edge of Roman London. In his *Historia* Geoffrey writes that late in the third century after Christ, when the Romans were fighting among themselves for control of Britain, a large Celtic army besieged London and forced the Roman garrison to surrender. In the aftermath the victors decapitated an entire Roman legion and threw their heads into a river called the "Galobroc." In the 1860s, dozens of skulls, with practically no other bones accompanying them, were excavated from the bed of the Walbrook by the archaeologist A.H. Pitt-Rivers, who wrote that it was clear that they had been severed from their bodies before being thrown into the river. As this incident appears in no other history, it may be that Geoffrey learned of it from a native source we no longer possess.

Several other manuscripts in Middle Welsh contain different versions of a work known as *Trioedd Ynys Prydain,* or *Triads of the Island of*

Britain, a collection of the names and exploits of dozens of ancient Welsh heroes and villains, all arranged in groups of three—a traditional Celtic format that allowed them to be easily memorized. After being recited in this pattern over the centuries by bards in the courts of Welsh kings, they were then written down in the same arrangement and sequence. The earliest-surviving manuscripts of the *Triads* were transcribed during the thirteenth and fourteenth centuries, but several are copies of material that was first brought together in the twelfth century or even earlier. None of the versions of the *Triads* provides a continuous narrative; they are, rather, a hodge-podge of unorganized episodes that refer to both legendary and historical characters from the beginning of British history to approximately AD 1200.

One of the names occurring in the *Triads* is Caswallawn, described as the foremost defender of Britain and betrothed to Fflur, a woman of legendary beauty, who is said to be a cause of contention between him and Caesar. One of the *Triads* suggests that it was Caesar's love for Fflur ("flower" in Middle Welsh) that led him to invade Britain, and another that she was abducted by a Gallic prince named Mwrchan Lleidr (Murchan the Thief) and delivered by him to the Emperor "Ul Kessar." Caswallawn then leads an army to the continent in search of Fflur. In one *Triad* he succeeds in bringing her back to Britain; in another he disguises himself as a cobbler and pursues her as far as Rome, where he disappears. Fflur is the only woman mentioned in any account of Caesar in Britain, and the notion that she was a motive for his invasion is an example of the custom in early sagas of attributing personal motives to historical events. The account of Britons crossing to the continent is thought to refer to the reinforcements sought and obtained by tribes in Gaul to defend themselves against Caesar. The *Triads* also contain fragments of the story of Mandubracius, the Trinovantian prince whose father was slain by Cassivellaunus.

The Welsh scholar Rachel Bromwich, in her definitive edition of the *Triads,* asserted that there was undoubtedly a connection between the historical Cassivellaunus and the legendary Caswallawn, and that the latter "had an independent existence in Welsh tradition" before his historical counterpart appeared in Geoffrey's *Historia.*[10] The confused and contradictory nature of the *Triads* and their mixture of what is thought to be true and thought to be mythical appear to be the result of an overlay of written history upon older and parallel oral versions.

Caswallawn also appears in *The Mabinogion*, a collection of twelve allegorical tales that is considered the foremost Welsh prose classic of the Middle Ages. The text is found in two medieval Welsh manuscripts—"The White Book of Rhydderch" and "The Red Book of Hergest"—the earliest remaining copies of which were transcribed between AD 1325 and 1400. However, internal evidence suggests that the tales were written down as early as 1060, and most scholars agree that several of the stories existed in oral or even written form long before that. The tales of *The Mabinogion* are a rich mixture of myth and history that relate the magical feats of gods and the ordinary activities of earthly men and women who lived in Britain between its earliest settlement and the Middle Ages. Much scholarly energy has been spent on unraveling the meaning of the episodes and finding the historical basis for the characters and their actions.

It is the story of Mandubracius, the Trinovantian prince, that provides the strongest connection between *The Mabinogion* and Caesar's account of his invasion. In an article published in 1987, John Koch of Harvard University identifies the historical Cassivellaunus with the Caswallawn of *The Mabinogion*.[11] He argues convincingly that one of the stories—"Manawydan"—is an allegory for the conflict between Caesar and Cassivellaunus in Britain in 54 BC. According to Koch, Manawydan, a disenfranchised Briton noble, represents Mandubracius, the Trinovantian who fled to Gaul and to Caesar, and then sought vengeance against Cassivellaunus, the slayer of his father.

Significant details in Caesar's narrative—the status of Cassivellaunus as chieftain or king, the use of the hidden stakes in the Thames, the driving of cattle into the woods by the Britons, the appropriation of grain by the Romans, the death of the British noble in the attack on the ship-camp, and the illegitimate (to the Catuvellauni) restoration of Mandubracius as ruler of the Trinovantes—are all represented allegorically in the story of Manawydan. Koch's thesis is that this tale in *The Mabinogion* was not taken from a Roman history or Geoffrey's *Historia*, but arose out of "a continuous native tradition" that had preserved it orally for centuries.

In support of his theory of the oral preservation of pre-Roman British history, Professor Koch writes: "One crucial piece of evidence puts it beyond all doubt that Welsh tradition has remembered something of the pre-Roman Iron Age independently of Latin history." In a medieval manuscript of Old Welsh genealogies there appears the sequence of names "Caratacos son of Cunobelinus son of Tasciovanus," referring to the dynasty of Celtic chieftains that began with Cassivellaunus, father or grandfather of Tasciovanus, and ended with Caratacos, who led an unsuccessful revolt against the Romans in AD 49.

Cunobelinus, known to readers of Shakespeare as Cymbeline, restored the domination of the Catuvellauni over the Trinovantes that was first imposed by his ancestor Cassivellaunus, and then broken by Caesar. Cunobelinus controlled a large part of southern Britain between AD 7 and 40, and called himself "*rex*" on coins minted at his capital, Camulodunum, modern-day Colchester. The significance of the series of names is that Caratacos and Cunobelinus are well known to history, but Tasciovanus, the father of Cunobelinus, is known to us only from coins on which his name appears. The medieval scribe who copied out his name could only have obtained it from a tradition that had preserved it for more than a thousand years.

Koch has also detected references to the same Catuvellaunian dynasty in the "Gododdin," a richly detailed lyric of more than a hundred stanzas that is one of the earliest-surviving examples of Welsh poetry. The "Gododdin," which, incidentally, contains the first extant reference to Arthur, is attributed to Aneirin, a Welsh bard who lived at the end of the sixth century. It describes the disastrous attack in about AD 600 by the Britons on a fort held by the Angles at Catraeth, today Catterick in Yorkshire. The poet himself participated in the battle and was one of a handful of survivors.

The actual age of the stories in these medieval Welsh manuscripts and their relationship to Geoffrey's *Historia Regum Britanniae* are puzzles that may never be solved. Short of the discovery of a manuscript with references to the invasion story that predates Geoffrey and his Latin sources, the theory that the legend of Caesar's invasion was orally preserved by Cymric bards may never be proven. Until such a discovery, we are without a version of Caesar's British campaigns produced by the defenders themselves.

Although some expressed doubts from the beginning, the English of Geoffrey's time, and for several centuries afterward, were more than willing to believe his tales of giants and dragons and the founding of Britain by Brutus and the Trojans. His story was all the more convincing because he named each king, and the dates of his reign, from Brutus in the mists of prehistory to Cadwallader, the traditional last King of the Britons, who fled to Aremorica in Gaul at the end of the seventh century.

Not one to leave anything unexplained, Geoffrey is the first writer to reveal the story of the building of Stonehenge. In the latter part of the fifth century AD, according to him, the Britons were planning a monument to commemorate the deaths of so many of their countrymen at the hands of the Saxons. They consulted the prophet Merlin, who was reputed to have great skill in "mechanical contrivances." Merlin told them about a monument that had been erected in Ireland from stones brought from Africa by giants, and suggested that they bring it to Britain. Fifteen thousand Britons, under the command of Uther Pendragon, then journeyed to Ireland, where they defeated the Irish in battle and, with the help of Merlin's magic, transported the huge stones to the plain of Salisbury. There Merlin "put the stones up in a circle around the sepulchre, in exactly the same way as they had been arranged on Mount Killaraus in Ireland, thus proving that his artistry was worth more than any brute strength."[12]

This tale has received more than passing attention from modern scholars because it reflects what has been shown by twentieth-century science—that the famous Bluestones at Stonehenge could only have come from the Prescelly Mountains in Wales, more than two hundred miles away. Stuart Piggott has pointed out an affinity between Geoffrey's account and the story of Branwen, daughter of Llyr, one of the tales in *The Mabinogion*. In this story Bran the Blessed, Branwen's brother, is killed in a battle in Ireland, and his head is brought to Britain by way of Wales over the course of nine decades to London, where it is buried with the face toward France in order to ward off foreign invasion. Other scholars have shown that echoes of certain trading patterns and religious practices from as far back as the Early Bronze Age have been preserved in *The Mabinogion* and in the religious conventions of the Britons during the Roman occupation. In either case, there is the possibility that Geoffrey based his information on a manuscript or, more likely, an oral tradition about the origin of Stonehenge that had been preserved by the inhabitants of Britain for as long as three thousand years.[13]

By the time of the Renaissance a new spirit of rigorous scholarship led some historians to dismiss the story of Trojans in Britain and even to cast doubt on some of Geoffrey's Arthurian tales. These opinions were strongly condemned by the majority of scholars, clerics and others familiar with the *Historia*. However, in 1485 there was a surge of patriotic enthusiasm for the book when Henry Tudor—of the Tudors of Anglesey—fought his way to the throne, becoming the first King of England of Welsh ancestry in eight hundred years. For the next century, the Tudor monarchs embraced and promoted Geoffrey's version of British history and proudly identified themselves as descendants of the illustrious Arthur.

Besides the controversy over the "Brut," the availability of a variety of classical texts spurred a new interest in history, particularly English history. Caesar's *Commentaries* were printed in Venice in 1511, and editions of Tacitus and Pliny soon followed. During the 1500s, the first English translations of many classical writers became available to the ordinary reader. These new sources of knowledge fueled the interest of the English in their past and in the ancient inhabitants of their island. The presence of countless barrows and ditches, monumental stones and ruins of all kinds in every part of the country stimulated them to discover what these were and who put them there. And they found that they had a great deal to learn.

One of the defenders of Geoffrey of Monmouth, and a supporter of the legend of the "Brut," was John Leland, a young scholar who obtained a commission from Henry VIII in 1533 to search the country for lost or forgotten manuscripts. As he traveled from place to place he made notes on everything he saw—every notable structure, every aspect of topography and every unusual or historical sight he came across. On his journey through Kent, he stopped at the seacoast town of Deal, near Sandwich, and inspected the terrain:

> Deale, half a myle fro the shore of the se, a fisscher village iii. myles or more above Sandwice, is apon a flat shore and very open to the se, wher is a fosse or a great bank artificial betwixt the towne and se, and beginneth about Deale, and rennith a great way up toward S. Margaret's Clyfe, yn so much that sum suppose that this is the place where Caesar landed *in aperto litore* [on an open beach]. Surely the fosse was made to kepe owte ennemyes there, or to defend the rage of the se; or I think rather the castinge up beche or pible.[14]

The most authoritative English antiquary of this period was William Camden, a teacher at the Westminster School in London, who published his *Britannia* in 1586. A serious researcher, Camden taught himself Old English and Welsh and roamed all over England examining ruins and searching libraries for manuscripts. His book was a summary of all that was known about the origin of the English people and the surviving evidence of their history. He described the invasions of Britain from the Romans to the Normans, and the societies of each period, and included a detailed account of the antiquities in each shire. *Britannia* was immensely popular. It was reprinted six times during Camden's lifetime, and by 1610 had become a copiously illustrated folio of 860 pages.

Although Camden depended on correspondents throughout England and abroad for some of his material, he went himself to the same beach in Kent where Leland thought Caesar might have landed:

> At Deal (which Nennius, and I believe rightly, calls Dole, a name still given by our Britans to an open plain on a river or the sea) tradition affirms Caesar landed, with which agrees Nennius, who, in his barbarous style writes, "Caesar batteled at Dole." A table also hanging in Dover castle proves the same, and Caesar himself gives it weight when he says he landed on an open plain shore and was warmly received by the Britans. . . .

After that general (to digress a little from the subject) had made himself master of all parts of the world by sea and land . . . he turned his views towards the Ocean, and as if the Roman world were not sufficient he entertained thoughts of another. In the year before Christ 54, and the following, with a fleet of 2000 sail . . . [he] invaded Britain either to be revenged on its inhabitants who had assisted the Gauls, as Strabo relates, or to get some of the British pearls, as Suetonius says, or, as others, fired with the love of glory. He had before informed himself of the harbours and passage. . . . For a considerable length under this shore are a number of heaps like banks, which some suppose to have been blown up by the wind; but I rather take them for the fortifications or defences for ships, which Caesar was ten days and nights throwing up to draw his shattered ships into, and secure them from storms and the Britans who attacked them in vain.

I understand that the inhabitants call these banks Romesworke, q.d. the work of the Romans. And I rather think Caesar landed here, because he says seven miles from hence . . . the sea is so confined by narrow mountains that a spear may be thrown from the high grounds upon the coast. Certain it is, that soon after you leave Deal, a ridge of cliffs (those *moles magnificae*, as Cicero calls them) covered with Crythmus, or samphire, runs on for about seven miles to Dover, where it divides and opens a passage, and the place exactly answers Caesar's description of it as admitting and confining the sea between two hills . . .[15]

Not every Elizabethan antiquary was as confident as William Camden about evidence of Julius Caesar, nor as interested. In *A Perambulation of Kent*, published in 1570, William Lambarde noted that he had been told there were vessels of old wine and salt in Dover Castle that were supposed to be part of Caesar's stores, and that the castle itself had been built by Caesar, but that he believed neither story. And Clement Edmonds, in his translation of *The Gallic War* in 1604, wrote that Caesar's expedition ". . . afoordeth little matter of discourse, being indeed but a scambling warre." [16]

Besides Leland and Camden, many fifteenth- and sixteenth-century English writers, as well as several in France, included an account of Caesar's invasions in their works. These were based mainly on Geoffrey's history, and each added an embellishment of his own. Edmund Spenser in *The Faerie Queene* and Raphael Holinshed in his *Chronicles* both mention Caesar. And in both *Richard II* and *Richard III* Shakespeare alludes to the mistaken tradition that Caesar built the Tower of London.[17] But Leland and Camden made the first serious attempts to locate Caesar in the British past, and the first attempts at historical accuracy, based not only on what had already been written, but also on what they saw.

The English now seized on these revelations about their past with astonishment and pride, and book after book appeared on the subject of ancient Britain. Caesar's on-the-scene account of his British invasion in *The Gallic War* was the first record of an event in English history. Speculations about what he did and where he did it began to appear in the standard histories of England, and of Kent and Surrey.

Interest in the origins of Britain was also stimulated by another development at this time: the European penetration of the New World and the discovery of the less-advanced societies of the Western Hemisphere. As early as 1502, the explorer Sebastian Cabot had brought three Eskimos clad in skin garments to show to Henry VII, and hundreds of captured Native Americans were exhibited in Europe during the following decades. William Camden made the first connection between the body decorations of American Indians and those recorded of the Celts, and near the end of the sixteenth century the first illustrations of "Ancient Britons" were published. They were based largely on drawings of Indians by John White, who accompanied Walter Raleigh on his expedition to Virginia in 1585.

Increasingly, during the next century the parallels between the American natives and the ancient inhabitants of Britain were too convincing to resist. In 1621, in *The Anatomy of Melancholy,* Robert Burton wrote: "See but what Caesar reports of us, and Tacitus of those Germans, they were once as uncivil as they in Virginia."[18] In 1659, John Aubrey, in an essay on prehistoric Wiltshire, wrote:

Let us imagine then what kind of countrie this was in the time
of the ancient Britons . . . a shady dismal wood: and the inhabitants almost as savage as the Beasts whose skins were their only
rayment. The language British, which for the honour of it was
in those days spoken from the Orcades to Italie and Spain. . . .
Their priests were Druids . . . their waie of fighting is lively
sett down by Caesar. . . . They knew the use of iron. . . . They
were two or three degrees, I suppose, less savage than the
Americans.[19]

Easier access to classical writers had one other result: the rediscov-
ery of the Druids. Caesar, Tacitus and Pliny had all described in detail
this mysterious class of priests and seers who administered the Celtic
religion. As early as the reign of Augustus, the Romans considered the
Druids a threat to their government, and in Gaul, at least, they executed as many as they could find and prohibited the practice of their
religion. Centuries later, Christianity absorbed elements of Druidism
and drove the rest of its priests to isolated pockets and fringes of
Europe. In search of an explanation for what they saw in front of
them, the antiquarians inevitably, and erroneously, concluded that
Stonehenge was constructed for the practice of Druid rites. It was not
until the twentieth century that archaeologists determined that
Stonehenge was built long before the time of the Druids, although
they may have used it for their ceremonies.

Early in the nineteenth century, Edward Williams, a Welsh scholar
and patriot, and two other Welshmen published *The Myvyrian
Archaiology of Wales*, the first appearance in print of any of the manuscripts of the "British Histories," some of which, unfortunately, were
Mr. Williams' own compositions. In the following decades the search
for Caesar's Britain began in earnest, and antiquarianism gradually
became archaeology. Claims and counterclaims about Caesar's landing-
places and battle-sites, and particularly about the spot where he crossed
the Thames, appeared in magazines such as *The Athenaeum* and
Gentlemen's Magazine. Full-length books began to appear in the 1850s.

Then, in 1865, there appeared in Paris the first volume of one of
the most remarkable works of history of the nineteenth century: the

Histoire de Jules César, by Louis-Napoleon III, nephew of Napoleon Bonaparte, and reigning Emperor of the French. (The title Napoleon II was reserved for the ill-fated son of Bonaparte; the so-called "King of Rome" died in 1832 at the age of twenty-one.) While in exile in Germany and Switzerland after Waterloo, Louis-Napoleon was a prolific writer on political and military subjects, and saw himself as a latter-day Caesar who would, as he thought Caesar had, create order and stability out of the confusion of popular rule in France. In 1840 he made an abortive attempt to seize the Bourbon throne by landing with a few dozen men near Boulogne. He was arrested, tried and sentenced to life imprisonment in the nearby fortress of Ham. Six years later, he escaped to England. Returning to France after the establishment of the Second Republic in 1848, he was elected to a seat in the Constituent Assembly. At the end of the same year, evoking the glories of the Napoleonic legend to gain broad popular support, Louis-Napoleon was overwhelmingly elected President of the Republic. Four years later, he proclaimed himself Emperor of the French and remained in power for nearly two decades.

Fascinated with Caesar's personality and career, and seeing in them numerous affinities with his own, Napoleon III undertook a full-scale investigation of Caesar's campaigns in ancient France and Britain. Using the enormous resources he had at his disposal as Emperor, he established an archaeological corps to conduct research and fieldwork, such as mapping Caesar's marching routes and searching for his camps and battle-sites. He had models made of Roman catapults that can be seen today in the National Museum of Antiquities, which he founded in 1862 to display the fruits of his interest in ancient France.

One of his most ambitious efforts was to order the design and construction of a full-size replica of one of Caesar's war galleys. A 130-foot trireme with a single mast and sail was built in a Paris shipyard, and in March 1861, the Emperor and Empress went on board for a short voyage between two bridges on the Seine. The ship carried a crew of twenty and used sixty-five oarsmen on each side, arranged at three levels. Some time later, it was towed down the Seine and along the coast as far as Cherbourg, but it apparently was never actually seaworthy.[20]

The Emperor then set about writing Caesar's biography. He sought the help of scholars, military experts and writers, such as Prosper Mérimée, but apparently wrote most of the book himself. By the time the second and final volume appeared in 1866, however, the work was considered by most to be an uneven work of history flawed by political propaganda. Nevertheless, by locating and excavating many of Caesar's battlefields and camps, Napoleon III and his assistants made important contributions to the study of Caesar's campaigns.

In 1907, Thomas Rice Holmes, an Irish schoolmaster, published his monumental *Ancient Britain and the Invasions of Julius Caesar,* the most comprehensive study of the subject that has yet appeared, and an inspiration to historians and archaeologists ever since. Holmes devoted his spare time for nearly thirty years to his book, and although superseded in some details by archaeological discoveries since his day, it remains the standard work on Caesar's invasions.

The most recent treatment of the subject is by C.F.C. Hawkes, one of the outstanding British archaeologists of this century. His *Britain and Julius Caesar* was first delivered as the Mortimer Wheeler Archaeological Lecture before the British Academy in 1975, and incorporated the latest research in archaeology, anthropology and Roman political history. He analyzes in detail Caesar's channel crossings, and examines the prevalent theories about his port in Gaul and his landing-places. His is the most thorough discussion of Caesar's motives for invading Britain, of his plan of conquest and of his exploitation of the antagonisms among the British Celts.

Hawkes' great contribution is his analysis of Caesar's motives, as distinguished from what was set down in *The Gallic War.* Although many writers have commented on the propagandist element in Caesar's work, Hawkes presents a convincing explanation of his intentions, as well as his reasons for including and excluding what he did from his book.

Each of the three aforementioned works of history brings a particular strength to the study of Caesar's invasions. Of all the investigators into the subject, Napoleon III was the most successful in locating and preserving Caesar's traces. Holmes digested and codified the mass of information accumulated by scholars and antiquarians in the centuries before him. Hawkes' book is the most comprehensive modern account of Caesar's expeditions to Britain, and he uses the results of the most recent research to set out not only what happened, but why.

Despite the intensive investigations and formidable scholarship brought to bear on the subject, it is clear that the English search for Caesar presents more mysteries than solutions. Many medieval Welsh manuscripts remain to be translated and interpreted, and sites in Kent, Surrey and Hertfordshire await archaeological excavation. Only when this is done will the whole story be told.

CITATIONS

Prologue

1. Korfmann, "The Sling as a Weapon," (1973).

Chapter I: Caesar in Rome

1. Origin and nature of Roman Republic: Bloch, *The Origins of Rome* (1960), p. 100; Crawford, *The Roman Republic*, 2nd ed. (1993), Appendix 1.
2. Roman population: Yavetz, "The Living Conditions of the Urban Plebs in Republican Rome" (1958).

   Roman diet: Lacey, *Cicero and the End of the Roman Republic* (1978), p. 184; Shelton, *As the Romans Did* (1988), p. 82.

   Slaves: Cunliffe, *Greeks, Romans and Barbarians* (1988), p. 77.
3. Salway, *Roman Britain* (1993), p. 21.
4. Suetonius, *Julius Caesar*, 49.
5. Keveaney and Madden, "Phthiriasis and Its Victims" (1982), pp. 87–99.
6. Suetonius, op. cit., 4.
7. Suetonius, op. cit., 45.
8. Suetonius, op. cit., 50.
9. Gelzer, *Caesar: Politician and Statesman* (1968), p. 30.
10. Hallett, *Fathers and Daughters in Roman Society* (1984), p. 6.
11. Cicero, *De Officiis,* I, 25.
12. Suetonius, op. cit., 59. Trans. J.C. Rolfe (1960).
13. Details of Catilinian conspiracy: Kaplan, *Catiline: The Man and His Role in the Roman Revolution* (1968); Hutchinson, *The Conspiracy of Catiline* (1966).
14. Suetonius, op. cit., 7; Cassius Dio, *Roman History*, 37, 52, 2; Plutarch, *Caesar,* 11.
15. Deutsch, "The Apparatus of Caesar's Triumph" (1924), pp. 257–66.
16. Cassius Dio, *Roman History,* 38, 2, 1–3.
17. Cicero, *Letters to Atticus,* II, 19. Quoted in Sabben-Clare, *Caesar and Roman*

Politics 60–50 B.C. (1971), p. 21.

18. Cicero, *Pro Flacco,* 26, 63.

Chapter II: The Celts in Europe

1. Livy, *History of Rome,* Book V, 48, pp. 8–9.

2. Renfrew, "The Origins of Indo-European Languages" (1989); Gamkrelidze and Ivanov, "The Early History of Indo-European Languages" (1990).

3. Herodotus: *The Persian Wars,* II, 33.
　　Hecataeus: Jacoby, *Fragmente der Griechischen Historiker* (1957), Vol. IA, p. 17.
　　Aristotle: *Nicomachean Ethics,* iii, 7, 7.

4. Wells, *Farms, Villages, and Cities* (1984), pp. 144–45.

5. Pliny, *Natural History,* 12, 5.

6. Polybius, *The Rise of the Roman Empire,* Book II, 29.

7. Braudel, *The Identity of France* (1988), Vol. I, p. 70.

8. Diodorus Siculus, *Historical Library,* V, 28. Trans. in Tierney, "The Celtic Ethnography of Posidonius" (1960), p. 249.

9. Athenaeus, *The Deipnosophists,* IV, 36, pp. 151E–152D; trans. in Tierney, op. cit., p. 247.

10. Diodorus Siculus, op. cit., V, 26; Tierney, op. cit., p. 249.

11. Ibid., V, 32; Tierney, op. cit., p. 252.

12. Ibid., V, 31; Tierney, op. cit., p. 251.

13. D.A. Binchy, quoted in Dillon, "Celtic Religion and Celtic Society" (1964).

14. Strabo, *Geography,* IV, IV, 2.
　　Xenophon, *Hellenica,* VII, i, 20 and 31.

15. Diodorus Siculus, op. cit., V, 29; trans. in Tierney, op. cit. p. 250.

16. Piggott, *The Druids* (1975), p. 100.

17. Diodorus Siculus, op. cit., V, 31; trans. in Tierney, op. cit., p. 251.

18. Piggott, op. cit., p. 110.

19. Caesar, *The Gallic War,* Book VI, 16. Trans. in Tierney, op. cit., p. 272.

20. Pliny, *Natural History,* XXX, 13; Diodorus Siculus, op. cit., V, 32; Pausanias, *Description of Greece,* X, xxii, 2; Solinus, *Collectanea Rerum Memorabilium* (Collection of Memorable Things), 23.

21. Cunliffe, *The Celtic World* (1979), p. 110.

22. Hubert, *The Rise of the Celts* (1934), p. 14.

23. Powell, *Prehistoric Art* (1966), p. 185.

24. Jacobsthal, *Early Celtic Art* (1944), p. 105.

25. Ibid., p. 103.

Chapter III: Caesar in Gaul

1. Rivet, *Gallia Narbonensis* (1988), p. 15.
2. Bonnet, "The Celtic Port of Geneva" (1991), pp. 522 and 697.
3. Suetonius, *Julius Caesar*, 57.
4. Legionary clothing: Webster, *The Roman Imperial Army in the 1st and 2nd Centuries AD* (1985), p. 121.

Legionary armor: Bishop and Coulston, *Roman Military Equipment* (1993), p. 17; Grant, *The Army of the Caesars* (1974), pp. xvii–xxi; Connolly, *Greece and Rome at War* (1981), pp. 130–33.
5. Delbrück, *Warfare in Antiquity* (1975), pp. 53–54; Judson, *Caesar's Army* (1888), p. 106.
6. Keegan and Holmes, *Soldiers* (1985), p. 24.
7. Delbrück, op. cit., p. 416.
8. Rice Holmes, *Caesar's Conquest of Gaul* (1971), pp. 617–20.
9. Funck-Brentano, *The Earliest Times* (1927), p. 88.
10. Connolly, op. cit., p. 241; Judson, op. cit., p. 63.
11. The best discussion of the possible site is in Delbrück, op. cit., pp. 483–87.
12. Beeson, "Text History of the Corpus Caesarianum" (1940), p. 113.
13. Hadas, *A History of Latin Literature* (1952), p. 91.
14. Cicero, *Brutus,* 262.
15. Grant, *The Ancient Historians* (1970), p. 190.
16. Delbrück, op. cit., pp. 461–63.
17. Montaigne, *Essays,* Vol. II, Chap. X, p. 77.
18. Hadas, op. cit., p. 91; Cunliffe and Wiseman, Introduction to *The Battle for Gaul* (1980), p. 9; Hastrup, "On the Date of Caesar's Commentaries on the Gallic War" (1957), p. 74; Adcock, *Caesar as a Man of Letters* (1956), pp. 77–89.

Chapter IV: The Rhine and the Channel

1. Wheeler and Richardson, *Hill-Forts of Northern France* (1957), pp. 12 and 129.
2. de Laet, *The Low Countries* (1958), p. 169.
3. Catullus, *Poems,* 57.
4. Plutarch, *Pompey,* 52.
5. Cicero, *Letters to Atticus,* IV, 5, in Sabben-Clare, *Caesar and Roman Politics 60–50 B.C.* (1971), p. 88.
6. Hawkes, *Britain and Julius Caesar* (1978), p. 145.
7. Lazenby, "The Conference of Luca and the Gallic War" (1959), p. 67; Stevens, "55 BC & 54 BC" (1947), passim.
8. Markale, *Celtic Civilization* (1976), p. 85.

9. Ibid., p. 88.
10. Plutarch, *Pompey*, 52; *Cato the Younger*, 43, 1–7; *Crassus*, 15, 3.
11. Rambaud (ed.), *Bellum Gallicum Liber Quartus* (1967), pp. 88–91.
12. Hawkes, op. cit., p. 151.
13. Ibid., pp. 153–54.

Chapter V: Expedition to Britain

1. Colvin, "On Dover Castle" (1959), pp. 125–27.
2. Halley, "Of the Time and Place of Caesar's Descent upon Britain" (1691), passim.
3. Catapults: Marsden, *Greek and Roman Artillery* (1969), pp. 86, 93, 169; Laffont (ed.), *The Ancient Art of Warfare* (1966), pp. 121 and 129.
4. Roman camp: Polybius, *The Rise of the Roman Empire*, Book VI, 27–38; Connolly, *Greece and Rome at War* (1981), Chap. 2.
5. Napoléon Bonaparte, *Correspondance* (1858–70), Vol. XXXI, p. 551.
6. Napoléon III, *The History of Julius Caesar* (1865–66), p. 187.
7. Suetonius, *Julius Caesar*, 47.
8. Mitchell, "Cornish Tin, Iulius Caesar, and the Invasion of Britain" (1983), p. 98.
9. Cunliffe, *Greeks, Romans and Barbarians* (1988), p. 77.
10. Rankin, *Celts and the Classical World* (1987), p. 216.
11. British chariots: Furger–Gunti, "The Celtic War Chariot" (1991), pp. 356–59; Lynch, *Prehistoric Anglesey* (1970), pp. 258–59; Fox, *A Find of the Early Iron Age from Llyn Cerrig Bach, Anglesey, Interim Report* (1945), pp. 12–13, 44.
12. Rivet, "A Note on Scythed Chariots" (1979), pp. 130–32.
13. Napoléon Bonaparte, *Précis des Guerres de César* (1984), p. 71.

Chapter VI: Invasion

1. Rivet and Smith, *The Place-Names of Roman Britain* (1979), p. 39.
2. Rice Holmes, *Ancient Britain and the Invasions of Caesar* (1936), pp. 459–61.
3. Catullus, 11, Trans. Gilbert Highet, *Poets in a Landscape* (1957), p. 24.
4. Suetonius, *Julius Caesar*, 56; Rice Holmes, *The Roman Republic and the Founder of the Empire* (1923), Vol. II, p. 310.
5. Gelzer, op. cit., p. 139.
6. P.T. Wiseman, *Roman Studies* (1987), p. 39.
7. Hawkes, *Britain and Julius Caesar* (1978), p. 152.
8. Ibid., p. 160, Note 2.
9. Hawkes, op. cit., pp. 157ff.
10. Holmes, *Ancient Britain and the Invasions of Caesar* (1936), p. 685.

11. Thompson, "Excavations at Bigberry, near Canterbury, 1978–80" (1983), pp. 237–78.

12. Hawkes, op. cit., p. 162.

13. Polybius, *The Rise of the Roman Empire,* Book VI, 34–38.

14. Suetonius, op. cit., 65–67.

15. Hawkes, op. cit., p. 162.

16. Polybius, op. cit., Book VI, 40; Josephus, *The Jewish War,* III, 89–92; Connolly, *Greece and Rome at War* (1981), pp. 238–39; Hyland, *Equus: The Horse in the Roman World* (1990), p. 88; Dodge, *Caesar* (1892), p. 357.

17. Davies, "The Roman Military Diet" (1971), passim.

18. Oldbury Hill: Perkins, "Excavations on the Iron Age Hillfort of Oldbury, near Ightham, Kent" (1944), p. 127.

Anstiebury, etc.: Thompson, "Three Surrey Hillforts: Excavations at Anstiebury, Holmbury and Hascombe, 1972–77" (1979), passim.

19. Coin hoards: Rodwell, "Coinage, Oppida and the rise of Belgic Power in South-Eastern Britain" (1976), p. 181.

Payments to Britons: Kent, "The Origins of Coinage in Britain" (1981), pp. 41–43.

Minting of gold coins: Haselgrove, "Warfare and Its Aftermath as Reflected in the Precious Metal Coinage of Belgic Gaul" (1984), passim.

Chapter VII: The Celts in Britain

1. Greene, "The Coming of the Celts: The Linguistic Viewpoint" (1983), pp. 131–33; Price, *Ireland and the Celtic Connection* (1987), pp. 6–7.

2. Hutton, *The Pagan Religions of the Ancient British Isles* (1991), pp. 18–19.

3. Fowler, *The Farming of Prehistoric Britain* (1983), pp. 4–5.

4. Sherratt: "The Emergence of Élites: Earlier Bronze Age Europe, 2500–1300 BC" (1994), p. 251.

5. Darvill, *Prehistoric Britain* (1987), p. 160.

6. Ibid.

7. Powell, *The Celts* (1980), p. 15.

8. Hanna, *Celtic Migrations* (1985), p. 17; Jackson, "Two Early Scottish Names" (1954), pp. 16–17.

9. Reynolds, *Farming in the Iron Age* (1976), pp. 6–11.

10. Ibid., pp. 37–43.

11. Darville, op. cit., p. 160.

12. Reynolds, *Iron Age Farm* (1979), p. 68.

13. Jones, *England Before Domesday* (1986), p. 59.

14. Tylecote, *Metallurgy in Archaeology: A Pre-History of Metallurgy in the British Isles* (1962), pp. 141 and 203.

15. Reynolds, op. cit.

16. Tylecote, op. cit., p. 202.

17. Wainwright, *Gussage All Saints* (1979), pp. 133–90.

18. Birchall, "The Aylesford-Swarling Culture: the Problem of the Belgae Reconsidered" (1965), p. 241.

19. Cunliffe, *Iron Age Communities in Britain* (3rd ed, 1991), pp. 108–10.

20. Kent, "The Origins of Coinage in Britain" (1981), p. 43.

21. Schmidt, "Insular Celtic: P and Q Celtic" (1993), p. 75.

22. Ibid., pp. 67 and 78.

23. Hanna, op. cit., pp. 26–27.

24. Rivet and Smith, *The Place-Names of Roman Britain* (1979), pp. 298–99.

25. Ross and Robins, *The Life and Death of a Druid Prince* (1989), Chaps. I–III; Stead, Bourke and Brothwell, *Lindow Man* (1986), pp. 177–80; Brothwell, *The Bog Man and the Archaeology of People* (1986), pp. 95–97.

26. Pyatt, et al.: "*Non Isatis sed Vitrum* or, the Colour of Lindow Man" (1991), pp. 61–73.

27. Wild, "Papyrus in Pre-Roman Britain?" (1966), pp. 139–41.

Chapter VIII: To the Thames

1. Stow, *Survey of London* (1956 ed.), p. 22.

2. Bede, *A History of the English Church and People* (1955 ed.), Book I, Chap. 2.

3. Camden, *Camden's Britannia: Surrey and Sussex* (1977 ed.), pp. 7 and 10.

4. Manning, *The History and Antiquities of the County of Surrey* (1804–14), Vol. II, p. 759.

5. Wheeler, "Old England,' Brentford" (1929), p. 20.

6. Stonebanks, *Coway Stakes at Walton-on-Thames* (1972), p. 9.

7. Milne, *The Port of Roman London* (1985), pp. 44–49.

8. Napoléon III, *The History of Julius Caesar* (1865–66), Vol. II, p. 201.

9. Hawkes, *Britain and Julius Caesar* (1978), p. 168, Note 1.

10. Thornhill, "A Lower Thames Ford and the Campaigns of 54 BC and AD 43" (1976), pp. 119–28.

11. Polyaenus, *Stratagems,* Book VIII, xiii, 5. Quoted in Stevens, "Julius Caesar's Elephant" (1959), p. 626.

12. Stevens, ibid.

13. Stead and Rigby, *Baldock* (1986), p. 51; Stead, "A La Tène III: Burial at the Tene, Baldock, Herts." (1968), p. 306.

14. Wheeler, "Britain Before the Romans: The Lost Cities of Herts" (1933), pp. 15–16.

15. Dyer, "Ravensburgh Castle, Hertfordshire" (1976), p. 153.

16. Burne, *The Art of War on Land* (1947), pp. 73–77.

17. Holmes, *Ancient Britain and the Invasions of Caesar* (1936), pp. 347–49 and 731–35.
18. Allen, "The British Epics of Quintus and Marcus Cicero" (1955), pp. 143–60.
19. Quoted by Cicero in *Letters to Atticus*, IV, 18, 5.
20. Home, *Roman London* (1948), p. 42.

Chapter IX: Turmoil in Rome

1. Julia's funeral: Gelzer, op. cit., pp. 147–48; Grant, *Julius Caesar* (1969), p. 124.
2. Cicero, *Pro C. Rabirio Postumo*, 42.
3. Lucan, *Pharsalia*, I, 120.
4. The best discussion of the subject is in G. Elton, "The Terminal Date of Caesar's Gallic Proconsulate" (1946).

Chapter X: Revolt in Gaul

1. Evans, *Gaulish Personal Names* (1967), p. 122.
2. Strabo, *Geography*, Book IV, II, 3.
3. Delbrück, *Warfare in Antiquity* (1975), pp. 499–501.
4. Plutarch, *Caesar*, 27.
5. Fuller, *Julius Caesar* (1965), p. 157.
6. Bénard, "César devant Alésia: les Témoins Sont dans le Sol" (1987), pp. 29–41.
7. Inscription quoted in Le Gall, *Alésia: Le Siège de la Forteresse* (1985), p. 22.
8. Harmand, "Une Question Césarienne Non Résolue: la Campagne de 51 contre les Bellovaques et Sa Localisation" (1959), pp. 271–72; Hatt, *Celts and Gallo-Romans* (1970), p. 138.
9. See Chap. III, Note 18.
10. Sutherland, *Roman Coins* (1974), pp. 74–77 and 88; Sydenham, *The Coinage of the Roman Republic* (1952), pp. xxxvi and 167–68.
11. Seager, *Pompey* (1979), pp. 3–5.
12. Gelzer, *Caesar: Politician and Statesman* (1968), p. 192; Caesar, *The Civil War*, 1, 5.
13. Caesar, *The Civil War*, 1, 7.

Chapter XI: Divus Julius

1. Gelzer, *Caesar: Politician and Statesman* (1968), p. 200.
2. Cicero, *Letters to Atticus*, IX, 16, quoted in *Letters of Cicero*, Trans. L.P.

Wilkinson (1968), p. 119.

3. Cicero, op. cit., IX, 18, in Wilkinson, ibid.

4. Plutarch, *Caesar,* 39.

5. Delbrück, *Warfare in Antiquity* (1975), pp. 542ff.

6. Plutarch, *Antony,* 27.

7. For arguments on both sides of the question, see Volkmann, *Cleopatra* (1953), pp. 73–80; Pomeroy, *Women in Hellenistic Egypt* (1984), pp. 25–26; Balsdon, "The Ides of March" (1953), pp. 86–87.

8. Suetonius, *Divus Julius,* 52.

9. Plutarch, *Brutus,* 20.

10. Plutarch, *Caesar,* 69.

11. Virgil, *Georgics,* I, 464–65.

12. Cicero, *De Officiis,* II, 84.

13. See especially Rambaud, *L'Art de la Déformation Historique dans les Commentaires de César* (1966).

14. Gelzer, op. cit., pp. 329–33.

Chapter XII: Aftermath

1. A.H.M. Jones, *Augustus* (1970), p. 42.

2. Wells, *Farms, Villages and Cities* (1984), p. 145.

3. Cunliffe, *Iron Age Communities in Britain* (3rd ed., 1991), p. 140.

4. Merrifield, *The Archaeology of London* (1974), pp. 43–44.

5. Suetonius, *Gaius (Caligula),* 46.

Postscript: The English Search for Caesar

1. Tacitus, *Dialogue on Oratory,* 17.

2. Nennius, *Historia Brittonum,* 19.

3. Leckie Jr., *The Passage of Dominion* (1981), p. 3.

4. Geoffrey of Monmouth, *The History of the Kings of Britain,* IV, 1.

5. Ibid., IV, 2.

6. Ibid., IV, 7.

7. Ibid., IV, 9.

8. Southern, "Aspects of the European Tradition of Historical Writing, etc." (1970), p. 194.

9. Griscom (ed.), *The Historia Regum Britanniae of Geoffrey of Monmouth* (1929).

10. Bromwich (ed.), *The Triads of the Island of Britain* (1978), p. 301.

11. Koch, "A Welsh Window on the Iron Age: Manawydan, Mandubracios" (1987), p. 17.

12. Geoffrey of Monmouth, op. cit., VIII, 12.

13. Piggott, "The Sources of Geoffrey of Monmouth, II: The Stonehenge Story" (1941), passim.

14. Leland, *Leland's Itinerary in England and Wales* (1964), Vol. IV, p. 48.

15. Camden, *Camden's Britannia: Kent* (1977), p. 62.

16. Edmonds, *The Commentaries of C. Julius Caesar* (1677 ed.), p. 100.

17. Spenser, *The Faerie Queene,* Book II, X, 49.

    Holinshed, *Chronicles: England, Scotland and Ireland* (1587), Vol. I, Book 3, pp. 464–477.

    Shakespeare, *Richard II,* V, i, 2; *Richard III,* III, i, 68–74.

18. Burton, *The Anatomy of Melancholy,* 2:2:4 "To the Reader."

19. Aubrey, *Hypomnemata Antiquaria A,* quoted in A. Powell (ed.), *Brief Lives* (1949), p. 1.

20. Lehmann, "A Trireme's Tragedy" (1982), pp. 145–51.

BIBLIOGRAPHY

ANCIENT SOURCES

Aristotle. *Nicomachean Ethics*. Trans. H. Rackham. London: W. Heinemann, 1926.

Athenaeus. *The Deipnosophists*. Trans. Charles B. Gulick. London: W. Heinemann, 1927–57.

Bede. *A History of the English Church and People*. Trans. Leo Sherley-Price. Harmondsworth, UK: Penguin Books, 1955.

Caesar. *The Battle for Gaul*. Trans. Anne and Peter Wiseman. Intro. Barry Cunliffe and Peter Wiseman. Boston: David R. Godine, 1980.

———. *The Civil War*. Trans. Jane F. Gardner. Harmondsworth, UK: Penguin Books, 1967.

Cassius Dio. *Dio's Roman History*. Trans. Earnest Cary. Cambridge: Harvard University Press, 1954.

Catullus. *Poems*. Trans. Charles Martin. Omaha: University of Nebraska Press, 1979.

Cicero. *Brutus*. Trans. G.L. Hendrickson. London: W. Heinemann, 1939.

———. *De Officiis*. Trans. Walter Miller. Cambridge: Harvard University Press. 1961.

———. *Pro C. Rabirio Postumo*. Trans. N.H. Watts. Cambridge: Harvard University Press, 1964.

———. *Letters of Cicero, A Selection in Translation*. Trans. L.P. Wilkinson. New York: W. W. Norton & Co., 1968.

———. *Letters to Atticus*. Trans. D.R. Shackleton-Bailey. Harmondsworth, UK: Penguin Books, 1978.

———. *Pro Flacco*. Trans. C. Macdonald. Cambridge: Harvard University Press, 1989.

———. *Selected Political Speeches*. Trans. and ed. Michael Grant. London: Penguin Books, 1989.

Diodorus Siculus. *Historical Library* (*Diodorus of Sicily*). Trans. C.H. Oldfather.

London: W. Heinemann, 1933–67.

Herodotus. *The Persian Wars.* Trans. George Rawlinson. New York: The Modern Library, 1942.

Josephus. *The Jewish War.* Trans. G.A. Williamson; rev. E. Mary Smallwood. Harmondsworth, UK: Penguin Books, 1981.

Livy. *The Early History of Rome.* Trans. A. de Sélincourt. Baltimore: Penguin Books, 1965.

Lucan. *Pharsalia.* Trans. Robert Graves. Harmondsworth, UK: Penguin Books, 1956.

Nennius. *British History and The Welsh Annals.* Trans. and ed. John Morris. London: Phillimore, 1980.

Pliny. *Natural History.* Trans. H. Rackham. Cambridge: Harvard University Press, 1938–63.

Plutarch. *Selected Lives and Essays.* Trans. L.R. Loomis. New York: Walter J. Black, 1951. Contains *Cato the Younger.*

———. *Fall of the Roman Republic.* Trans. Rex Warner. Harmondsworth, UK: Penguin Books, 1958. Contains *Caesar, Pompey, Crassus.*

———. *Makers of Rome.* Trans. Ian Scott-Kilvert. Harmondsworth, UK: Penguin Books, 1965. Contains *Brutus, Antony.*

Polyaenus. *Stratagems.* Trans. R. Shepherd. Chicago: Ares Publishers, 1974.

Polybius. *The Rise of the Roman Empire.* Trans. I. Scott-Kilvert. Harmondsworth, UK: Penguin Books, 1979.

Strabo. *Geography.* Trans. H.L. Jones. London: W. Heinemann, 1917–32.

Suetonius. *Lives of Eminent Grammarians.* Trans. Alexander Thomson; rev. T. Forester. London: G. Bell, 1906.

———. *The Twelve Caesars.* Trans. Robert Graves; rev. Michael Grant. Harmondsworth, UK: Penguin Books, 1979.

Tacitus. *Complete Works.* Trans. A.J. Church and W.J. Brodribb. New York: The Modern Library, 1942.

Terence. *Phormio.* Trans. Frank O. Copley. New York: Liberal Arts Press, 1958.

Virgil. *The Eclogues and Georgics of Virgil.* Trans. T.F. Royds. London: J.M. Dent & Co., 1907.

Vitruvius. *On Architecture.* Trans. Frank Granger. London: W. Heinemann, 1934.

Xenophon. *Hellenica.* Trans. C.L. Brownson. London: W. Heinemann, 1918–21.

MODERN BOOKS

Adcock, F.E. *Caesar as a Man of Letters.* Cambridge, UK: Cambridge University Press, 1956.

Adkins, Lesley and Roy. *Introduction to the Romans.* Secaucus, NJ: Chartwell Books, Inc., 1991.

Ashbee, Paul. *The Ancient British.* Norwich, UK: Geo Abstracts Ltd., 1978.

Aubrey, John. *Brief Lives and Other selected writings by John Aubrey.* A. Powell, ed. London: Cresset Press, 1949.

Ball, M.J., and J. Fife, eds. *The Celtic Languages.* London: Routledge, 1993.

Balsdon, J.P.V.D. *Roman Women, Their History and Habits.* New York: Barnes and Noble, 1962.

Birch, C.M. *Concordance and Index to Caesar.* New York: Hildesheim, 1988.

Bishop, M.C., and J.C. Coulston: *Roman Military Equipment.* London: Batsford, 1993.

Bloch, R. *The Origins of Rome.* New York: Praeger, 1960.

Bonaparte, Napoléon. *Correspondance.* Paris: H. Plon, J. Dumaine., 1858–70.

————. *Précis des Guerres de César.* Napoli: Jovene, 1984.

Branigan, Keith. *The Catuvellauni.* Gloucester, UK: A. Sutton, 1985.

Braudel, F. *The Identity of France.* London: Collins, 1988.

Bray, Warwick, and David Trump. *The Penguin Dictionary of Archaeology.* Harmondsworth, UK: Penguin Books, 1972.

Bromwich, Rachel, ed. *The Triads of the Island of Britain.* Cardiff: University of Wales Press, 1978.

Bromwich, Rachel, A.O.H. Jarman, and B.G. Roberts, eds. *The Arthur of the Welsh.* Cardiff: University of Wales Press, 1991.

Brothwell, D. *The Bog Man and the Archaeology of People.* London: British Museum Publications, 1986.

Bunbury, E.H. *History of Ancient Geography.* New York: Dover Publications, 1959.

Burne, A.H. *The Art of War on Land.* Harrisburg, PA: Military Service Publishing Co., 1947.

Burton, Robert. *The Anatomy of Melancholy.* Floyd Dell and Paul Jordan-Smith, eds. New York: Tudor Publishing Co., 1955. Originally published 1621.

Calder, Nigel. *The English Channel.* New York: Penguin Books, 1986.

Cambridge Ancient History. Vols. VII–IX. Cambridge, UK: Cambridge University Press, 1932–94.

Camden, William. *Camden's Britannia: Kent.* G.J. Copley, ed. London: Hutchinson of London, 1977. Originally published 1586.

————. *Camden's Britannia: Surrey and Sussex.* G.J. Copley, ed. London: Hutchinson of London, 1977. Originally published 1586.

Chadwick, Nora. *The Druids.* Cardiff: University of Wales Press, 1966.

———. *The Celts.* Harmondsworth, UK: Penguin Books, 1971.

Chevallier, R. ed. *Présence de César.* Paris: Société d'Édition "Les Belles Lettres," 1985.

Clarendon, Edward. *The History of the Rebellion and Civil Wars in England.* Oxford: The Clarendon Press, 1807. Originally   published 1674.

Collis, John. *The Iron Age in Britain.* Sheffield, UK: University of Sheffield, 1977.

Connolly, Peter. *Greece and Rome at War.* London: Macdonald, 1981.

Constans, L.-A. *Guide Illustré des Campagnes de César en Gaule.* Paris: Société d'Édition "Les Belles Lettres," 1929.

Cornell, Tim and John Matthews. *The Roman World.* Alexandria, VA: Stonehenge Press, 1991.

Cottrell, Leonard. *Seeing Roman Britain.* London: Pan Books, 1967.

Crawford, Michael. *Coinage and Money under the Roman Republic.* London: Methuen, 1985.

———. *The Roman Republic.* Cambridge: Harvard University Press, 1993.

Cunliffe, Barry. *The Celtic World.* London: The Bodley Head, 1979.

———, ed. *Coinage and Society in Britain in Gaul: Some Current Problems.* London: Council for British Archaeology, 1981.

———. *Danebury: Anatomy of an Iron Age Hillfort.* London: Batsford, 1983.

———. *Greeks, Romans and Barbarians.* London: Methuen, 1988.

———. *Iron Age Communities in Britain.* London: Routledge, 3rd ed., 1991.

———. *Wessex to AD 1000.* London: Longman, 1993.

———, ed. *The Oxford Illustrated Prehistory of Europe.* Oxford: Oxford University Press, 1994.

Cunliffe, Barry, and T. Rowley, eds. *Lowland Iron Age Communities in Europe.* Oxford: British Archaeological Reports, 1978.

Cunliffe, Barry, and T. Rowley, eds. *Oppida: The Beginnings of Urbanisation in Barbarian Europe.* Oxford: British Archaeological Reports, 1976.

Curley, Michael J. *Geoffrey of Monmouth.* Toronto: Twayne Publishers, 1994.

Darvill, Timothy. *Prehistoric Britain.* New Haven: Yale University Press, 1987.

Davies, Roy W. *Service in the Roman Army.* David Breeze and Valerie Maxwell, eds. Edinburgh: Edinburgh University Press, 1989.

Delaney, Frank. *The Celts.* London: BBC Publications, 1986.

Delbrück, Hans. *Warfare in Antiquity.* Lincoln, NB: University of Nebraska Press, 1975. Originally published 1900.

Dimbleby, G. *Plants and Archaeology.* New York: Humanities Press, 1967.

Dodge, T.A. *Caesar.* Boston: Houghton-Mifflin, 1892.

Dorey, T.A., ed. *Latin Historians.* New York: Basic Books, Inc., 1966.

Drewett, P., D. Rudling, and M. Gardiner. *The Southeast to AD 1000.* London: Longman, 1988.

Dyer, James. *Ancient Britain*. Philadelphia: Univ. of Pennsylvania Press, 1990.

Ebel, C. *Transalpine Gaul, The Emergence of a Roman Province*. Leiden: E.J. Brill, 1976.

Edmonds, Clement. *The Commentaries of C. Julius Caesar*. London: Jonathan Edwin, 1677. Originally published 1604.

Ellis, P.B. *The Celtic Empire*. London: Constable, 1990.

Evans, D. Ellis. *Gaulish Personal Names*. Oxford: The Clarendon Press, 1967.

Evans, J.K. *War, Women and Children in Ancient Rome*. London: Routledge, 1991.

Forster, E.M. *Alexandria*. Garden City, NY: Anchor Books, 1961.

Foster, Jennifer: *The Lexden Tumulus*. London: British Archaeological Reports, 1986.

Fowler, P.J. *The Farming of Prehistoric Britain*. Cambridge, UK: Cambridge University Press, 1983.

Fraser, P.M. *Ptolemaic Alexandria*. Oxford: The Clarendon Press, 1972.

Frere, Sheppard S., ed. *Problems of the Iron Age in Southern Britain*. London: University of London, Institute of Archaeology, 1958.

———. *Britannia, A History of Roman Britain*. London: Routledge and Kegan Paul, 3rd ed., 1987.

Fuller, J.F.C. *Julius Caesar: Man, Soldier and Tyrant*. Minerva Press, 1965.

Funck-Brentano, Fr. *The Earliest Times*. London: W. Heinemann, 1927.

Gabba, Emilio. *Republican Rome*. Berkeley: University of California Press, 1976.

Gabriel, Richard A., and Karen S. Metz. *From Sumer to Rome: The Military Capabilities of Ancient Armies*. New York: Greenwood Press, 1991.

Gantz, Jeffrey, trans. *The Mabinogion*. Harmondsworth, UK: Penguin Books, 1976.

Gelzer, Matthias. *Caesar: Politician and Statesman*. Cambridge: Harvard University Press, 1968 ed.

Geoffrey of Monmouth. *The History of the Kings of Britain*. Trans. Lewis Thorpe. Harmondsworth, UK: Penguin Books, 1966.

Grant, Michael. *Julius Caesar*. New York: McGraw Hill, 1969.

———. *The Ancient Historians*. London: Weidenfeld and Nicolson, 1970.

———. *Cleopatra*. London: Weidenfeld and Nicolson, 1972.

———. *The Army of the Caesars*. New York: Charles Scribners, 1974.

———. *The Twelve Caesars*. New York: Charles Scribner's Sons, 1975.

Gregor, Douglas B. *Celtic: A Comparative Study of the Six Celtic Languages*. Cambridge, UK: Oleander Press, 1980.

Grimal, Pierre. *The Civilization of Rome*. New York: Simon and Schuster, 1963.

Grimes, W.F., ed. *Aspects of Archaeology in Britain and Beyond*. London: H.W. Edwards, 1951.

Griscom, Acton, ed. *The Historia Regum Britanniae of Geoffrey of Monmouth*. London: Longmans, Green, 1929.

Hackett, Sir John, ed. *Warfare in the Ancient World.* London: Sidgwick and Jackson, 1989.

Hadas, Moses. *A History of Latin Literature.* New York: Columbia University Press, 1952.

Hallett, J.P. *Fathers and Daughters in Roman Society.* Princeton: Princeton University Press, 1984.

Hanna, W.A. *The Celtic Migrations.* Belfast: Pretani Press, 1985.

Harding, D.W., ed. *Hillforts: Later Prehistoric Earthworks in Britain and Ireland.* London: Academic Press, 1976.

Harley, J.B., and D. Woodward. *The History of Cartography.* Chicago: University of Chicago Press, 1987.

Harris, W. *War and Imperialism in Republican Rome, 327–70 B.C.* Oxford: The Clarendon Press, 1979.

Harrison, Shirley. *The Channel.* Glasgow: Collins, 1986.

Harvey, Sir Paul. *The Oxford Companion to Classical Literature.* Oxford: Oxford University Press, 1984.

Hatt, Jean-Jacques. *Celts and Gallo-Romans.* Trans. James Hogarth. London: Barrie and Jenkins, 1970.

Hawkes, C.F.C. *Pytheas: Europe and the Greek Explorers.* Oxford: Oxford University Press, 1977.

———. *Britain and Julius Caesar.* Oxford: Oxford University Press, 1978 ed.

Healy, J.F. *Mining and Metallurgy in the Greek and Roman World.* London: Thames and Hudson, 1978.

Herm, Gerhard. *The Celts.* New York: St. Martin's Press, 1975.

Highet, Gilbert. *Poets in a Landscape.* New York: Alfred A. Knopf, 1957.

Holinshed, R. *Chronicles: England, Scotland and Ireland.* New York: AMS Press, 1965. Originally published 1577.

Holloway, R.R. *Archaeology of Early Rome and Latium.* London: Routledge, 1994.

Holmes, T. Rice. *The Roman Republic and the Founder of the Empire.* Oxford: The Clarendon Press, 1923.

———. *Ancient Britain and the Invasions of Caesar.* Oxford: The Clarendon Press, 1936. Originally published 1907.

———. *Caesar's Conquest of Gaul.* Oxford: Oxford University Press, 1971. Originally published 1899.

Home, Gordon C. *Roman London.* New York: George H. Doran Co., 2nd ed., 1948.

Howard, Philip. *London's River.* London: Hamilton, 1975.

Hubert, Henri. *The Greatness and Decline of the Celts.* London: Bracken Books, 1993. Originally published 1934.

———. *The Rise of the Celts.* London: Bracken Books, 1993. Originally published 1934.

Hughes, H. Stuart, ed. *Teachers of History*. Ithaca, NY: Cornell University Press, 1954.

Humez, Alexander and Nicholas. *A•B•C et Cetera*. Boston: David R. Godine, 1987.

Hutchinson, L. *The Conspiracy of Catiline*. London: Blond, 1966.

Hutton, Ronald. *The Pagan Religions of the Ancient British Isles*. Oxford: Blackwell, 1991.

Hyland, Ann. *Equus: The Horse in the Roman World*. New Haven: Yale University Press. 1990.

Ireland, S. *Roman Britain*. London: Croom Helm, 1986.

Jackson, Kenneth. *Language and History in Early Britain*. Cambridge: Harvard University Press, 1953.

Jacobsthal, Paul. *Early Celtic Art*. Oxford: The Clarendon Press, 1944.

Jacoby, Felix. *Die Fragmente der Griechischen Historiker*. Leiden, The Netherlands: Brill, 1957.

Jesson, Margaret, and D. Hill, eds. *The Iron Age and Its Hillforts*. Southampton: Southampton University Archaeological Society, 1971.

Jones, A.H.M. *Augustus*. New York: W. W. Norton, 1970.

Jones, Martin. *England Before Domesday*. New York: Barnes and Noble, 1986.

Judson, H.P. *Caesar's Army*. New York: Biblo and Tannen, 1888.

Kahn, A.D. *The Education of Julius Caesar*. New York: Schocken Books, 1986.

Kaplan, Arthur. *Catiline: The Man and His Role in the Roman Revolution*. New York: Exposition Press, 1968.

Keegan, J., and R. Holmes. *Soldiers*. London: Hamilton, 1985.

Kendrick, T.D. *British Antiquity*. London: Methuen, 1950.

Kruta, Venceslas. *The Celts of the West*. Trans. Alan Sheridan. London: Orbis, 1985.

de Laet, Sigfried. *The Low Countries*. London: Thames and Hudson, 1958.

Laffont, Robert, ed. *The Ancient Art of Warfare*. London: Barrie and Rockliff, 1966.

Laing, Lloyd, and Jennifer. *The Origins of Britain*. London: Granada, 1982.

———. *Art of the Celts*. London: Thames and Hudson, 1992.

Laistner, M.L.W. *The Greater Roman Historians*. Berkeley: University of California Press, 1966.

Lambarde, William. *A Perambulation of Kent*. Bath: Adams and Dent, 1970. Originally published 1576.

Leckie, Jr., R.W. *The Passage of Dominion: Geoffrey of Monmouth and the Periodization of Insular History in the Twelfth Century*. Toronto: University of Toronto Press, 1981.

Le Gall, Joël. *Alésia: Le Siège de la Forteresse Gauloise par César*. Paris: Ministère de la Culture, Impr. Nationale, 1985.

Legg, Rodney. *Romans in Britain*. London: Heinemann, 1983.

Leland, John. *Leland's Itinerary in England and Wales*. L.T. Smith, ed. Carbondale, IL: Southern Illinois University Press, 1964. Originally published 1549.

Lewin, Thomas. *The Invasion of Britain by Julius Caesar*. London: Longman, Green, Longman and Roberts, 1859.

Lintott, A.W. *Violence in Republican Rome*. London: The Clarendon Press, 1968.

Longworth, Ian H. *Prehistoric Britain*. London: British Museum Publications, 1985.

Lynch, Frances. *Prehistoric Anglesey*. Llangefni, Anglesey, Wales: The Anglesey Antiquarian Society, 1970.

Mabey, Richard. *Food for Free*. London: Collins, 1972.

MacAulay, Donald, ed. *The Celtic Languages*. Cambridge, UK: Cambridge University Press, 1992.

MacCana, Proinsias. *The Mabinogi*. Cardiff: University of Wales Press, 1977.

MacEoin, G., ed. *Proceedings of the Sixth International Congress of Celtic Studies*. Dublin: Dublin Institute for Advanced Studies, 1983.

MacLennan, Gordon W., ed. *Proceedings of the First North American Congress of Celtic Studies*. Ottawa: University of Ottawa, 1988.

Mallory, J.P. *In Search of the Indo-Europeans*. London: Thames and Hudson, 1989.

Manning, Owen. *The History and Antiquities of the County of Surrey*. William Bray, ed. London: J. White, 1804–14.

Markale, Jean. *Celtic Civilization*. London: Gordon and Cremonesi, 1976.

Marsden, E.W. *Greek and Roman Artillery*. London: The Clarendon Press, 1969.

McEvedy, C., and R. Jones. *Atlas of World Population History*. New York: Facts on File, 1978.

Merrifield, Ralph. *Roman London*. New York: F.A. Praeger, 1969.

———. *The Archaeology of London*. Park Ridge, NJ: Noyes Press, 1974.

Milne, Gustav. *The Port of Roman London*. London: B.T. Batsford, 1985.

Montaigne, Michel de. *Essays*. Trans. Jacob Zeitlin. New York: Alfred A. Knopf, 1935.

Moscati, S., gen. ed. *The Celts*. New York: Rizzoli, 1991.

Napoléon III. *The History of Julius Caesar*. London: Cassell, Peter, and Galpin, 1865–66.

Nash, Daphne. *Coinage in the Celtic World*. London: Seaby, 1987.

Nelson, R.B. *Warfleets of Antiquity*. Goring-by-Sea, UK: Wargames Research Group, 1973.

Nennius. *British History and The Welsh Annals*. Edit. and trans. John Morris. Totowa, NJ: Phillimore, 1980.

Parry, Thomas. *A History of Welsh Literature*. Trans. H.I. Bell. Oxford: The Clarendon Press, 1957.

Partridge, Clive. *Skeleton Green: A Late Iron Age and Romano-British Site*. London: Society for the Promotion of Roman Studies, 1981.

Piggott, Stuart. *The Neolithic Cultures of the British Isles*. Cambridge, UK: Cambridge University Press, 1954.

———. *Celts, Saxons and the Early Antiquaries*. Edinburgh: Edinburgh University Press, 1967.

———. *The Druids*. New York: Thames and Hudson, 1968.

———. *The Earliest Wheeled Transport*. Ithaca, NY: Cornell University Press, 1983.

———. *Ancient Britons and the Antiquarian Imagination*. London: Thames and Hudson, 1989.

———. *Wagon, Chariot and Carriage*. London: Thames and Hudson, 1992.

Piggott, Stuart, Glyn Daniel, and Charles McBurney, eds. *France Before the Romans*. Park Ridge, NJ: Noyes Press, 1973.

Pollini, John. *Roman Portraiture*. Los Angeles: University of Southern California, 1990.

Pomeroy, Sarah. *Women in Hellenistic Egypt*. New York: Schocken Books, 1984.

Potter, T.W. *Roman Italy*. Berkeley: University of California Press, 1987.

Potter, T.W., and Catherine Johns. *Roman Britain*. Berkeley: University of California Press, 1992.

Powell, T.G.E. *The Celts*. London: Thames and Hudson, 1980. Originally published 1958.

———. *Prehistoric Art*. New York: Praeger, 1966.

Price, Glanville. *The Languages of Britain*. London: E. Arnold, 1984.

———. *Ireland and the Celtic Connection*. Gerrards Cross, UK: Smythe, 1987.

Raftery, J., ed. *The Celts*. Cork, Ireland: Mercier Press, 1964.

Rambaud, Michel, *L'Art de la Déformation Historique dans les Commentaires de César*. Paris: Société d'Edition "Les Belles Lettres," 1966.

———, trans. and ed. *Bellum Gallicum Liber Quartus*. Paris: Presses Universitaires de France, 1967.

Rankin, H.D. *Celts and the Classical World*. London: Croom Helm, 1987.

Renfrew, Colin. *Before Civilization*. Cambridge, UK: Cambridge University Press, 1979.

———. *Archaeology and Language: The Puzzle of Indo-European Origins*. London: Jonathan Cape, 1987.

Reynolds, Peter. *Farming in the Iron Age*. Cambridge, UK: Cambridge University Press, 1976.

———. *Iron Age Farm: The Butser Experiment*. London: British Museum Publications, 1979.

Rivet, A.L. *Gallia Narbonensis*. London: B.T. Batsford, 1988.

Rivet, A.L., and C. Smith. *The Place-Names of Roman Britain*. Princeton:

Princeton University Press, 1979.

Rodgers, W.L. *Greek and Roman Naval Warfare.* Annapolis: United States Naval Institute Press, 1937.

Rolt, L.T.C. *The Thames from Mouth to Source.* London: B.T. Batsford, 1951.

Ross, Anne. *Everyday Life of the Pagan Celts.* London: B.T. Batsford, 1986.

Ross, Anne, and Don Robins. *The Life and Death of a Druid Prince.* New York: Simon and Schuster, 1989.

Sabben-Clare, James. *Caesar and Roman Politics 60–50 BC.* London: Oxford University Press, 1971.

Salway, Peter. *Roman Britain.* Oxford: Oxford University Press, 1993.

Schmidt, Karl H., and R. Kodderitzsch, eds. *History and Culture of the Celts.* Heidelberg, Germany: Carl Winter Universitätsverlag, 1986.

Scullard, H.H. *The Elephant in the Greek and Roman World.* London: Thames and Hudson, 1974.

Seager, Robin. *Pompey, A Political Biography.* Berkeley: University of California Press, 1979.

Shelton, Jo-Ann. *As the Romans Did.* New York: Oxford University Press, 1988.

Starr, C.G. *The Roman Imperial Navy, 31 BC–AD 324.* New York: Barnes and Noble, 2nd ed., 1960.

———. *The Influence of Sea Power on Ancient History.* Oxford: Oxford University Press, 1989.

Stead, I.M. *Celtic Art in Britain Before the Roman Conquest.* London: British Museum Publications, 1985.

Stead, I.M., and V. Rigby. *Baldock.* London: Society for the Promotion of Roman Studies, 1986.

Stead, I.M., J.B. Bourke, and D. Brothwell. *Lindow Man.* Ithaca, NY: Cornell University Press, 1986.

Stephens, Meic, ed. *The Oxford Companion to the Literature of Wales.* Oxford: Oxford University Press, 1986.

Stevenson, V., ed. *Words.* London: Macdonald, 1983.

Stonebanks, John A. *Coway Stakes at Walton-on-Thames.* Walton-on-Thames, UK: Walton and Weybridge Local History Society, 1972.

Stow, John. *Survey of London.* London: J.M. Dent & Sons, 1956. Originally published 1598.

Sutherland, C.H.V. *Roman Coins.* London: Barrie and Jenkins, 1974.

Sydenham, E.A. *The Coinage of the Roman Republic.* London: Spink, 1952.

Syme, Ronald. *The Roman Revolution.* Oxford: Oxford University Press, 1952.

Taylor, Lily Ross. *Party Politics in the Age of Caesar.* Berkeley: University of California Press, 1961.

Todd, Malcolm. *Roman Britain 55 B.C.–A.D. 400.* Brighton: Harvester Press, 1981.

Treggiari, S. *Roman Freedmen During the Late Republic.* Oxford: The Clarendon Press, 1969.

Tylecote, R.F. *Metallurgy in Archaeology: A Pre-History of Metallurgy in the British Isles.* London: E. Arnold, 1962.

Volkmann, Hans. *Cleopatra.* Trans. T.J. Cadoux. London: Elek Books, 1958.

Von Hagen, V.W. *The Roads That Led to Rome.* Cleveland: The World Publishing Co., 1967.

Wacher, John. *The Roman World.* London: Routledge and Kegan Paul, 1987.

Wainwright, G.J. *Gussage All Saints.* London: H.M.S.O., 1979.

———. *The Henge Monuments.* London: Thames and Hudson, 1990.

Warry, J.G. *Warfare in the Classical World.* London: Salamander Books, 1980.

Watson, G.R. *The Roman Soldier.* Ithaca, NY: Cornell University Press, 1969.

Webster, G. *The Roman Imperial Army in the 1st and 2nd Centuries AD.* London: A. & C. Black, 1985 ed.

Wells, P.S. *Farms, Villages and Cities.* Ithaca, NY: Cornell University Press, 1984.

Wheeler, Sir Mortimer, and Katherine M. Richardson. *Hill-Forts of Northern France.* London: Research Reports of the Society of Antiquaries, 1957.

Wightman, Edith. *Gallia Belgica.* Berkeley: University of California Press, 1985.

Wilson, C.A. *Food and Drink in Britain from Stone Age to Recent Times.* London: Constable, 1984.

Wiseman, T.P. *Roman Studies.* Liverpool: F. Cairns, 1987.

Woodell, S.R.J., ed. *The English Landscape: Past, Present and Future.* Oxford: Oxford University Press, 1985.

ARTICLES

Allen, D.F. "The Origins of Coinage in Britain: A Reappraisal," in S. Frere, ed., *Problems of the Iron Age in Southern Britain* (1958).

———. "British Potin Coins: A Review," in Margaret Jesson and D. Hill, eds., *The Iron Age and Its Hill Forts* (1971).

Allen, W. "The British Epics of Quintus and Marcus Cicero," in *Transactions of the American Philological Association,* Vol. LXXXVI (1955).

Anderson, J.K. "Homeric, British and Cyrenaic Chariots," in *American Journal of Archaeology,* Vol. LXIX (1965).

Balsdon, J. "The Ides of March," in *Historia,* Vol. VII (1953).

Barrington, Daines. "Observations on Caesar's Invasions of Britain, and More Particularly His Passage Across the Thames," in *Archaeologia,* Vol. II (1809).

Beeson, C. "Text History of the Corpus Caesarianum," in *Classical Philology,* Vol. XXXV (1940).

Bénard, Jacky. "César devant Alesia: les Témoins sont dans le Sol," in *Revue*

Historique des Armes, No. 167 (June 1987).

Birchall, A. "The Aylesford-Swarling Culture: The Problem of the Belgae Reconsidered," in *Proceedings of the Prehistoric Society*, Vol. XXXI (1965).

Collins, John H. "Caesar and the Corruption of Power," in *Historia*, Vol. IV (1955).

Colvin, H.M. "On Dover Castle," in *Antiquity*, Vol. XXXIII (1959).

Cornell, Tim. "Rome and Latium to 390 BC," in *Cambridge Ancient History*, Vol. VII, Part II (1989).

Cunliffe, Barry. "Settlement and Population in the British Iron Age: Some Facts, Figures and Fantasies," in B. Cunliffe and T. Rowley, eds. *Lowland Iron Age Communities in Europe* (1978).

———. "Man and Landscape in Britain 6000 BC–AD 400," in S.R.J. Woodell, ed., *The English Landscape: Past, Present and Future* (1985).

Davies, Roy W. "The Roman Military Diet," in *Britannia*, Vol. II (1971).

Dawkins, W. Boyd. "On Bigbury Camp and the Pilgrim's Way," in *Archeological Journal*, Vol. LIX (1902).

Deutsch, Monroe. "The Apparatus of Caesar's Triumph," in *Philological Quarterly*, Vol. III (1924).

DeWitt, N.J. "The Druids and Romanization," in *Transactions of the American Philological Association*, Vol. LXIX (1938).

Dillon, Myles. "Celtic Religion and Celtic Society," in J. Raftery, *The Celts* (1964).

Dumville, David. "The Historical Value of the *Historia Brittonum*," in *Arthurian Literature*, Vol. VI (1986).

Dyer, James. "Ravensburgh Castle, Hertfordshire," in D.W. Harding, ed., *Hillforts: Later Prehistoric Earthworks in Britain and Ireland* (1976).

Elton, G.R. "The Terminal Date of Caesar's Gallic Proconsulate," in *Journal of Roman Studies*, Vol. XXXVI (1946).

Forsyth, P.Y. "In the Wake of Etna, 44 B.C.," in *Classical Antiquity*, Vol. VII, No. 1 (April 1988).

Furger-Guntis, Andres. "The Celtic War Chariot," in S. Moscati, ed. *The Celts* (1991).

Greene, D. "The Coming of the Celts: The Linguistic Viewpoint," in G. MacEoin, ed., *Proceedings of the Sixth International Congress of Celtic Studies* (1983).

Greep, S.J. "Lead Slingshot from Windridge Farm, St. Albans, and the Use of Sling by the Roman Army in Britain," in *Britannia*, Vol. XVIII (1987).

Hachmann, R. "The Problem of the *Belgae* Seen from the Continent," in *Institute of Archaeology Bulletin*, Vol. XIII (1976).

Halley, Edmond. "Of the Time and Place of Caesar's Descent upon Britain," in *Philosophical Transactions of the Royal Society of London*, Vol. III (1683–94).

Harmand, Jacques. "Une Question Césarienne Non Résolue: la Campagne de 51contre les Bellovaques et Sa Localisation," in *Bulletin de la Société Nationale des Antiquaires de France* (1959).

———. "Un Refus du Témoignage Césarien: l'Iconographie de la Reddition de Vercingétorix depuis Cent Ans," in R. Chevallier, ed., *Présence de César* (1985).

Haselgrove, C.C. "Warfare and Its Aftermath as Reflected in the Precious Metal Coinage of Belgic Gaul," in *Oxford Journal of Archaeology*, Vol. III, No. 1 (1984).

Hastrup, T. "On the Date of Caesar's Commentaries on the Gallic War," in *Classica et Mediaevalia*, Vol. XVIII (1957).

Helbaek, H. "Early Crops in Southern England," in *Proceedings of the Prehistoric Society*, Vol. XVIII (1952).

Hussey, R.C. "The British Settlement in Bigbury Wood," in *Archaeologia Cantiana*, Vol. IX (1874).

Jackson, Kenneth. "Two Early Scottish Names," in *Scottish Historical Review*, Vol. XXXIII (1954).

Jessup, Ronald F. "Bigberry Camp, Harbledown, Kent," in *Archaeological Journal*, Vol. LXXXIX (1932).

Jessup, Ronald F., and N.C. Cook. "Excavations at Bigbury Camp, Harbledown," in *Archaeologia Cantiana*, Vol. XLVIII (1936).

Jones, Thomas. "The Early Evolution of the Legend of Arthur," in *Nottingham Mediaeval Studies*, Vol. VIII (1964).

Kent, J.P.C. "The Origins of Coinage in Britain," in B. Cunliffe, ed., *Coinage and Society in Britain in Gaul: Some Current Problems*. CBA Research Report No. 38 (1981).

Klein, W.G. "Roman Temple at Worth, Kent," in *Antiquaries Journal*, Vol. VIII (1928).

Koch, John. "The Laureate Hero in the War-chariot: Some Recollections of the Iron Age in the *Gododdin*," in *Etudes Celtiques*, Vol. XXIV (1987).

———. "A Welsh Window on the Iron Age: Manawydan, Mandubracios," in *Cambridge Medieval Celtic Studies*, No. 14 (1987).

Korfmann, M. "The Sling as a Weapon," in *Scientific American*, Vol. CCXXIX, No. 4 (1973).

Kranzberg, M. "An Emperor Writes History," in H. Stuart Hughes, ed., *Teachers of History* (1954).

Lawrence, G.F. "Antiquities from the Middle Thames," in *Archaeological Journal*, Vol. LXXXVI (1929).

Lazenby, J.F. "The Conference of Luca and the Gallic War," in *Latomus*, Vol. XVIII (1959).

Lehmann, L.Th. "A Trireme's Tragedy," in *International Journal of Nautical*

Archeology, Vol. XI, No. 2 (May 1982).

Lipke, Paul. "Trials of the Trireme," in *Archaeology*, Vol. XLI, No. 2 (March/April 1988).

Lord, L.E. "The Date of Julius Caesar's Departure from Alexandria," in *Journal of Roman Studies*, Vol. XXVIII (1938).

Mitchell, Stephen. "Cornish Tin, Iulius Caesar, and the Invasion of Britain," in *Studies in Latin Literature and Roman History*. Collection Latomus, Vol. CLXXX (1983).

Perkins, J.B. Ward. "Excavations on the Iron Age Hillfort of Oldbury, near Ightham, Kent," in *Archaeologia*, Vol. XC (1944).

Petrie, Sir W.M. Flinders. "Neglected British History," in *Proceedings of the British Academy*, 1917–18.

Piggott, Stuart. "The Sources of Geoffrey of Monmouth, II: The Stonehenge Story," in *Antiquity*, Vol. XV, No. 60 (1941).

———. "Celtic Chariots on Roman Coins," in *Antiquity*, Vol. XXVI (1952).

———. "The *Carnyx* in Early Iron Age Britain," in *Antiquaries Journal*, Vol. XXXIX (1959).

———. "The Coming of the Celts: The Archaeological Argument," in G. MacEoin, ed., *Proceedings of the Sixth International Congress of Celtic Studies* (1983).

Pyatt, F.B., et al. "*Non Isatis sed Vitrum* or, the Colour of Lindow Man," in *Oxford Journal of Archaeology*. Vol. X, No. 1 (1991).

Renfrew, Colin. "The Origins of Indo-European Languages," in *Scientific American*, Vol. CCLXI, No. 4 (October 1989).

Rivet, A.L. "A Note on Scythed Chariots," in *Antiquity*, Vol. LIII (1979).

Roberts, Brynley. "Geoffrey of Monmouth's *Historia* and *Brut Y Brenhinedd*" in R. Bromwich, A.O.H. Jarman, and B. Roberts, eds., *The Arthur of the Welsh* (1991).

Rodwell, W.J. "Coinage, Oppida and the Rise of Belgic Power in South-Eastern Britain," in B. Cunliffe and T. Rowley, eds., *Oppida: The Beginnings of Urbanisation in Barbarian Europe* (1976).

Schmidt, K.H. "Insular Celtic: P and Q Celtic" in M.J. Ball and J. Fife, eds., *The Celtic Languages* (1993).

Sharpe, Montagu. "The Great Ford Across the River Thames," in *Archaeological Journal*, Vol. LXIII (1906).

Sherratt, Andrew. "The Emergence of Élites: Earlier Bronze Age Europe, 2500–1300 BC," in B. Cunliffe, ed., *The Oxford Illustrated Prehistory of Europe* (1994).

Southern, R.W. "Aspects of the European Tradition of Historical Writing: 1. The Classical Tradition from Einhard to Geoffrey of Monmouth," in *Transactions of the Royal Historical Society*, 5th Series, Vol. XX (1970).

Stead, I.M. "A la Tène III: Burial at the Tene, Baldock, Herts.," in *The Antiquaries Journal*, Vol. XLVIII (1968).

Stebbing, W.P.D. "Discoveries in the Neighborhood of Deal in 1936," in *Archaelogia Cantiana*, Vol. XLVIII (1936).

Stevens, C.E. "55 BC and 54 BC," in *Antiquity*, Vol. XXI (1947).

———. "The 'Bellum Gallicum' as a Work of Propaganda," in *Latomus*, Vol. XI (1952).

———. "Britain and the *Lex Pompeia Licinia*," in *Latomus*, Vol. XII (1953).

———. "Julius Caesar's Elephant," in *History Today*, Vol. IX (1959).

Thompson, Frederick H. "Three Surrey Hillforts: Excavations at Anstiebury, Holmbury and Hascombe, 1972–77," in *Antiquaries Journal*, Vol. LIX (1979).

———. "Excavations at Bigberry, Near Canterbury, 1978–80," in *Antiquaries Journal*, Vol. LXIII (1983).

Thornhill, Patrick. "A Lower Thames Ford and the Campaigns of 54 BC and AD 43," in *Archaeologia Cantiana*, Vol. XCII (1976).

Tierney, J.J. "The Celtic Ethnography of Posidonius," in *Proceedings of the Royal Irish Academy*, Vol. LX, Section C (March 1960).

Watson, G.R. "The Army of the Republic," in J. Wacher, *The Roman World* (1987).

Wheeler, Mortimer. "'Old England', Brentford," in *Antiquity*, Vol. III (1929).

———. "Britain Before the Romans: The Lost Cities of Herts," in *The Times* (London), Feb. 24, 1933.

Wilford, J.M. "Remaking the Wheel: Evolution of the Chariot," in *The New York Times*, Feb. 22, 1994.

Yavetz, Z. "The Living Conditions of the Urban Plebs in Republican Rome," in *Latomus*, Vol. XVII (1958).

ILLUSTRATION
ACKNOWLEDGMENTS

The publishers would like to express their deepest appreciation to the following individuals and organizations for material reproduced in this book.

The campaign maps and "Gaul in Caesar's Time" are by Tom Stalker-Miller and are reproduced through the courtesy of the copyright holder, Professor Barry Cunliffe of Oxford University. The map of Eastern Kent is by Ramon L. Jiménez, adapted from Sonia and C.F.C. Hawkes.

Illustration numbers 1, 3, 4, 9, 12, 15, 20 and 27 are reproduced through the courtesy of David R. Godine, Publisher Inc., Boston, MA, from *The Battle for Gaul*, Julius Caesar translated by Anne and Peter Wiseman (1985). Sources include: the Mansell Collection (1, 3, 4 and 27); Roger Agache, photographer (9); Musée des Antiquities Nationales (12); Ron Bowen, artist (15); René Goguey, photographer (20); and Jeremy Ford (the diagrams accompanying 12 and 15).

Numbers 2, 5, 6, 21 and 26 are courtesy of the Musée Alésia, France. Number 7 is from Aylett Sammes, *Britannia Antiqua Illustrata,* 1676. Numbers 10, 11, 13 and 14 are courtesy of the Museum of Roman Civilization, Rome, Italy. Numbers 22 and 23 are courtesy of the Musée Crozatier, City of Puy-en-Velay, France. Number 17 is courtesy of the Musée des Arts Décoratifs, Paris, France. Number 24 is courtesy of the Museo Capitolino, Rome. Number 25 is courtesy of the Ny Carlsberg Glyptothek, Copenhagen, Denmark. Numbers 8, 16, 18 and 19 are photographs courtesy of Ramon L. Jiménez. The maps accompanying numbers 9 and 20 were created by Tom Stalker-Miller and made available through the kind courtesy of Professor Barry Cunliffe of Oxford University.

INDEX